SCREAMING
FOR PLEASURE

COAL CRACKER PRESS

Coal Cracker Press
PMB 800 1250 Fairmont Dr., Ste. A
San Leandro, CA 94578

coalcrackerpress.com

ISBN: (print) 978-0-692-19335-8
ISBN: (ebook) 978-0-692-19336-5

Ordering Information:
Special discounts are available on quantity purchases by corporations, associations, and others. For details, contact Coal Cracker Press at the address above.

SCREAMING FOR PLEASURE

HOW HORROR MAKES YOU HAPPY AND HEALTHY

S. A. BRADLEY

SAN LEANDRO, CA

DEDICATED TO

Harlan Ellison (1934-2018)

Harlan Ellison's writing saved me as a teen. His attitude and outspokenness convinced me that I didn't have to hide my intelligence or my love of genre, but I always needed to be able to back my words up with substance, and never back down from a fight.

"You must not be afraid to go there."
– Harlan Ellison

"I want to tell you, everyone that is dreaming of a parable, of using genre and fantasy to tell the stories about the things that are real in the world today, you can do it. This is a door. Kick it open and come in."

– Guillermo del Toro, upon receiving the Best Picture Oscar for *The Shape of Water* (2017)

CONTENTS

CHAPTER ONE
Your First Kiss: How Horror Hooks You / 1

CHAPTER TWO
We Bond Over Popcorn: Watching Horror with an Audience / 15

CHAPTER THREE
Big Bad Books: How Horror Literature Can Empower You / 39

CHAPTER FOUR
Screaming for Pleasure: Exorcise Your Demons Through Devil Music / 59

CHAPTER FIVE
My Outer Demons: Fighting Your Phobias with Phantasms / 91

CHAPTER SIX
Killed by Death: Facing Mortality Through Horror Movies / 105

CHAPTER SEVEN
Picking at the Scabs: When Horror Echoes Real Life / 123

CHAPTER EIGHT
You Will Deny Horror Three Times Before the Dawn:
My Horror Manifesto / 149

CHAPTER NINE
Welcome to the New Tension: Women Horror Directors / 173

CHAPTER TEN
Things That Go Bump and Grind in the Night: Sex and Horror / 199

CHAPTER ELEVEN
Shut Up and Watch the Movie: Time for Your Horror Therapy / 225

CHAPTER TWELVE
Horror Can Make You Happier and Healthier, and I'm Living Proof / 255

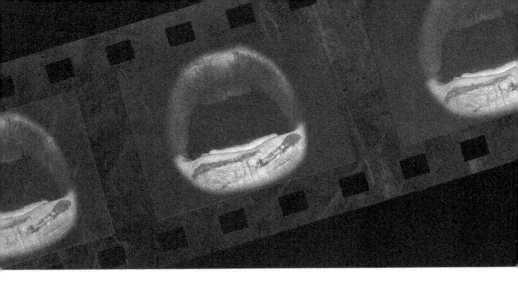

CHAPTER ONE

YOUR FIRST KISS:
HOW HORROR HOOKS YOU

I remember my First Kiss like it was yesterday. I was eight years old, and it was with an older woman named Julie. It happened in her backyard. It happened right next to the corpse of her daughter.

I should probably explain.

I'm talking about my First Kiss with horror.

Don't Look Now (1973) hooked me into a lifetime obsession with getting scared. It starred actress Julie Christie. Like my physical first kiss, the experience was scary, overwhelming, and thoroughly exhilarating. And just like my physical first kiss, I wasn't supposed to be doing that kind of thing at such a young age.

But I did it anyway.

Whether you're a die-hard horror fan, or you absolutely hate the genre, chances are that the first time you were exposed to a horror movie was when you were just a kid. And it may be that something in that first viewing was so powerful that you formed a lifelong opinion about the genre.

I was shaken to my core when I saw my first horror movie. I had nightmares. I was terrified to walk upstairs in my house alone at night because of the full-length mirror at the end of the hallway. I couldn't stare at my reflection because I was afraid I'd see the monster from the movie appear out of one of the dark rooms behind me and advance on me while I was paralyzed with fear.

My first horror movie traumatized me.

And yet, I found myself attracted to that intense feeling.

What Makes a Horror Movie a Horror Movie Anyway?

I consider horror to be one of the most diverse and beautiful storytelling styles that we have. Because it's so diverse, there can be a big difference in the look and feel of horror films; and this sometimes causes debates among fans and critics about what constitutes a "horror movie."

I like to keep it simple. The definition of *horror* is "an intense feeling of shock, dread, repulsion, or terror." So, a *horror movie* tells a story that gives the viewer an intense feeling of shock, dread, repulsion, or terror. I think the definition needs to be loose because what it takes to give each viewer those intense feelings is subjective. Horror is about emotion first.

Breaking the Rules Is Half the Fun

I think breaking the rules is part of the appeal of horror, especially when you're a kid. It's that intoxicating buzz of the forbidden. When you watch a scary movie, you know you're safe, but you don't *feel* safe. You get an uneasy charge from jumping into the unknown.

When I got that charge for the first time, it was an intimate moment. It felt like my First Kiss, one that was made just for me, like it had been waiting for me. Up until that point, I had only watched what I was allowed to watch. But this one I picked for myself. Even though the movie gave me nightmares, it was liberating.

Serving Time in Parent Prison with Court-Appointed Horror

I'll bet good money that most kids in the world probably got scared by the Wicked Witch of the West, or the flying monkeys in the *Wizard of Oz* (1939), or the Wicked Stepmother in *Snow White* (1937). But I never hear anyone cite those movies as a First Kiss.

That's because those scares wash off easily, even for little children. They are in movies that are safe, and in the end, life-affirming. Safe and life-affirming are *not* scary.

If your childhood was anything like mine, your parents didn't want you getting freaked out by horror movies because they needed to get you to sleep at night. As a result, any scary movies you begged to watch had to go through a gauntlet of scrutiny. And when a good night's sleep was at risk, most parents would err on the side of caution. So, the only horror you got to see was parent-approved. It was court-appointed horror.

My parents were my first teachers. I inherited their values, and I also inherited their entertainment, by default. I watched what they watched. My parents were the Deans of my first film school—they picked the curriculum.

Then when I was a little older, my dad was my horror movie professor, and that means I watched the films he loved as a kid. He loved the Atomic Age horror movies of the 1950s, so I saw a lot of giant insects. Many of those movies had exclamation points built into their titles. He introduced me to the giant ants in *THEM!* (1954), and the slow-motion horrors of *TARANTULA!* (1955).

My dad also introduced me to *his* First Kiss, Howard Hawks' *The Thing from Another World* (1951). In that film, a military research facility at the North Pole discovers a UFO buried under the ice. The ship is destroyed, but the team of soldiers and scientists find a body trapped under the ice that they assume to be the alien pilot. Of course, someone accidentally defrosts the ice block enough for the creature to escape. The humans are then in a fight to the death with the alien—who looks a lot like the Frankenstein monster with thorny hands.

I loved the movie, but it wasn't scary. I jumped a few times, but the film was more thrilling than frightening. Even as a seven-year-old kid, I knew that the heroic Air Force guys were going to win in the end. It was also slow, there was a *lot* of talking, and the monster was trapped in a block of ice so it took a long time to melt that damn ice. *The Thing from Another World*, my dad's First Kiss, was not *my* First Kiss.

There was a pattern to all of the horror movies my dad let me watch. They had one, maybe two, scary moments, and in the end the military or the police conquered the monster and order was restored. For me, the parts I liked and remembered were the one or two scary scenes, and I definitely wanted more.

For a while, I thought the only horror movies were *monster* movies. Then one Saturday night during a family card game, my uncle found out that I loved horror movies, and he decided to share with me the movie that had scared *him* as a teenager—Alfred Hitchcock's *Psycho* (1960). As soon as my uncle said the name of the movie, my dad coughed loudly and gave him a harsh stare. My uncle smiled at me and changed the subject. Luckily for me, my older cousins were more than happy to freak me out, so when I asked them about the movie, they gave me all the gory details. I had to sleep with the light on just from their descriptions of *Psycho*.

Now I knew that there was *more* horror and *scarier* horror out there than the predictable monster movies I had watched. Even though I knew I'd have nightmares, I was attracted to the rush of being scared. My dad, my movie professor, was holding me back—obviously he was hiding the good stuff.

Your First Corruptor Walked Right in the Front Door

Television and comic books are time-honored corrupters that go all the way back to the Baby Boomers. They had *Creature Features* on television, or EC Comics like *Tales from the Crypt* or *Vault of Horror* to give them nightmares. Both things were dismissed as kid stuff and underestimated by the parents.

Just like whatever corrupted *you*.

In my case, my corrupter was the first pay cable television station in the United States.

Home Box Office (HBO), The Fifth Horseman

It's hard to fathom now, but HBO used to be considered an oddball idea that would never take off. To be fair, the original Home Box Office was nothing like the channel that gives us *Game of Thrones* today.

Home Box Office was the first paid subscription channel. That idea was met with a lot of skepticism, since up until then the only thing you had to pay for was the television set. Paying for a television channel seemed absurd.

In his 2013 article, *It's Not TV: HBO, The Company That Changed Television:*

The Green Channel, Bill Mesce chronicled how, in 1971, HBO targeted the residents of six US cities to research if the residents would subscribe to a pay television channel. Five of the six cities polled were uninterested, but the city of Allentown, Pennsylvania was receptive, and it was decided that Northeastern Pennsylvania would beta-test the channel. HBO hooked people by advertising that it would show movies uncut and uninterrupted by commercials, and I was lucky enough to be exposed to the very early days of HBO.

HBO would put anything on to get people to watch.

The service was on the air nine hours a day, and in that nine hours I got to watch *The Poseidon Adventure* (1972) and *White Lightning* (1973) with my mom and dad. But after a while my parents would get bored watching movies and they would go and do other things. They never expected me to turn the channel back on when they weren't around.

So, I watched *Dirty Mary, Crazy Larry* (1974), *The Life and Times of Judge Roy Bean* (1972), *The Seven-Ups* (1973), *The Getaway* (1972), and *The Stone Killer* (1973).

Blood! Bullets! Cursing! Women in tight, tight T-shirts! I was hooked.

For long stretches of the day, I was unsupervised. Television was a babysitter that kept me out of sight and out of mind, as with most kids of my generation.

Also, at that time my parents were in the process of getting a divorce, so I was not the center of attention.

I didn't know exactly what was happening, but the tension in the house was palpable and I knew something was wrong. Something terrible. I would hear the arguments, and I was anxious a lot and didn't sleep well.

I became obsessed with sitting in front of the TV. I watched Home Box Office to keep myself busy and lose myself in the movies.

Then just when the anxiety of real life got to be too much, I got my First Kiss.

My First Kiss

My First Kiss was Nicolas Roeg's *Don't Look Now* (1973). It starred Donald Sutherland and Julie Christie as a husband and wife who suffer a tragedy that leads them to the supernatural.

Nicolas Roeg isn't a director that springs to mind for most horror fans. I find it humorous that of all the legendary horror movies I have seen, Nicolas Roeg's *Don't Look Now* was the one to change my life and begin my lifelong obsession with horror movies.

Nicholas Roeg was at his most popular in the '70s, and he's considered a cult figure with art-film aesthetics. He started as a cameraman, and his movies are celebrated for their foreboding atmosphere—that he created using unusual, and often disturbing, visual imagery and a non-linear narrative.

His movies were like anxiety-filled puzzles that typically didn't come into full focus until the final shots.

As a child, *images* in movies connected with me more than plot or narrative. And I think it was the way Roeg visually told his story that hit me so hard that day.

Don't Look Now wasn't like any movie I had ever seen. There was no music in the background to tell me what to feel and this movie didn't have that bright stage lighting that my dad's favorite '50s monster movies did.

In fact, it didn't look like a movie at all. It looked *real.*

I only saw the first 10 minutes of the movie that day. But every second of it, and how I felt while I watched it, is burned into my memory.

Don't Look Now

The first shot opens on the English countryside. A little girl in a red raincoat plays with a wheelbarrow. She pushes it around the field. She's all alone, and we don't know where she is.

It turns out that she's out playing on the land of a large English home that sits on a small hill. It's wet and wintery, and everything is a little misty.

Then we cut to a shot of a boy who is slightly older than her. He rides his bicycle around some trees on the property. He must be her brother.

Then we see the girl walking alone carrying a little talking doll. Nicolas Roeg shoots this image so that the sun goes into the camera lens, making the girl a shadowy figure. The camera sits low to the ground. She's distorted. Twigs and weeds obscure her. The camera shakes a little.

I didn't know why, but I started to get nervous. The little girl walks towards a red ball in the foreground. She picks it up and throws it. The ball lands in a nearby pond. She walks out onto a small embankment to get the ball. She leans over, stretching out her arm, trying to reach the ball. She leans over so far that all we can see is the back of her red raincoat. The only sound is the birds in the trees.

We cut to the boy on the bicycle. He's oblivious to everything, speeding around the trees.

We cut back to the girl, still reaching out. We see the house in the background. She seems so far away from it. The camera pans down to the water and the girl is reflected in it.

The scene cuts to inside the house. It is very quiet. The only sound is the crackle of the fireplace. The girl's mother and father are in the den. The mother, played by Julie Christie, reads a book. The father, played by Donald Sutherland, looks at slides of the interior of a Gothic church with a large stained-glass window over the altar.

Something in one of the slides catches his eye. The picture itself is rather ominous. It's shot at a low angle, from the floor of the church, to capture the entire stained-glass window. Because of the angle, the pews are distorted in size. They look menacing and shadowy.

In one of the pews sits a figure in a red hooded raincoat. We can only see the back of the hood, and the figure is hunched forward.

He takes the slide out of the projector and puts it on a lightbox under a magnifier to get a closer look. Under magnification, the image distorts even more. The only sound we hear is the whirring fan on the slide projector.

I'm taking this in, and I'm frightened. And I don't know why.

We cut back outside. We see the upside-down reflection of the girl in the mirrored surface of the pond. She walks on the bank of the pond with the red ball in her hand. She starts to run. The camera tries to keep up with her reflection. The shot makes me a little dizzy.

We cut to the boy on his bicycle. He speeds up as he passes by.

There's a quick cut to the girl's red boot stomping through a big puddle. At the same moment, the boy runs over a pane of glass hidden in the grass, and he falls off his bike.

As soon as he falls, we cut to inside the house. The father jerks his head up from the slide he has been studying, as if he has just heard something.

At this point, Roeg cuts to a shot of a cigarette burning in an ashtray sitting right next to dirty dishes and unfinished food on the dinner table. The camera stays on that shot for a long time—too long.

Why are we looking at this? What is happening to the kids?

Instead of letting us see what's happening to the kids, we cut to the mother searching for her cigarettes. She looks under the pillows and cushions on the couch. There is no time for this, I think to myself, and I'm barely breathing while I watch.

We finally cut back outside, and we see the boy checking the tires on his bicycle for a leak. He looks back and sees his sister standing at the edge of the pond; she seems very far away. He cuts his finger on the glass that's embedded in the tire.

We cut back into the house and the father is reaching over the lightbox to fetch the cigarettes his wife is looking for. He tosses them into her hands. At the same moment, there's a quick cut to the little girl at the edge of the pond, throwing her red ball into the water.

As the ball hits the water, there's a cut to the father knocking a glass of water onto the slide that's on the lightbox. He rushes over with a towel and tries to dry it.

We cut to a shot of the ball in the pond, spinning silently.

We cut back to the father. He looks under the magnifier to see if the slide has been damaged by the water. We look at the slide through the magnifier, and what we see makes my throat clamp up.

The head of the red hooded figure begins to distort. A red tendril begins to stretch out of it towards the stained glass, like a ghostly finger. Or a demonic soul. It is blood—red and black—and as it spreads, it grows.

What we are literally seeing is the emulsion disintegrating on the slide because of the moisture. But what I am seeing, what I am feeling in my heart, is that I am watching something evil being born. Something horrible has been set free.

The father suddenly looks up, horrified. It's as if he's feeling what I'm feeling. Something is wrong. He walks silently out of the room towards the door. He's so quiet that his wife doesn't notice him leave.

What happens next, happens quickly.

We see a shot of the boy running fast towards the house. There's no sound. The father runs outside towards him.

We cut to a slow motion shot of the girl in the pond, sinking under the water, face up, eyes closed. We see her face disappearing into the darkness below as she sinks deeper. The last thing to disappear is the red of her raincoat.

The boy runs towards the house yelling, "Dad! Dad!" The boy slips and falls. The father runs down the hill and his body compresses at the impact of hitting the uneven land. He's falling forward more than he's running, and he is pale and terrified. Like he already knows.

When he gets to the pond, he sees the red ball floating all alone. He staggers into the water and pushes himself to where his daughter sank. The boy watches from the shore, blood on his fingers, a shard of glass in his hands. The father takes a horrified breath and dives under the water.

Inside the house, the mother looks at the ruined slide. The hooded figure is completely gone; there is only the expanding red blob.

While we look at the slide, there is this unholy whooshing sound, like thunder in reverse. And there is the loud, deep strain of cellos, music that sounds like pure evil. The red tendril explodes into life, growing, moving as if it's alive, circling the stained glass.

This was pure evil, and it was loose in God's house—where you're supposed to be safe and protected. And the evil was growing.

The next shot is the one that truly terrified me. This was the moment of my First Kiss.

Nicolas Roeg knew this shot had to be terrifying, and he made sure it was. He shot the pond in the dark, with a bright light on Donald Sutherland as he rises out from under the water with his dead daughter in his arms. This made everything else outside of the father and daughter fall off into a darkness that you *feel* as much as you see. He shot it in slow motion, and the bright light makes the water spray look like shards of glass. It has all the qualities of my real nightmares.

Donald Sutherland's hair is matted over his face. You can only see the open "O" of his mouth as he lets out a moan so terrible that it makes me cover my ears. This is sheer grief in horrible slow motion.

Then Julie Christie comes out of the house. She doesn't know what has happened. She turns the corner of the house, and then she looks directly into the camera and lets out a deafening scream.

The Important Lesson Learned from My First Kiss

I sit cross-legged in front of the TV, frozen in place. I realize I have stopped breathing, and when I gulp in some air, I start to tremble. I'm alone in the room and that terrifies me. It's as if Donald Sutherland's moan and Julie Christie's scream have coated the walls and I'm surrounded by them.

I go outside, but no matter where I go in my backyard, I can't shake off the horrible sounds that those parents made in the movie. The green grass around me reminds me of the drowned girl. I'm afraid to look at the tree in the corner of the yard because I might see a body in a red raincoat slumped underneath it. It is midafternoon, and I don't know why I'm so scared in broad daylight.

At night, the images visit me. My father tells me he wakes me from nightmares where I'm crying out, "She's dead, she's dead!"

Why did *Don't Look Now* affect me so much? The emotions and situations being shown were adult themed. Nicolas Roeg did his job well, and I just caught everything he wanted to convey.

But that wasn't really what got me. I had watched a family get destroyed, just like mine. I realized that I wasn't scared because the little girl died. I was scared because I was watching a mother and a father, two adults, fall completely apart. I saw my parents in the movie's parents. The father and the mother couldn't stop it from happening; they were powerless. Even when they felt safe, even when they were supposed to be protected, evil could wrap its tendrils around their lives and smother them.

My world was coming apart. I had no idea what would happen to me if there was no more family, if my mother or father went away forever. I was helpless against whatever fate my parents chose for me. And because of that, I was scared all the time.

But I wasn't helpless when I watched a scary movie. I could feel the fear, I could even scream out loud, and that would be okay. In a time when I feared everything, this was one fear I could control.

Don't Look Now scared me. But I got over it. I felt myself get over it. I felt a relief and I felt a strength. It felt like I had conquered something, that I came out alive. And I realized that I liked getting scared that way.

I had just had my First Kiss, and I couldn't wait to get my second one.

FIVE ACCLAIMED DIRECTORS WHO DIRECTED A GREAT HORROR FILM

Nicolas Roeg is critically praised for dramas like *Performance* (1970), *Walkabout* (1971), and *Bad Timing* (1980). He also made the horror film *Don't Look Now* (1973). He's not the only acclaimed director who has a great horror movie on his resume. Here are five others:

1. Robert Wise (*West Side Story, The Sound of Music*) – *The Haunting* (1963)

2. William Friedkin (*The French Connection*) – *The Exorcist* (1973)

3. Stanley Kubrick (*2001: A Space Odyssey, Paths of Glory*) – *The Shining* (1980)

4. Jonathan Demme (*Philadelphia, Melvin and Howard*) – *Silence of the Lambs* (1991)

5. Danny Boyle (*Trainspotting, Slumdog Millionaire*) – *28 Days Later* (2002)

CHAPTER TWO

WE BOND OVER POPCORN:
WATCHING HORROR
WITH AN AUDIENCE

Nothing brings a group of strangers together better than a little hysteria. There's something freeing about being in a crowd that bonds through uncontrollable emotional outbursts that defy logic. Support can be beautiful.

A movie theater brings people from all kinds of backgrounds together and gives them a shared experience. A movie can cut through all the superficial differences and find an emotional core that unifies them.

Art allows groups of people who are angry, frustrated, or scared to feel represented and to feel heard. Sometimes art gives us what we need, even when we had no idea we needed it.

Communion at the Church of Cinema Will Save your Soul

All of us, even the most introverted, have a deep-seated need to belong, to be part of a like-minded community. There's a story out there somewhere that will connect you with your tribe.

Your "First Kiss" was an intimate and personal event that turned you into a horror fan. But the experience isn't entirely personal. It's also communal.

We can stream any movie we want from the comfort of our couches, and we can even watch them on our cell phones. But something special happens when we're part of a live audience and that can't happen if we're home alone. When you go to a movie theater, you can be part of history when a movie legend is born.

The original *Star Wars* (1977) was released in only 32 theaters on May 25, 1977. But there was also a test screening for the general public on May 1.

That screening was at the tiny Northpoint Theater in San Francisco's Fisherman's Wharf. It was the last chance for the movie to prove it could find an audience. Fox executives didn't understand *Star Wars*, and they didn't know how to market it.

What do you think it was like to be in that audience?

Sometimes a movie strikes a nerve or taps into the mood of the culture at just the right time. The audience then goes from serving as spectators to acting as part of the experience.

The screen disappears. The sticky floor melts away. The audience forgets they're watching a movie. Everyone gets caught up in the energy. Inhibitions disappear. It gets loud and boisterous.

The first horror movie I saw in a cinema as a kid was a Vincent Price movie called *Theatre of Blood* (1973). The plot revolves around Price as a washed-up Shakespearean actor who is mocked by film critics at a prestigious award ceremony. Despondent, he commits suicide by jumping from a skyscraper into the Thames. Two years later, however, he reappears and starts to murder the critics in poetic ways taken straight from Shakespeare's plays.

I watched movies in my house with the lights on, but I watched *Theater of Blood* in the dark, in unfamiliar surroundings, surrounded by strangers. The movie screen was huge, and so were Vincent Price's eyes. *Theatre of Blood* was a campy horror film but, at eight years old, it still scared me.

There's a scene in the film where Price sneaks into the bedroom of one of his critics. He's dressed like a surgeon, and he's flanked by a crazy assistant who carries a tray full of surgical instruments. Price drugs both of the people in the bed. Then he pulls out a tube of red lipstick and draws a dotted line on the critic's neck.

And then he pulls out a scalpel.

I'm horrified because, in my child's mind, someone sneaking into your room and cutting off your head was a distinct possibility.

And then, right when I'm about to completely freak out, something amazing happens. All of the adults in the movie theater start laughing. When Vincent Price starts to cut his victim's throat, the blood spurts straight up, like a fountain. His assistant panics and tries catching the blood in a nearby chamber pot. Price rolls his eyes. There's so much blood that it becomes absurd.

If it was just me watching that scene alone, I would never have seen the comedy and I would have been terrified. But when everyone else started laughing, I suddenly felt safe and I began to relax. The spell was broken.

Nonetheless, I made sure my covers were tucked firmly under my chin when I went to bed that night.

If you're in a crowded movie theater, the audience can influence how you react to a film. When a film gives an audience precisely what it didn't know it needed, it's a religious experience. We laugh as one, and we cry as one, and we cheer as one.

We know it's just a movie. But we suspend our disbelief because *we want to believe miracles are still possible.* Belief is powerful magic, and from the beginning, cinema tapped into our desire to witness a miracle. If you're in the audience when a movie legend is born, it's no longer a screening. It's a church revival.

The Magic of Movies Is Powerful, and Unpredictable

In 1895, the Lumiere Brothers premiered their silent film, *Arrival of a Train at La Ciotat Station.* It's nothing more than a train coming into the station, but the audience thought there was an actual train coming at them and people ran out of the theater.

You might think that kind of extreme response to a movie could only happen when the motion picture was a brand new technology, right?

Not so fast.

The Blackboard Jungle (1955) was the first film to have a rock-and-roll soundtrack. Bill Haley and the Comets' "Rock Around the Clock" played over the opening credits, and teenagers went crazy and danced in the aisles, and tore the bolted seats out of the floor.

Almost eighty years after *Arrival of a Train at La Ciotat Station,* the Lumiere Brothers' silent film, *The Exorcist* (1973) was released. People fainted or ran from the theater, and some claimed to have been possessed. *The Journal of Nervous and Mental Disease* discussed *The Exorcist's* possible role in triggering mental illness.

In his book, *American Exorcism: Expelling Demons in the Land of Plenty*, sociologist Michael Cuneo chronicles how Catholic priests were inundated with claims of possession from their parishioners.

Both *The Blackboard Jungle* and *The Exorcist* tapped into the anxieties that simmered just below the surface at the times when they were made. *The Blackboard Jungle* gave an outlet to the smoldering teenage rebellion of the '50s, and *The Exorcist* tapped into the fear of revered institutions collapsing in the early '70s.

How *Saint Rocky* Delivered Us from the Era of the Bummer Endings

Sometimes a movie connects so strongly with the audience that it becomes part of popular culture.

I saw the original *Rocky* (1976) in the theater when it first came out.

Rocky was a small, low budget, independent film about a down-and-out boxer in down-and-out Philadelphia. Rocky Balboa is a simple man who believes in loyalty, and he keeps his dream of being a heavyweight champion alive, even when the only person interested in his fighting skills is the local mobster who needs a debt collector.

Balboa gets an unexpected shot at the heavyweight title when the reigning champion, Apollo Creed, needs a last-minute opponent for his highly publicized fight. Creed decides to give a local contender a chance at glory, and he picks Rocky because he likes the sound of his nickname: "The Italian Stallion." Even though nobody, not even his friends, thinks he has a chance, Rocky is compelled to take the challenge. He doesn't expect to win; all he wants to do is prove to everyone, including himself, that he can go the distance.

The movie played in the tiniest theater in my town. That night it played to a packed house of blue-collar families. We had no idea what was about to happen.

Before I tell you what happened to that crowd of blue-collar families at the cinema on that fateful night, I want to give some context to what it was like going to the movies in the 1970s, right before *Rocky* was released.

It was the second Golden Age of Hollywood Cinema, with movies like *M.A.S.H.* (1970), *The French Connection* (1971), *The Godfather* (1972), *The Exorcist* (1973), and *Taxi Driver* (1976) revolutionizing movie storytelling. However, it was also the age of the Bummer Ending.

It felt like every movie that came out was bleak, and the endings were all downers. Movies would routinely end without a tidy resolution, or they would end suddenly with everyone dying.

A great example of this was *Dirty Mary, Crazy Larry* (1974), a counterculture car-chase movie where a fun-loving NASCAR driver, his mechanic, and his girlfriend stick up a supermarket to fund their racing habit. The heist sets up a car chase that lasts for the entire duration of the film. The happy-go-lucky trio race dozens of goofy police officers to the state line, and there are plenty of car crashes where the only things that get bruised are the egos of the patrolmen.

It's all fun and games until literally the last minute of the film. Dirty Mary, Crazy Larry, and Larry's mechanic have escaped the clutches of the tenacious sheriff's pursuit, and it looks like they are driving off into the sunset. One of the characters actually says, "Nothing can stop us now!"

Suddenly, their car is hit by a freight train that comes out of nowhere. The car bursts into flames and they are killed instantly. Roll the credits.

In the 1970s, it was common to go to a movie where, towards the end of the film, somebody in the audience would yell, "That better not be the end!"

And it would be the end. The whole audience would groan and boo. It was relentless. It was a sign of the times.

Rocky was different. The fight happens in the last quarter of the film. The first three quarters of the film exposes us to a world of bleakness and cynicism. And yet, Rocky remains hopeful. When nobody believes he has any worth, Rocky still dreams and he still tries.

Even as a kid, I felt the emotion building—as if the theater was a pressure cooker. We love Rocky, but we're afraid to hope. We're waiting for Apollo Creed to knock him out. We're waiting for Rocky to suffer a heart attack or an aneurism. We are nervous. We are invested.

All this tension and dread sets up one of the purest and most amazing experiences I've ever had watching a film.

At the beginning of the fight, Rocky gets the stuffing knocked out of him. The match is a promotional exhibition for the arrogant Apollo Creed. The plan all along is for him to pummel Rocky into the ground.

We hear the incessant snap of boxing gloves, the crowd, the announcers… and Rocky's wounded grunts.

Then Rocky knocks Apollo Creed down!

That bell starts to ring on the soundtrack and we hear the Rocky theme music, a wall of blaring trumpets that emit a sound that seems to pull everyone upward by their breastbone. The emotion that has built up in the theater, all the tension and the cock-eyed hope, explodes! The entire audience jumps out of their seats as if they've been electrocuted, and we all cheer at the same time!

As the fight goes on, we stay on our feet. We lean forward and yell at the screen! We feel every hit Rocky takes; we shout for him to get back up before the 10-count finishes. We are Rocky, and Rocky is us!

After the movie ends, everyone still cheers and claps. It doesn't even matter that Rocky has lost. If we had the chance, we'd be back tomorrow to watch Rocky lose again.

The Emotional Contract Between Audience and Filmmaker

I had never seen grown men cry over a movie until I saw *Rocky*. The adults were so elated that after the film they ran down the street like kids! I'd seen an entire audience *laugh* at movies before, but laughing is like a reflex. You're surprised, and then you laugh. But in this case, the audience chose to clap and cheer for 10 minutes after the movie ended.

People allowed themselves to be vulnerable. They let their defenses down and allowed the story in, and they let the magic charge them. Sounds like a spiritual experience, doesn't it?

When that rare movie moment happens, the audience enters into a contract with the filmmaker, even if they don't know it. They say, "I'll allow myself to be vulnerable; I'm going to trust you, and if my trust is rewarded, you'll be rewarded...."

Of course, we're talking about a feel-good movie like Rocky. What about making that same contract for a horror movie—where, by the nature of horror movies, trust is a shaky proposition? Now we're talking high stakes!

The Art of Horrible/Beautiful

Good horror movies scare you, but great horror movies leave you awestruck. When a horror movie reaches a palpable level of awe, I call it "horrible/beautiful."

When an image is horrible/beautiful, it is disturbing, brutal, even repulsive, but it also taps into something that makes you keep looking. Maybe you look in disbelief. Maybe you look out of morbid fascination. Perhaps what you see is so rare and so unusual that it has a weird beauty.

A great example of horrible/beautiful is a scene from *Alien* (1979). Not only is the scene itself full of images that inspire awe, but we see a character in the throes of a horrible/beautiful moment.

Harry Dean Stanton, playing Brett, is looking for Jonesy, the ship's cat. We see something he doesn't. We see the fully-grown xenomorph creature curled up on dangling chains behind Brett. The phallic, exoskeleton head uncurls from its body in one smooth, organic twist. It is wet, and fluid drips out of its mouth. We can almost smell the humidity of the body. Brett senses something, and he turns to see the alien beast tower above him. Brett doesn't run or scream; he can only stare.

Because he mirrors our own response, we are also transfixed, taking in every detail. There is a moment of placidity before the alien strikes and splits his face open.

That is horrible/beautiful.

The Religious Experience of *Jaws*

Jaws (1975) is one of the few horror movies I can think of where the first 30 minutes is back-to-back iconic horrible/beautiful sequences. Even if director Steven Spielberg had messed up the rest of the movie, the opening scene would still rank with the greatest sequences in film history.

I went to see *Jaws* with a friend of mine without my parents' permission. Because of the movie's reputation and a poster that stated "MAY BE TOO INTENSE FOR YOUNGER CHILDREN," we were scared before the film started. In fact, when seaweed brushed up against the camera, everybody in the audience jumped.

The contract was signed.

The terrifying death of Chrissy, the first victim, is horror at its most primal. The attack happens at dusk. The sun quickly sets behind Chrissy and darkness grows as she pulls off her clothes and goes for a swim. A teenage boy tries to follow her, but he's too drunk to get his pants off, and he passes out on the beach. The only sound is the ocean as she swims out further from the shore. She looks so alone.

And then, she gets tugged down, just a little, just like a bobber when a fish nibbles. But the look on her face! She's trying to register what's happening. She gets tugged down again, and she starts to panic.

Then all hell breaks loose. She's dragged across the surface of the water, screaming. She grabs hold of a nearby buoy and whimpers The Lord's Prayer. The beast pulls her away from the buoy, and she cries, and she pleads with God. Then she disappears under the water.

Silence.

We never even see a fin.

At that moment, Spielberg introduces a beast that is very real—in a way that evokes every monster we've ever imagined. We know sharks exist. But by not showing the shark, he makes it an archetype of primal horror. He makes the entire ocean the dark closet, or the basement, or the space under the bed that holds our boogeyman.

But it's the death of the Kitner boy that is genuinely horrible/beautiful. It takes place in broad daylight. Crowds of people surround the boy while he floats on an inflatable raft. He's barely in the water.

The initial attack is stunning. We see it from a long shot, and…we're not quite sure what we observe. We get an almost surreal image, brief and silent, of what looks like two pectoral fins in a belly roll with the boy and the twisting raft in the center. The kids right next to him in the water don't even notice when it happens. Somebody on shore does.

"Did you see that?" the man on the beach asks in a flat voice.

I don't know how many times I've rewound and freeze-framed that sequence over the years, trying to see how it was done and what it shows—but it's a lot of times. A gout of blood spews from the Kitner boy and shoots out of the water. I can still see the nearby football floating in the blood.

How Spielberg got away with the shot of the boy flailing and the blood spewing up like a fountain is beyond me. That shot of blood and bubbles means the kid's torso and chest cavity has ripped open. That air is *coming from inside his body.*

My friend and I watch bug-eyed as we see a shot of the boy underwater, screaming, drowning, bleeding, devoured. Someone runs up the aisle of the movie theater and into the lobby. Horrible/beautiful isn't for everyone.

While we are still in shock, there's another punch. We see an attack in an estuary. It's not even the ocean; it's tamed marina water where they let little kids and old people go. It's where kids are taught to swim and dive.

We see a fin. We see Sean Brody, the son of the main character, swimming with his friends. Between the boys and the approaching fin is a man in a small boat. The boat is capsized by the shark, which is still only a dorsal fin on the surface, and the guy tries to swim back to his boat.

The camera moves to an aerial view. We see the man swimming, and we can see the shadow of his legs kicking under water. We see a big, silent, graceful, grey-and-white shape right below the water. We see just enough definition to realize this shape has a mouth. That mouth closes around the man's leg, and he gets pulled under the water.

When the man's severed leg hits the ocean floor, my friend jerked his head back in fright—so violently that his glasses flew off.

However, it wasn't the horrible/beautiful moments in the film alone that made *Jaws* the premiere religious experience for the Summer of 1975. It was because Spielberg gave us an ending that allowed all of us to release the tension we built up.

The end of the movie is absurd. The shark gets blown up by an air tank lodged in its mouth. But it's the *perfect* end. We needed the explosion to give us release. The ridiculous ending wouldn't have worked if the intensity and horrors weren't as strong as they were.

Just like *Rocky* would do the next year, Spielberg rang the bell. He honored the contract with the audience, and the reward was a record-breaking summer of return visits to *Jaws*. People still went to the beach, but they didn't go in the water. *I* sure didn't.

I don't think anyone went to see *Jaws* for the ending. But that ending made it safe even for non-horror fans to see it. There was a resolution; the tension they felt would stay behind in the theater seat.

As scared as we were watching *Jaws* in the theater, we knew something special was happening with this film. We collectively screamed, and then we collectively laughed at how scared we had been. We weren't alone in the water like Chrissy, the shark's first victim. We were all in it together, getting legitimately scared was a community event.

The Sacrilegious Experience of John Carpenter's *The Thing* (1982)

There are plenty of movies that audiences hate, and usually people forget those films. But sometimes the audience goes in expecting a religious experience and instead they get something else entirely. It can be an uncomfortable and visceral experience when an audience loses *faith* in the movie they're watching. It becomes a *sacrilegious* experience.

That's precisely what happened on June 25, 1982, the opening day for the eagerly-anticipated premiere of John Carpenter's *The Thing*.

The story takes place at an isolated US research base in Antarctica on the cusp of another ruthless winter. The 12 men of Outpost 31 are a little stir crazy from tedium and they are bored with each other's company. Their ennui is disrupted when a helicopter from a Norwegian research camp located several miles away enters their air space shooting rifles and dropping live hand grenades. Their target seems to be a lone Siberian Husky that then escapes into Outpost 31.

During the violent chaos and the lack of a common language, the Norwegian helicopter pilot and his armed passenger are killed by the Americans shooting in self-defense. Clark, the Outpost's kennel master, takes the orphaned Husky and adds the dog to their sled team.

The Americans can only speculate that these Norwegian researchers went stir crazy, and Dr. Copper convinces the American helicopter pilot, MacCready, to fly out to the Norwegian base so they can see if anyone there needs medical attention.

Copper and MacCready arrive too late to help anyone. The Norwegian camp is a smoldering ruin. The men stumble upon the body of someone who committed suicide by slashing his wrists and throat, and they find what looks like a funeral pyre with burned human remains in it.

They discover videotapes revealing that the scientists had found a large circular object trapped underneath the ice. They also discover a massive block of ice that looks like it had once had something encased inside of it.

MacCready and Copper return to the outpost with the videotapes, and also one of the burned bodies so they can do an autopsy.

I now consider this movie a masterpiece. To me, it is the personification of *horrible/beautiful*. I put it on the same level as *Jaws* as a perfect horror film. And I'm not alone—you'll find *The Thing* on most critics' 10 Best Horror Films list.

At least, it's on those critics' lists *now*. It sure as hell wasn't in 1982.

Why was *Jaws* allowed to push the limits of onscreen violence and gore in a PG-rated film and be celebrated, whereas *The Thing* was considered *pornographic* even though it was rated R, which gave audiences advanced warning that there would be violence not suitable for people under the age of 17?

As with most things, there are probably multiple reasons why *The Thing* was trashed and why director John Carpenter had his promising career severely damaged.

I went to see *The Thing* on Opening Day with my dad.

By 1982, my dad and I had a strained relationship. We were two different people and we rarely seemed to agree on anything anymore, but we both loved John Carpenter movies.

My dad loved John Wayne movies and Westerns, whereas I was more of a Steve McQueen guy, and I preferred movies like Sam Peckinpah's *The Getaway* (1972). As it turned out, Carpenter's *Assault on Precinct 13* (1974) was a perfect hybrid between those two types of films.

That was the appeal of Carpenter's early work. His films, at the time, were a bridge between two different generations of movie fans. I liked him because he was imaginative and his movies had cool ideas and cooler antiheroes. My dad liked him because he thought Carpenter had "class" and "style."

"Class" meant that Carpenter's movies had the same kind of moral core that Westerns had. They featured plain-spoken people who might be reluctant heroes, but they still did the right thing in the end. To my dad, "style" meant that the movies were violent, but not too violent. People swore, but they weren't bucket-mouths.

My dad loved *Halloween* (1978), John Carpenter's breakout low-budget hit about a masked killer stalking teenagers, and *The Fog* (1980), an old-fashioned ghost story. He thought *Escape From New York* (1981), a dystopian action film that cast the island of Manhattan as a maximum security prison, was "okay" but he didn't like the ending. Nevertheless, John Carpenter was his favorite "modern director."

My dad's favorite horror movie of all time was the Howard Hawks/Christian Nyby classic, *The Thing from Another World* (1951), and John Carpenter's *The Thing* was actually a remake of that film. My dad was almost as excited as I was to see what Carpenter would do with his remake of *The Thing from Another World*. We knew the director was a fan of the original film because he paid homage to it in *Halloween* with a scene that showed characters watching the movie on TV. The combination of Carpenter and *The Thing* seemed to be a slam-dunk.

I'm sure my father wasn't the only one in the theater whose favorite film was the 1951 version of *The Thing*. Fathers and sons ready to bond over this movie made up most of the audience. The place buzzed before the lights went down.

My dad and a whole bunch of other dads signed the contract with John Carpenter before they got into the theater parking lot. They trusted him with their favorite movie.

The lights went down and the movie began. An alien spacecraft hurtles towards Earth, and the movie recreates the iconic burning title from the original film. I sense the excitement in the theater. My dad sits so straight in his seat he seems 10 feet tall. I'm getting chills.

But the excitement is short lived.

The uneasiness starts small, but you can feel it. The first problem is that the movie is set in a military outpost in Antarctica, but the guys stationed there are unshaven and long-haired. In the Hawks version, the Air Force personnel are solid, clean-cut professionals who work together. The guys in Carpenter's version are lazy whiners by comparison.

Then comes Dr. Copper, a middle-aged man who wears an earring and a nose ring. On a 50-foot movie screen, the nose ring is the size of a bowling ball; you can't miss it. These might have been an expression of Copper's rebelliousness, but an earring and a nose ring meant something else entirely to my dad's generation. I hear my dad sigh, and I suddenly feel embarrassed to look at the character on the screen.

Then comes the first death from the opening sequence, where one of the crazed Norwegian researchers is shot dead by the commanding officer of Outpost 31. The death is clean and fast, but then there's a cut to the dead body on a slab. There's a lingering shot of the man with his eye shot out.

The audience lets out a collective "Ewww."

Seconds after, there's a close-up of Dr. Copper sewing up a leg wound on one of the American scientists. Dads all around the theater start to grumble.

And it wasn't just the dads. It was the kids too.

By the time the movie was over, I was in a state somewhere between shock and awe. That was saying something, because I was already a jaded horror junkie by the time I saw *The Thing*.

I'd seen the chest-burster scene in *Alien*, I'd seen John Cassavetes explode in

Brian DePalma's *The Fury* (1978*)*, I saw the werewolf transformations in *The Howling* (1981), and I saw a guy get his nose cut off in *The Sentinel* (1977).

And I saw *Suspiria* (1977). I was no cream puff.

But the effects in John Carpenter's *The Thing* were next-level shit. I still believe that special effects artist Rob Bottin's creature makeup and cinematographer Dean Cundey's creepy lighting has never been surpassed on film. It's not gore; it transcends gore.

By 1982, elaborate special makeup effects had become a standard in horror films, but the focus was on making the effects as graphic and realistic as possible. They may have reveled in gallons of blood, but the effects artists were still tethered to the laws of physics and human physiology. On the set of *The Thing*, Rob Bottin was not.

The creature in the script was not only a shape-shifting alien that could make an exact replica of anything it consumed; it was also composed of separate shape-shifting entities *at a cellular level*. The Thing's true form and mass was unknown. If you cut the creature in two, you now had two monsters to deal with. When The Thing was under attack, its camouflage would break down, and it would explode into a swirling mass of every species it ever assimilated—sometimes all at once—to defend itself.

There had been horror movies with bigger body counts, with more severed body parts, and much more red blood splattering the screen, but none of them were as disturbing as *The Thing* was when it premiered.

I think the reason *The Thing's* effects were so revolting and so unsettling was that other horror films showed the gruesome things that could happen to the human body, but *The Thing* showed you stuff happening to bodies that shouldn't be able to happen—things that were impossible.

Other horror films showed you the desecration of the human body. *The*

Thing showed you the abomination of it. The violence in this film defied physics and dove into the realm of the surreal.

Heads split open and shoot out whip-like tendrils. Instead of familiar red blood, bodies tear apart to reveal sickening yellow and green fluid squirting out of stretched tendons and arteries. Viscous, unidentifiable bodily fluids splash the walls and ceilings. Tongues sprout canine teeth. The violence to the body doesn't stop until the body is burned into ash. It's a vision of hell as a biological event.

This stuff slithered into nightmarish Hieronymus Bosch territory. This was an evolutionary jump in horror. This was genre-changing. And it took balls.

We weren't ready for it.

The tipping point happens when, in one scene, a dog's head splits open like a blooming flower to reveal a rapidly expanding creature made up of a glistening mass of tentacles, crab legs, dog parts, raw meat, and sinew. Eyeballs sprout out of the ruined flesh.

People shouted out, revolted. Hostile energy filled the room. It was amazing and scary. Some people walked out, but most stayed, holding out hope that something, anything would happen to rectify the horror.

That hope ended when the character Norris appears to suffer a heart attack and collapses. The team rushes him to the medical ward and puts him on the examination table. Dr. Copper tries to restart Norris' heart with defibrillation while MacCready and the others watch with concern.

When Dr. Copper brings the charged paddles down on Norris' bare chest, his hands rip through the man's flesh as if it were made out of rice paper. Norris is ripped open from sternum to navel, leaving a vagina-shaped hole devoid of internal organs, and air hisses into the body cavity. Copper's arms sink into the man up to his elbows, and then the ribcage forms into bony, jagged teeth. The wound snaps closed like a giant mouth and amputates the doctor's forearms in an instant. Copper screams in horror and agony, waving his stumps in the air before he collapses backward. This is the first and last red blood that we see, but it is just the beginning of the carnage.

All the men are in shock, and they stare as Norris' chest flaps open, and a mass of slimy yellowish tendrils whip out of the wound right before a green geyser of gooey matter shoots up to the ceiling. MacCready grabs a flamethrower and looks up. The ceiling is covered with hanging droplets of something the consistency of snot. A thick rope of sinew runs from Norris' shell to the ceiling where it is attached to a grotesque creature that is part crab, part spider, with a caterpillar-like neck. The creature has a vicious, bastardized version of Norris' head with jagged teeth. It growls at the men.

MacCready uses the flamethrower to set the creature and Norris' body on fire. The body on the table screeches, and the head starts to move independently away from the burning torso. Norris' mouth opens obscenely wide, the tongue flails, and his neck stretches until the skin tears and exposes what looks like a mass of green cords. They snap, and the head frees itself from the body, slides off the edge of the table, and lowers slowly to the floor.

When the head hits the floor, Norris' eyes open. His mouth also opens, and his tongue stretches into a long, thrashing flagella. It latches to a chair leg and slowly reels the head across the floor to hide under a desk. As MacCready and the others put out the fire, the head under the desk sprouts spindly, crablike legs and rises off the ground.

All of this happens within 90 seconds of screen time.

When I saw that scene, I got dizzy. I remember thinking, "I might be going into shock."

Any single moment of that sequence would be shocking, but one aberrant image after another was devastating. That scene broke the back of the audience. After that, they were quiet, really quiet.

After the movie, we shambled out in stunned silence. My dad didn't say anything. Like most of the audience, he was repulsed, and he erased the experience from his mind. We never talked about it.

We Either Bond Over Popcorn or We Riot Over Popcorn

John Carpenter's *The Thing* was marketed as one of Universal Studio's tentpole summer blockbusters for 1982, along with *Poltergeist* and *E.T. the Extra-Terrestrial*. *The Thing* cost an estimated 15 million dollars to make, and it only grossed 13 million dollars in its initial domestic theatrical release. To put that into perspective, *Poltergeist* had an estimated budget of 10.5 million dollars, and it made 76.6 million in its initial US run. *ET* also cost 10.5 million dollars to make and went on to gross *359 million* domestically.

The box office returns for *The Thing* were disappointing, but *The Thing* was also savaged by the critics. *New York Times* film critic Vincent Canby wrote, "It is too phony to be disgusting. It qualifies only as instant junk." Roger Ebert, the critic for the *Chicago Sun Times* called it "a great barf bag movie."

But the critical venom didn't come only from the mainstream critics. Influential genre magazines also denigrated the film. *Starlog Magazine* was an early champion of Carpenter and his films, but critic Alan Spencer wrote, "*The Thing* smells, and smells pretty bad. It has no pace, sloppy continuity, zero humor, bland characters, on top of being totally devoid of either warmth or humanity." Spencer didn't stop at criticizing the film; he had invectives for Carpenter himself. "Here's some things he'd be better suited to direct: traffic accidents, train wrecks, and public floggings."

Another influential genre magazine, *Cinefantastique*, ran a cover story on

The Thing. The title of the story was, "Is This the Most Hated Movie of All Time?"

Carpenter laid most of the blame for the failure of his film on a prevailing shift in the culture at the time, one that he hadn't anticipated. That cultural shift was typified by the success of Steven Spielberg's *E. T. the Extra-Terrestrial* (1982), which was released two weeks before *The Thing* and was a runaway hit.

In a 2008 interview with Joshua Rothkopf for *Time Out New York*, Carpenter said, "But 1982 was the summer of *E.T.* You don't realize what a big deal that was. Spielberg had this uncanny knack of knowing what the audience wanted. He thought they wanted a big cry, and he was absolutely right. We came out two weeks later."

I think the popularity of *E.T.* played a small piece in what happened to *The Thing*, but it's an oversimplification. I think Carpenter failed to fulfill the contract with the audience because he and the audience had different expectations.

The audience and the movie executives expected a reasonably faithful update of *The Thing* with a little more edginess, and that was a mistake. That assumption was a misreading of the ambitions and career choices Carpenter had already made.

After Carpenter changed the course of horror with *Halloween* (1978), he wasn't interested in making the sequels, despite the money he would probably have made. He refused to repeat what had already been done. Carpenter was going to use *The Thing*, his big Hollywood break, to alter the course of horror again by freeing us from the old rubber-suit monster and giving us one we'd never forget.

I'm sure Carpenter thought that's what everyone wanted: something unforgettable and game-changing. Maybe it would have worked if he hadn't decided to remake *The Thing*. He forgot that, unlike with *Jaws* or *Alien*, the audience already had an emotional history with the story of *The Thing*.

In my dad's mind, Carpenter squandered the goodwill that he built with all his previous films when he trashed a sacred memory from his childhood. Whether it was fair or not, the audience felt that Carpenter broke their trust. They were vulnerable, so the stakes were higher, and the anger was deeper.

One Person's Sacrilege Is Another Person's Religious Experience

The response to the movie was so strong and visceral that I couldn't get *The Thing* out of my head. A film that could generate that much hatred had power. It may have been offensive, but it was not an inept, sloppy, or boring movie. It was well-crafted and thought-provoking.

Carpenter's version of *The Thing* was too revolutionary, transgressive and surreal for mainstream cinema at that time. But once the shock wore off, many of us kids in the audience realized that it was special. While our parents insisted that they wanted a refund, us kids huddled together in the playground with a copy of Issue #21 of *Fangoria Magazine* because it had a pictorial section on the special effects from *The Thing*.

Everyone who showed up to the theater in 1982 helped birth the legend of *The Thing*. But some of us couldn't forget the movie. We carried the torch for it; we recommended it to people for decades. Eventually, the movie was reappraised by critics, and it is now considered one of the greatest horror films ever made. In 2007, the *Boston Globe* ranked it number one in the article "Top 50 Scariest Horror Movies of All Time," and also in 2007, C. Robert Cargill ranked *The Thing* as the fifth best movie released in 1982. Even though Roger Ebert dismissed the film as a "barf bag movie," Matt Zoler Seitz, the editor-in-chief of RogerEbert.com, wrote on the website in 2016, "[*The Thing*] is one of the greatest and most elegantly constructed

B-movies ever made, serious yet subtle in exploring themes of paranoia, mistrust, identity, and camaraderie, and aces at scaring the hell out of you. Carpenter is one of the great film stylists of the second half of the twentieth century."

In 2014, *The Thing* was ranked ninth in a *Rolling Stone* reader's poll for "The 10 Best Horror Movies of All Time." Another generation found the film and embraced it.

When I go to horror conventions, I talk to fans from different generations about their favorite films. There can be huge differences of opinion about many horror films, but the two movies that are almost always on their favorites list are *Jaws* and *The Thing*. For some of us, the sacrilegious experience is our religious experience too.

We are Rocky; Rocky is us. We are MacCready; MacCready is us. We bond over popcorn.

Or not.

FIVE NOTORIOUS SACRILEGIOUS HORROR MOVIE EXPERIENCES

It's probably no surprise that Horror has more than its fair share of movies that have outraged audiences. Here are five that found themselves in the halls of infamy:

1. *Rosemary's Baby* (1968): The Catholic League protested that the movie mocked their religious beliefs.

2. *The Texas Chain Saw Massacre* (1974): Its perceived violence got the film banned for 25 years in the UK, and it was banned twice for inciting riots in France.

3. *Cannibal Holocaust* (1980): The first "found footage" horror movie had real animal mutilation and fake human mutilation. However, the fake stuff looked real, and director Ruggero Deodato was brought up on murder charges until the actors turned up in court to prove they were alive.

4. *Silent Night, Deadly Night* (1984): A killer dressed like Santa with a release date during the Christmas season got the movie ads pulled.

5. *Irreversible* (2002): When the film premiered at Cannes, the graphic 10-minute rape sequence had 250 people walk out, and 20 people had to be given oxygen.

CHAPTER THREE
BIG BAD BOOKS:
HOW HORROR LITERATURE
CAN EMPOWER YOU

When I was eight years old, I stole *Alfred Hitchcock's Spellbinders in Suspense* from my elementary school library. It was a collection of classic mystery and suspense stories.

After flipping through the illustrations and stories, I decided I had to keep it forever. The illustrations by Harold Isen were the scariest drawings I had ever seen. They showed a man buried alive, a knife-wielding maniac standing atop a pile of victims, and a man being attacked by birds. My imagination put me in each of those predicaments, and I needed to read the stories to find out what happened.

I just walked out of the library with it when the bell rang.

It was the perfect crime.

That book allowed me to indulge in my darkest thoughts and emotions in total safety and privacy. I could personalize the monsters in a way I couldn't do with movies. Books have a way of letting you do that.

A good book can change your life if you read it at the right moment. There may be a story out there that relates to a struggle that you're going through, and that book may connect with you on a deeply personal level and bring some relief in a way that only art can.

When I stole the book, it was a dark period in my young life. My parents were on the verge of divorce, and I was trapped in a religion that believed the world was going to end within the next year. I could relate to stories where everything was falling apart, and if things got too scary in the story, I could close the book. I longed for that kind of control.

This book gave me monsters that sparked my imagination when I needed to get away from my life, and they could never hurt me.

Alfred Hitchcock's Spellbinders in Suspense (1967)

Yours Truly, Jack the Ripper (Robert Bloch)

Yours Truly suggests that Jack the Ripper is immortal, and all his victims are sacrifices to help keep him that way. The story takes place in modern day Chicago, and the protagonist is the only person who suspects that the Ripper may somehow still be plying his trade. Being a kid who lost a lot of friends by saying the world was coming to an end, I could relate to being the only person who sees the danger.

Man from the South (Roald Dahl)

An old man proposes a wager that a brash young man's lighter can't light 10 times in a row. If the lighter performs the task, the young man wins a Cadillac. If the lighter misses, the man chops off the young man's pinky.

The Man from the South has a collection of 47 fingers.

As a third-grader, I couldn't get the idea of a guy traveling with a suitcase full of fingers out of my head.

The Most Dangerous Game (Richard Connell)

A man hunts other men for sport with real guns and real death. I related to the theme of predator and prey because bullies were already a tangible threat in third grade. There was even a rich kid who got other people to bully for him.

When I realized I had been reading horrible stuff in view of everybody, I raised my head in guilt and looked around the room. Nobody was staring at me. The book hadn't drawn any attention. I realized reading a book allowed me to be naughty without anybody knowing. So, I stole the book and hid it in my room.

Sex and Violence Promote Healthy Reading Habits

The library is where they hide all the good stuff. Thanks to being brought up in a religion that believed the end of the world was nigh, a morbid curiosity and an attraction to the forbidden were natural rites of passage for me. Those alleged bad habits drew me to books, and I reaped the benefit of a lifetime of self-education.

Reading puts words right in your brain, unfiltered by anyone else's suggestions. The images you imagine while you read are yours alone. Those unconscious decisions, like whether the bad guy looks like the bully at school or your uncle, can be powerful.

Reading horror stories lets us experience emotions we normally wouldn't dare access. When we snuggle up with a novel about serial killers, we get to briefly acknowledge the shadow within us, and nobody gets hurt.

Books are also portable. You don't have to go to a movie theater or bring a laptop charger with you for a dose of primal scream. You can get the instant gratification of experiencing a brutal murder right there on your crowded commuter bus, or at your work desk.

I Prefer My Horror Double-Spaced

Horror movies may not be your thing. The intensity, the noise, and the expressionistic visual style might leave you cold. Horror *literature* is different. It moves at its own pace that delivers chills in a style that might be perfect for you.

Books allow you to form an image that works for you. You know exactly what scares you. That's also the bad news.

Perhaps you've watched a horror movie based on an acclaimed novel and you walked away hating the film and wondering why anyone thought that story was any good in the first place. You may have just found the perfect novel to read. It may be that the beauty of the story is in how it is told, and that may be a style that only a novel can accommodate.

A Tale of Two Stephen Kings

Some great novels never get read because everyone saw the lousy movie adaptation.

Perhaps no other popular novelist's work reveals the disparity between movie adaptations and novels better than that of Stephen King. Most of King's novels have a huge fan base, whereas the movie versions of his novels often disappoint.

Why are there so many bad Stephen King movie adaptations? Most of the movies are faithful to the plots of the book and they include the scary set pieces and the monsters.

But the truly engrossing elements of King's novels aren't plot points and monsters. What makes his books rich, gripping, and disturbing is the internal dialogue of the main characters. The scariest things happen inside the characters' heads.

King's novels are full of conflicted and unreliable narrators. Many times, their internal discussions tell us what the character doesn't want us to know. That's hard to capture on film.

Pet Sematary is the best example of this.

Pet Sematary (novel, 1983)

The movie *Pet Sematary* (1989) was a faithful adaptation of the novel, and it's one of the few that I appreciate. It includes all the big set pieces that were in the story, and Stephen King wrote the screenplay.

Yet I think it misses the dark stuff that makes *Pet Sematary* the most disturbing book King ever wrote. It's missing the dark heart of a man.

Louis Creed, the main character, is a doctor who has moved to rural Maine with his wife, Rachel, and their two young children, Ellie and Gage. Louis acts like a wholesome family man. But he secretly resents his wife, his daughter, and his in-laws, and the choices he has made in his life.

He blames his family for interfering with who he could have been. He did all the right things for all the wrong reasons, and he's only good because he feels he had no other choice.

Louis adores his son Gage, and he sees in Gage a younger version of himself.

He fantasizes about leaving his wife and daughter, and taking Gage with him to start a new life.

Then when tragedy takes his beloved son away from him, evil calls with a supernatural solution to his grief. When he succumbs to the temptation, the result is horrible, and he knows he is responsible.

Stephen King originally shelved the book because he and his wife, Tabitha, who is also a novelist, thought the book went too far.

In Lisa Rogak's book, *Haunted Heart: The Life and Times of Stephen King,* King expressed his feelings about *Pet Sematary.*

"That book *came out of a real hole in my psyche,"* he said. "If I had my way about it, I *still* would not have published *Pet Sematary.* I don't like it. It's a terrible book, not in terms of the writing, but it just spirals down into darkness. It seems to say that nothing works and nothing is worth it, and I don't really believe that."

However, King was embroiled in a legal battle with his former publisher, Doubleday, to remove a boilerplate clause in his original contract. Douglas E. Winter's 1983 book review in *The Washington Post* stated that King delivered *Pet Sematary* "as ransom for substantial money, earned by King's early novels, that had been withheld from him."

Pet Sematary was a major hit, much to King's surprise. "I couldn't imagine ever publishing *Pet Sematary*—it was so awful. But the fans loved it. You can't gross out the American public—or the British public, for that matter, because they loved it too."

For me, the death of children wasn't the darkest part.

The evil of Louis is cold, indifferent, and all too real. It's frighteningly relatable. There is no redemption possible for Louis. Those horrible inner thoughts don't translate well to film, and the movie only hints at the darkness.

Two *Birds* Are Better Than One

Sometimes a book and the corresponding movie are both great, but they elicit different emotions.

The Birds (1963) is a good example of how a *medium* can change the mood of a story. Alfred Hitchcock directed the movie *The Birds* and Daphne du Maurier wrote the original novella *The Birds*.

They share a setting, and they both take place in a seaside town. In both, birds start to attack people for no apparent reason. Then they go inexplicably dormant, and then they attack again. Neither version of the story offers an explanation.

It sounds silly until you take a walk alone in a park after reading the story or watching the movie. When I did so, I watched flocks of birds darting in the air in unison, following some impulse I didn't understand. I was unaware that hundreds of birds were quietly hiding in a tree until they suddenly all took flight as I walked by. I felt unaware, unprepared, and outnumbered.

I think it's one of the simplest and purest horror ideas ever written.

Daphne Du Maurier's *The Birds* (1952)

Du Maurier's version is much darker than Hitchcock's. It's told as a first-person narrative by Ned, a farmhand working on a farm in Cornwall, England, who notices the birds acting strangely. Slowly, he, his family, and the nearby community come under attack. Then we learn that the attacks aren't isolated to the farm, the peninsula, or even England.

The attacks are happening everywhere....

Du Maurier's story quietly builds into a siege. The first attack on Ned's home happens at night. He can only imagine how many birds there are. By dawn, the birds are gone. Ned walks to the beach and sees what he thinks are white-caps. When he looks more closely, he sees that they are seagulls, covering the water and waiting for the tide to rise.

The story becomes apocalyptic. Jet fighters fall from the sky. The BBC radio reports attacks across Britain right before the station goes off the air. A panicked herd of cows tramples a farmer into a gooey paste. Bodies lie in the streets, gouged thousands of times by birds.

Du Maurier creates a quiet terror using the power of suggestion. She makes you imagine the worst. The sense of doom and dread is palpable to the last crushing paragraph.

Alfred Hitchcock's *The Birds* (1963)

Where Du Maurier used suggestion, Hitchcock had to show us what the frenzied bird attacks looked like. That changed the tone and the mood of the story. Du Maurier gave us quiet dread; Hitchcock gave us chaos and shock.

Hitchcock builds suspense with minor incidents between birds and the residents of Bodega Bay, California. He cranks up the tension through the first half of the film. When the attacks happen, the release is a tumultuous barrage of brutal images.

Even though the bird attacks are the centerpiece of the film, I think the most powerful scene involves the mother of one of the characters visiting a neighbor.

The woman knocks on the front door and finds it unlocked. She walks in and calls out for the neighbor. No one answers. She wanders through the house calling for him. Everything looks normal until she walks into his bedroom.

There is a dead bird stuck in the glass of the broken window. The room is torn apart, and furniture and broken lamps litter the floor. It's eerily quiet.

She finds the neighbor, still in his pajamas, slumped in a corner on the floor. His eyes have been pecked out.

It is the scene that is the most evocative of the mood of Du Maurier's original story, and it is also the most grotesque and disturbing in the movie.

That scene gave me nightmares for three nights in a row. I woke up screaming. After my dad had to stagger into my room in the middle of the night for the third time, he laid down the law. No more horror movies unless he watched them first.

I didn't like that rule, so I started smuggling horror books home in my stacks of school books, camouflaged by classics like *Of Mice and Men*.

I learned then that books can be just as terrifying as movies, if not more so. Some of my favorites include:

I Am Legend (Richard Matheson, 1954)

The story is credited by authors like Stephen King, Ray Bradbury, and Dan Simmons, as well as the Horror Writer's Association, with inspiring the apocalyptic horror genre, and the modern interpretations of vampires and zombies. In *I Am Legend*, a pandemic creates a worldwide apocalypse, where those who are infected show symptoms similar to vampirism.

Carrie (Stephen King, 1972)

King writes with an understanding of the pain of loneliness that comes with being an outsider. He also understands that a victimized outsider can carry monstrous rage inside. If you have read no other Stephen King, start at the beginning with *Carrie*.

The Haunting of Hill House (Shirley Jackson, 1959)

The story revolves around four paranormal investigators who travel to the mansion to prove the existence of the supernatural. But the shy and sensitive Eleanor is the focal point of both the reader and Hill House itself, and her experiences make the book sublimely terrifying.

The Body Snatchers (Jack Finney, 1955)

It's a story of aliens in seed form landing in Mill Valley, California. They germinate into perfect replicas of the humans they parasitically consume. It is the ultimate identity paranoia story.

Ghost Story (Peter Straub, 1979)

Four elderly friends create an exclusive club to share ghost stories with each other. However, they live a true ghost story based on a tragedy that has linked them since their college days. *Ghost Story* puts a spin on the traditional notions of the supernatural revenge tale by proposing that the ghost and the haunted have a symbiotic dependence on each other that will ultimately destroy them.

The Exorcist (William Peter Blatty, 1971)

This book deserves special attention. It's one of the most groundbreaking novels of the twentieth century. It brought international attention to the horror genre and created its own subgenre. It also had a huge effect on me.

My parents were devout fundamentalist Christians. They took the Bible literally; it was the word of God. They believed that there was a burning bush, that there was an ark, and that Armageddon was coming soon. They even knew the calendar year it was going to happen. They also believed that the devil and demons were real and could possess weak souls.

It was fire and brimstone daily. Unfortunately, this wasn't contained to the household. They believed that all other religions, including other Christian sects, had been corrupted, and that their followers had thus been duped into idolatry and blasphemy. It was *our* job to set them straight.

One of the key tenets of this religion was that followers were obligated to convert as many people as possible before the end of days. The stakes were high, so aggressiveness was forgiven. We were ostracized by most of our neighbors, and our attempts to convert our relatives left us alienated from most of them.

It was a dramatic childhood. We converted after I was born, so I had to go through a rule change early on. I remember my dad using flash cards to teach me historical dates and scripture passages that proved the new doctrine.

I believed what my mom and dad taught me. I'd go to school and unintentionally insult every kid there by telling them that their parents believed in false gods. It didn't take long for me to be labeled a weirdo. Even early on, I had doubts about this religion. If I was right, I couldn't understand why I was miserable and alone.

What the Funk and Wagnall's Were They Thinking?

My behavior in this regard didn't make me popular at school, so I had a lot of time to read. My dad knew I was lonely, so as a consolation, he bought me a set of Funk and Wagnall's Encyclopedias. I was immediately hooked, and I read *all* the volumes.

I learned a lot through what I call the "potato chip effect." I would look something up in the encyclopedia, usually something dirty, and when I found it, the definition would mention another subject, so I looked that up too. Then something else on the opposite page would catch my eye. I couldn't stop with just one page—just like I couldn't stop with one potato chip—I kept reading.

The day I decided to research Satan, I believed I was taking a real risk.

My parents believed demonic influence caused all the evil in the world. They believed demons tempted you with sex, alcohol, drugs, Ouija boards, and rock music.

They believed if you gave in to temptation, you could get possessed. Demons could wear you like a cheap suit.

If my church was right, researching Satan would roll out the welcome mat for a possession. Something about that didn't feel true. Why would this be any different than anything else I looked up? Still, my heart raced as I turned the pages.

I was surprised to discover how many different versions of Satan there were in religions across the world. My parents' church didn't teach that.

Cue the potato chip effect.

I looked up Judgment Day and Armageddon, and that led me to an entry on Doomsday religions and cults. These people sounded like they were nuts, and I saw a long list of religions in that category.

As I read down the list, I saw my church.

It was listed as a cult. I looked up what a cult was.

A cult, strictly speaking, is a particular system of religious worship, especially with reference to its rites and ceremonies. A cult is a relatively small group of people having (esp. religious) beliefs or practices regarded by others as strange or sinister, or as exercising excessive control over members. A "Doomsday cult" is an expression that is used to describe groups that believe in apocalypticism and millenarianism, and it can also be used to refer both to groups that predict disaster and to groups that attempt to bring it about.

This wasn't a total shock. Even in third grade, I was skeptical. Every time I brought up some of my church's teachings at school, my pronouncements were met with belly laughs and mockery from other kids. The encyclopedia entry was more of a confirmation than a revelation.

The final confirmation was when the date for Armageddon came and went and nothing happened. The faithful, including my parents, believed that this just meant that the time was up and it would happen any time now.

I no longer believed.

But I still had to live in my parents' house and I had to follow their rules. It was a strict household with a black-and-white mentality around good and bad. I started a quiet revolution under their noses. Book smuggling became very important.

And this is where the Demon Pazuzu became my personal savior.

I brought *The Exorcist* into the house when I was 13. My parents considered it very dangerous stuff. They believed demons were all around us.

They weren't alone. The novel was an international bestseller that started a worldwide conversation about the struggles of faith and more than a little hysteria around belief in demonic possession. Truth be told, I still believed in it too.

Ultimately, the book helped me figure out what I believed.

When William Friedkin's film version of *The Exorcist* (1973) came out, demons became a part of popular culture. Suddenly, the next-door neighbor and my dad had something to talk about.

Friedkin and Blatty collaborated to create a movie faithful to the novel. It's the story of the demonic possession of a 12-year-old girl and the trial of her single mother who goes from agnosticism to horrified belief when medicine and psychiatry fail to help her daughter. She finds help in the form of two priests who risk their lives to exorcise the demon.

Both the movie and the novel are intense, draining, and terrifying experiences. But I think the novel is darker and more frightening, partly because of the different experience it offers.

In the film, the exorcism takes place in one spectacular night. It is climactic and cinematic, but the speed lessens the sense of desperation and futility Blatty creates to show the seemingly insurmountable struggle of faith.

In the novel, the possession of Regan goes on for *months*. The priests perform their rites and they are constantly rebuffed. Whenever the priests seem to make progress, the demon threatens Regan's life. The demon takes her to the edge of death. It slows down her pulse at will, or it keeps her wide awake and screaming for days.

How do you overcome something so brutal? Each chapter has you asking this question because Blatty's writing spares you nothing. You feel the futility that the characters feel. When Damien Karras, the younger and inexperienced priest, asks the elderly exorcist why this is happening, Father Merrin responds:

> *"I think the demon's target is not the possessed; it is us...the observers...every person in this house. And I think—I think the point is to make us despair; to reject our own humanity, Damien: to see ourselves as ultimately bestial; as ultimately vile and putrescent; without dignity; ugly; unworthy."*

The novel will have you nodding in exhausted agreement.

Running with the Devil

I read the book in my bedroom, late at night, after I was sure everyone was asleep. That made the whole thing scarier.

I had a first edition copy of the novel. The cover showed a blurry picture of a little girl looking up at you. The combination of the blur and the shadows cast by my overhead light made it look like the girl had no pupils. It was unnerving. I couldn't help but wonder if I'd look like that in the morning.

There's a particularly horrific passage in the book where Sharon, a close friend who has been tending to the sick girl, is stalked by the child. As Sharon stands in a hallway, she is unaware that the girl silently crawls towards her on all fours, upside down. She skitters like a spider and licks Sharon's ankle. When I read that for the first time, I felt that tongue. I had to stifle a scream. I could visualize my bedroom door crashing open, and the bowed body of Regan skittering up the foot of my bed, hissing as she dropped on top of my chest.

I thought about hiding the book in my closet until I remembered that the door had a faulty latch. I knew that if the door came loose and creaked open I'd have a heart attack. Leaving the door cracked open, exposing the dark cave of the closet with that book lurking in there was no better. Finally, I hid it under my bed. I set it with the front cover facing down, but I could still feel the pupil-less eyes staring at me.

I tried to sleep. But the only thing worse than hearing a creak somewhere in the house was the dense, suffocating silence. My throat was dry and my heart pounded.

What if there was a demon in the corner, toying with me, waiting until I relaxed before he attacked? What if my parents were right? What if I was so foolishly arrogant that I damned myself? I realized that I was afraid to have my parents find me possessed. If I were possessed, they would know. *They would know I had sinned*, that I brought danger into the house. They would know I brought them shame.

I fell asleep. I didn't realize I did until my alarm went off. It took me a minute to realize why falling asleep even mattered to me. I looked under the bed, and the novel was right where I left it, face down on the carpet.

I woke up, unpossessed. A wall came down. On the other side of that wall was a much bigger world.

Healing Old Wounds with Horror Literature

Horror books go far beyond the monsters in the pages. They can tap into real issues in people's lives. If you're grieving, you may find that you empathize with Louis Creed from *Pet Sematary* as much as you hate his selfishness. If you resent making sacrifices for loved ones, you may relate completely to Eleanor in *The Haunting of Hill House*. If you still have grief and regret over something you did in your past that haunts you, the elderly gentlemen in *Ghost Story* may show you that resolving indiscretions is better than a lifetime of self-hatred.

For those who don't like the energy and style of modern horror movies, there are centuries worth of books that delve into introspective horror. It may surprise you how much you identify with the characters.

Books allow people to explore new feelings, encounter scary situations, and deal with problems without drawing a lot of outside attention. Books let you break taboos and entertain new ideas. Sometimes the most powerful thing a book can do is to let you know that you're not alone in the world.

There are thousands of horror novels out there. You can enjoy a story in a single novel, or you can dive into a series where the universe and the story expand over the course of several books. There are a wide variety of styles, from comedic horror novels, to gothic horror, to splatterpunk gore, to psychological horror, to erotic horror.

It's all a matter of taste. Here are some of my favorite writers, whom I endorse for the caliber of their writing and their story ideas…and my beliefs.

Shirley Jackson, *The Haunting of Hill House* (1959)

Ray Bradbury, *Something Wicked This Way Comes* (1962)

Mary Wollstonecraft Shelley, *Frankenstein; or The Modern Prometheus* (1818)

Algernon Blackwood, *The Wendigo* (1910)

Robert Bloch, *Psycho* (1959)

Ray Nelson, *Time Travel for Pedestrians* (1972)

Harlan Ellison, *I Have No Mouth, and I Must Scream* (1967)

Stephen King, *The Stand* (1978)

Jack Finney, *The Body Snatchers* (1955)

William Golding, *Lord of the Flies* (1954)

Daphne Du Maurier, *The Birds* (1952)

Roald Dahl, *Man from the South* (1948)

William Peter Blatty, *The Exorcist* (1971)

Ramsey Campbell, *The Doll Who Ate His Mother* (1976)

Peter Straub, *Ghost Story* (1979)

Carmen Maria Machado, *The Husband Stitch* (2014)

Clive Barker, *The Hellbound Heart* (1986)

Edgar Allen Poe, *The Fall of the House of Usher* (1839)

H.P. Lovecraft, *At the Mountains of Madness* (1936)

F. Marion Crawford, *The Upper Berth* (1926)

Dan Simmons, *The Terror* (2007)

Lauren Beukes, *Broken Monsters* (2014)

Joe Hill, *Horns* (2010)

Neil Gaiman, *American Gods* (2001)

Dean Koontz, *Intensity* (1995)

Justin Cronin, *The Passage* (2010)

Joe R. Lansdale, *The Night They Missed the Horror Show* (2006)

Thomas Harris, *Red Dragon* (1981)

David Wong, *John Dies in the End* (2007)

I reserve a special place in hell for Cormac McCarthy for writing *Blood Meridian* (1985) and Jack Ketchum for *The Girl Next Door* (1989). I was furious with them for the way they so clearly and precisely wrote despair that I felt complicit in the carnage in the story and carried that despair for days afterwards.

But I sincerely thank every one of these authors for being the corruptors I needed at just the right time, and I hope you enjoy finding yours.

GREAT HORROR STORY COLLECTIONS AND ANTHOLOGIES

Sometimes the best way to get a sense of what horror fiction you enjoy is to pick up a collection of short stories instead of investing in a novel. Here are three anthologies (collections from various authors) and three collections (all by the same author) to give you a horror story primer.

Anthologies:

1. *Great Tales of Terror and the Supernatural* **(Edited by Phyllis Cerf Wagner & Herbert Wise):** Published in 1944, there's probably not a better collection of the masters: Edgar Allen Poe, H.P. Lovecraft, Henry James, Algernon Blackwood, H.G. Welles, E.M. Forster, Edith Wharton, Nathaniel Hawthorne, to name a few. The 52 stories give you a broad palette of horror.

2. *Prime Evil* **(Edited by Douglas E. Winter):** A great collection of contemporary horror masters, including Stephen King, Clive Barker, Peter Straub, Whitley Streiber, and Dennis Etchison, demonstrating that they can write tight short fiction. Standout: Ramsey Campbell's "Next Time You'll Know Me."

3. *Dark Forces* **(Edited by Kirby McCauley):** This is the pure horror story version of Harlan Ellison's epic "Dangerous Visions" sci-fi/horror anthology. McCauley got established writers to send stories that were previously rejected, stating that they would run without any edits. What we get is the uninhibited side of Ray Bradbury, Richard Matheson, and Robert Bloch, and they out-shock Stephen King, T.E.D. Kline, and Ramsey Campbell.

Collections:

1. *The Lottery and Other Stories* **(Shirley Jackson):** If there's only one book you decide to pick up and read, let it be this one. "The Lottery" and "The Daemon Lover" are enough for you to realize why she is considered one of the greatest horror writers. And there are still 23 more stories in the book.

2. *Night Shift* **(Stephen King):** His first collection is his best, and this is King when he was still lean and hungry. These stories are powerhouse reminders of the diversity of his imagination. The standout for me is "The Boogeyman."

3. *The Call of Cthulhu and Other Weird Stories* **(H.P. Lovecraft):** How could this collection not be on this list? In 18 stories, Lovecraft invents "Cosmic Horror" and influences every horror author after him. He's the one master of horror nobody disputes, and this collection shows why.

CHAPTER FOUR

SCREAMING FOR PLEASURE:
EXORCISE YOUR DEMONS
THROUGH DEVIL MUSIC

The Gregorian Monks invented devil music. Stop blaming Ozzy Osbourne.

The term "Diabolus in Musica," or "The Devil in Music," was coined in the ninth century, when the Gregorian Monks accidentally stumbled upon a combination of three tones that created a dissonant, unsettling sound when they were played together.

These three notes came to be known as the *tritone*, better known as the *diminished fifth* in music theory. A tritone uses three whole tones—a starting tone and then the third and fifth tones on the "Do-re-mi-fa-so-la-ti-do" scale. So, the tritone sounds like this:

"Do, Mi, So."

The Monks discovered the tritone, and when they heard that dark sound they promptly banned it from being used in compositions. Except for their own.

The Gregorian Monks understood what every musician knows: the devil has the best tunes.

Music from the Dark Side

Confession is good for the soul, but so is rock and roll. Music is the one real magic that exists in the world. It's a universal enchantress. The spell it casts reaches the subconscious part of us that words can't touch. It's the only time we as adults allow ourselves to feel emotions so profoundly that we need to dance, jump, or sing to release them. Like we did when we were kids.

Devil Music Can Be Good for You

Music can change our mood in an instant. There's a song for every emotion. Music that feels dark and dangerous finds a way to pull you into dark and dangerous emotions. With music, you don't need to articulate how you feel.

The right song can exorcise personal demons we didn't even know we had. The right song can push the envelope and let us indulge our inner demons, even if it's just for a few minutes. That experience can be empowering and cleansing.

That's right; devil music can be good for you.

There are plenty of musical styles to get your dose of empowering and cleansing shock therapy, even if you would never listen to Slayer's *Reign in Blood*. There has always been music that embraces horror. Let's go back to when the church gave evil a sound.

Devil Music and the Fear of God

In a 2006 interview with the *BBC*, Professor John Deathridge, King Edward professor of music at King's College London, explained that the tritone was consistently used by the church as a link to evil. "In medieval theology you have to have some way of presenting the devil."

It makes sense that the church would use the tritone to announce the arrival and presence of the devil in their songs and sermons—it was a memorable representation in a superstitious and fundamentally illiterate world. It seems that scaring the audience was the most effective way to drive the point home about the power of evil.

The diminished fifth became the voice of the devil in the church's Mystery Plays, which were traveling sermons set up as stage plays and based on Bible stories.

The clergy and musicians would travel to villages by way of a horse-drawn cart that doubled as a small stage. The plays covered the Creation, Adam and Eve, and the murder of Abel. The combined cycle of shows could last for days.

One of the most popular Mystery Plays was *The Last Judgment*, which dramatized the expected Second Coming of Christ. There would be an actor at the center of the stage who represented the common man. On one side of the stage, an actor would be introduced as God.

God had a theme song too. This was the "perfect fifth," also called the "Amen chord." It's the uplifting harmony you hear when someone sings the word "amen" in a choir. The devil would be announced with the tritone on the other side of the stage. The man in the center of the stage would face his judgment, and for each sin, the stage would tilt towards the devil, and for each pure action, it would tilt towards God. The play ended with the man in the center sliding one way or the other. Most of the time, the man would slide towards the devil, screaming while the tritone played.

Ah, show business…

Classical Music: Satan Goes Secular

During the Middle Ages, the church was the main owner and producer of music, because the music that was written down in manuscripts was written by church clerics. Troubadour songs, an early form of secular music that dealt with nonreligious themes, had been popular in France since the eleventh century, but secular music wasn't allowed to be played in churches.

Then with the invention of music printing around 1500 A.D., secular music manuscripts could travel wherever minstrels and troubadours went. Churches were no longer the main musical venue for the populace (Elliot Jones, *Secular Music—Troubadours, MUS 101,* Santa Ana College, 2017). Once music broke out of the church's domain, musicians began to explore society's fascination with the dark side. Classical musicians were the first to do this.

Classical musicians embraced elements of Gothic horror—like goblins, Pagan rituals, and even the end of the world—and many composers used the tritone to heighten the mood. Beethoven, Franz Liszt, Brahms, Stravinsky, Paganini, and Edvard Grieg all used tritones in their compositions.

But, in my opinion, the king of the tritone and horror in classical music is Richard Wagner. I think the best example would be his apocalyptic opera *Gotterdammerung.* The music was ominous and frightening, but it also told the story of the Norse war between the gods that destroys the world.

I think it's significant that, in 1876 during a decidedly Christian time in history, Wagner uses his opera to loosely tell the heathen story of Ragnarok. In Norse Mythology, Ragnarok is a series of events that culminate in a great war among the Norse gods, which causes a series of natural disasters and leads to the earth being submerged completely underwater. Essentially, Ragnarok is the end of our world, a big reset button. The good news is that the earth rises from the water, cleansed, and ready to start over. Wagner broke free from church dogma and created art from legend, lore, and even the supernatural.

Wagner was *metal* before there was metal. ♪

Murder Ballads: Bloody Folk Tales

Music doesn't need to be bombastic or use the tritone to give you chills. Sometimes, all you need is a guitar and a story. There is a rich vein of the macabre in a subgenre of the traditional folk ballad that did more than just announce the presence of evil. Murder ballads reveled in it.

Murder ballads told graphic stories of brutal deaths and dismemberment, sometimes based on actual events, like "Pretty Polly," a famous murder ballad:

> *Thus, I deluded her again,*
> *Into a private place,*
> *Then took a stick out of the hedge,*
> *And struck her in the face.*
> *But she fell on bended knee,*
> *For mercy she did cry,*
> *'For heaven's sake don't murder me,*
> *I am not fit to die.'*
> *From ear to ear I slit her mouth,*
> *And stabbed her in the head,*
> *Till she, poor soul did breathless lie,*
> *Before her butcher bled.*
> *And then I took her by the hair,*
> *To cover the foul sin,*
> *And dragged her to the riverside,*
> *And threw her body in.*

In his book, *Savage Pastimes: A Cultural History of Violent Entertainment* (2005), Harold Schechter writes that during the Renaissance, minstrels and balladeers put stories of murders to music and sang them to illiterate peasants. The same basic story would show up in different regions with alterations to suit a new audience.

For example, the popular Appalachian murder ballad, "The Knoxville Girl" (1924 - earliest recording), is derived from a nineteenth century Irish ballad, "The Wexford Girl," which is derived from the English ballad, "The Bloody Miller," from the seventeenth century.

Murder ballads have a standard structure. The victim and the killer are introduced to us. Sometimes the story is told from the killer's point of view, sometimes from the victim's. The victim usually gets lured to the murder site. Then the murder is described in graphic detail.

It might seem like murder ballads are an archaic cultural oddity, but they're still around today. Old songs get re-recorded by artists. There are modern stories as well, like "Tom Dooley," "Folsom Prison Blues," "Mack the Knife," and "Stagger Lee."

Evil Goes Electric

Folk singers spread horror across the world one acoustic guitar strum at a time. But things heated up fast when guitars went electric. The Birth of Rock and Roll in the 1950s and the increased use of the electric guitar gave the tritone sharp fangs. It paved the way for a new evolution of devil's music: heavy metal.

As a first-generation metalhead, I can say that metal sounded like nothing else at the time, nor did it want to. It was defiant and in-your-face. It came with the threat and danger of something forbidden. I got the same rush and exhilaration from a heavy metal album as I got from horror movies. To me, the songs were almost like mini-horror movies.

Heavy metal combines horror and music. Like horror, heavy metal isn't known for its subtlety. And, like horror, heavy metal embraces our darkest shadows, which makes it a lightning rod for controversy.

Black Sabbath: Highway to...Metal

It's hard for anyone born in the new millennium to understand, but during the '70s and '80s, people were seriously concerned that rock music, especially heavy metal, was a conduit to Satan.

There is room for debate on who was the first heavy metal band. Bands like Vanilla Fudge, Blue Cheer, and Deep Purple played loud and aggressive music as early as 1966. However, as author Tom Larson states in his book, *History of Rock and Roll* (2004), when Black Sabbath released its first album on Friday the 13th of 1970, they became the first band to clearly define the conventions of early heavy metal.

The group made music that reflected the dark side of life they saw. They used occult images, and lower tuning and distortion on their guitars, and they looked scary wearing black outfits and steel crosses.

In the beginning, four friends from Birmingham, England formed a heavy blues-rock band named Earth. They were playing gigs in and around Birmingham, England and not making an impact, when inspiration hit.

In a 2002 interview for *New York Rock*, Ozzy Osbourne talked about the first steps toward the creation of their image and sound, "Right across the road from our rehearsal room was a cinema that showed mainly horror movies. One day I thought about how it seemed strange that a lot of people spent so much money to see scary movies. Nobody really wanted to listen to us, so we decided to play slightly scary music. We liked it, and, yeah, that's how it all got started."

Osbourne got the idea to write a song with bassist Geezer Butler based on the work of horror author Dennis Wheatley (*The Devil Rides Out; To the Devil, a Daughter*). Butler included a vision he had as a child of a dark figure standing at the foot of his bed.

The band liked this new direction. Guitarist Tony Iommi started the song with the tritone. He played it slowly, like he was calling up the devil.

The music stood in stark contrast to acts like The Carpenters, whose song, "(They Long to Be) Close to You" was the #1 song on US Billboard on August 8, 1970. Black Sabbath's music felt dangerous. The band had found their calling card; they would make the musical equivalent of horror movies.

They renamed the band after the movie that served as Butler's inspiration: the horror anthology *Black Sabbath* (1963), starring Boris Karloff and directed by the legendary Mario Bava (*Blood and Black Lace, Black Sunday*).

The cover for the album *Black Sabbath* showed an English country farm with a creepy woman in black standing at the edge of the woods. She stares right at you.

I was freaked out before I even heard one note.

Music critics hated the album, but it hit #23 on the Billboard Top 200 and was a commercial success. (George-Warren, Holly, ed. [2001]. *The Rolling Stone Encyclopedia of Rock and Roll* [2005 ed., p. 463]). It seems there were a few people who felt disconnected from the mood of pop culture, and Black Sabbath's sound resonated with them.

Social watchdogs labeled Black Sabbath as devil worshippers, even though the opposite was true. In a 2011 interview with Jamie Blaine for *Classic Rock Magazine*, Geezer Butler, the primary lyricist for the band, explained that all the members of the band were raised as Christians, and he added, "We all believe in God."

"People like to find the negative in everything," said Butler. "We weren't interested in writing songs about the 'nice' things in the world—everyone else was writing about that. We wanted to inject some reality into music. I think," and at this point he laughed, "if we'd been called White Sunday we'd have had a totally different reaction!"

The album's success paved the way for other artists to explore the scarier side of music.

Alice Cooper: We Welcomed His Nightmare

Alice Cooper combined the visual flair of old Universal horror movies, the theatricality of 1950s rock and roll performer Screaming Jay Hawkins, and the anything-goes live energy of the traveling Midnight Spook Shows of the 1930s and 1940s—to give heavy metal one of its first larger-than-life villains.

The distorted guitars and Cooper's voice made every song on 1971's *Love It to Death* sound scary. There's even an homage to horror movies in the song, "The Ballad of Dwight Fry," named after the actor who played the insane servant, Renfield, in Tod Browning's *Dracula* (1931).

But it was the stage show, which featured Cooper being tortured, beheaded, and electrocuted, only to have him come back to life, that created horror theater. These antics were reminiscent of the Midnight Spook Shows, which were live horror shows that traveled from town to town in the days before television.

In his 2013 article entitled, "Before TV, Kids Would Flock to Midnight Ghost Shows," *Gizmodo* editor Matt Novak chronicled how in the 1930s and 1940s these shows specialized in performing seances and showing optical illusion ghosts to a live audience. However, in the 1960s and 1970s, the showrunners found baby boomers harder to scare. They had to switch to bloodier fare that featured guillotines and dismemberments.

Even though Spook Shows had played across the country for decades, the similar antics of an Alice Cooper show were considered too shocking. In 1972, Alice Cooper performed four songs on the premiere episode of ABC Television's *In Concert* series. Lawrence H. Rogers II, owner of Cincinnati's WKRC-TV Channel 12, was watching the show and he ordered his station to pull it off the air immediately. At the same time in Britain, *Top of the Pops* came under fire from Mary Whitehouse, the president of the National Viewers and Listeners Association, for giving Cooper's single, "School's Out," the opportunity to promote a philosophy of violence and anarchy to school children.

On a personal level, my parents' fundamentalist religion accused Cooper of being a devil worshipper. Alice Cooper's shows included cartoonish violence and questionable taste (Cooper kicked a pile of plastic baby dolls around the stage during the song, "Dead Babies,") but his shows didn't include nudity or profanity. The only recognizable difference between his concerts and the Midnight Spook Shows was the inclusion of heavy metal music.

Hidden Messages and Charles Manson

Even the most popular band in the world wasn't immune to controversy associated with the devil's music. Concern escalated when The Beatles recorded hidden messages in the songs "Revolution 9" and "I'm So Tired" on *The White Album* (1968).

The Beatles accidentally stumbled upon the process of backmasking (which is the recording of a message backward on a track) while working on their album *Revolver* (1966). Depending on which book you read, *The Beatles Illustrated Lyrics* (Alan Aldridge, 1991), or *Glass Onion: The Beatles in Their Own Words* (Geoffrey Guiliano, Vrnda Devi, 1999), the backmasking effect was either an experimental discovery by producer George Martin, or a recording error made by a stoned John Lennon on the song, "Rain."

The first line of the song, "Sunshine…Rain…When the rain comes, they run and hide their heads," was recorded in reverse to the fade-out. The band thought it sounded cool, so it stayed in the song.

In the days of LSD, trances and meditation, turntables and headphones, backmasking was psychedelic pop art. The Beatles experimented more with this on subsequent albums, and that's when things got weird.

On October 10, 1969, DJ Russ Gibb of WKNR-FM in Dearborn, Michigan received a phone call from a student at Eastern Michigan University who proclaimed that the strange conspiracy theory—Paul McCartney died in 1966 and had been replaced with a lookalike to keep the band together—was in fact true, and there was evidence of McCartney's death hidden in the songs, "Revolution 9" and "I'm So Tired," from *The White Album* (1968).

Author Andru J. Reeve's *Turn Me On, Dead Man: The Beatles and the "Paul-Is-Dead" Hoax* (2004) chronicles this moment as the start of one of the strangest conspiracies in rock and roll history. While live on the air, Gibb played the song "Revolution 9" in reverse by slowly rotating his turntable counterclockwise. As the eerie song played over the air, the repeated phrase "Number 9, Number 9" sounded like a garbled "Turn me on, Dead Man."

The station phones lit up, and Gibb spent hours shredding his copy of *The White Album*. When he played the song, "I'm So Tired," in reverse, Gibb found what he believed was a message from John Lennon that said, "Paul is dead, man. Miss him, miss him." After that, Gibb started spending time on his show talking about "The Great Cover-up" with his listeners (Yoakum, Jim "The Man Who Killed Paul McCartney," *The Gadfly* [May–June 2000]).

As word spread, other radio stations jumped into the game, and soon the rumor was worldwide. The phenomenon was so intriguing and the publicity was so big, that other bands, like Electric Light Orchestra and Deep Purple, experimented with backmasking.

Enter Charles Manson, who single-handedly ends the '60s and forever links backmasking with evil incarnate.

Charles Manson was a criminal and a cult leader who formed a desert commune of disciples, mostly comprised of college-age women with middle-class upbringings, that he called "The Family."

In Vincent Bugliosi's book, *Helter Skelter—The True Story of the Manson Murders,* Manson used hallucinogens, sex, and an isolated commune life to convince his followers that he was a manifestation of Jesus who prophesied about an upcoming apocalyptic race war.

He named this apocalyptic race war after a song on The Beatles' *White Album: Helter Skelter.* Manson believed that The Beatles also knew of the coming apocalypse and had sprinkled subliminal clues for Manson and his Family throughout the *White Album.* Although there is no mention of race in the song ("helter skelter" is British slang for being "confused"), Manson interpreted the lyrics as a message sent directly to him announcing that the war was imminent.

Within the framework of this delusion, Manson convinced four members of The Family to drive out to a mansion in the Hollywood Hills on August 9, 1969. That evening culminated in the brutal murder of five people, including actress Sharon Tate, who was pregnant at the time. The next night, The Family struck again and murdered Leno and Rosemary LaBianca in their home. ("Charles Manson is Dead: What Was His 'Helter Skelter' Race War Plan?" By Lindley Sanders, *Newsweek* 11/20/17).

The words "Healter Skelter" [*sic*] were found on the LaBiancas' refrigerator, written in the victims' blood. Nobody knew the significance of those words until the trial, when Manson told prosecutor Bugliosi, "It's The Beatles, the music they're putting out, these kids listen to this music and pick up the message. It's subliminal." ("Charles Manson: How Cult Leader's Twisted Beatles Obsession Inspired Family Murders" by Kory Grow, *Rolling Stone*, 8/9/2017).

And that's when the religious and civic leaders saw a new threat in rock music from an old source: the subliminal message.

A Pedigree of Paranoia

The concern, and the controversy, around the use of subliminal messages dates to the 1957 book, *The Hidden Persuaders*, by journalist and social critic Vance Packard. His target was advertising and marketing. Packard believed that ad firms used what he called "subliminal projection," where messages that were imperceptible to the viewers flashed on television and movie screens and influenced their unconscious minds.

Packard cited a test of "invisible commercials" by market researcher James M. Vicary at a New Jersey drive-in. The words "eat popcorn" were flashed on the screen for a split second to boost concession sales, and Vicary claimed that popcorn sales increased by 57.5 percent (O'Barr, William M. "Subliminal Advertising." *Advertising & Society Review*, vol. 13, no. 4, 2013).

Packard also exposed an unsuspecting public to the research techniques advertisers used on test audiences. Analysts monitored pupil dilation during commercials, recorded changes in voice pitch when subjects discussed products, and wired theater seats to monitor restlessness.

He put a sinister touch to it all when he wrote, "Many of us are being influenced and manipulated, far more than we realize, in the patterns of our everyday lives."

In her article "The Hidden Persuaders: Then and Now" for *The Journal of Advertising* (2013), Michelle R. Nelson states that criticism from academics and the advertising industry was widespread, in part for Packard's "sensationalist, unsubstantiated writing." Nonetheless, the book was very popular with audiences and it remained on the US bestseller list for a year. Nelson states that it "…helped shape public opinion, advertising regulation, and advertising research and practice."

Packard's theories were resurrected and expanded upon in 1974 with Wilson Bryan Key's book *Subliminal Seduction*. The cover photo shows a cocktail glass half full of a martini on the rocks with a lemon twist. Written above it is the question, "Are You Being Sexually Aroused by This Picture?"

Key, who had a PhD in communications, claimed that advertisers hid subliminal images of taboo subjects around sex, violence, death, even bestiality, to stimulate the unconscious and manipulate people to buy their products. He claimed that there was the image of a man with an erection in one of the ice cubes on the book cover (O'Toole, P., 1989. "Those sexy ice cubes are back." *Advertising Age*, October 2, p. 26).

Key didn't stop at the visual image. He introduced music into the mix. "Backward masking, or metacontrast, is another technique which, though not purely subliminal, does affect both conscious and unconscious perception." (*Subliminal Seduction*, p. 38).

Key went on to claim in his book that the conscious and unconscious mind works independently of each other, and information that passes through the unconscious can go undetected as it influences the brain. In the book, *Psychological Sketches* (1994), professor John R. Vokey, PhD states that Key also claimed that the "unconscious brain" comprehends advertisements "at the speed of light," which is a "direct contradiction to basic neurophysiology and brain function."

Key doesn't give any evidence or case studies to back up any of his scientific claims and, as Julie Sedivy, PhD wrote in *Psychology Today*, "Claims like these quickly gave birth to cottage industries of consumer education programs, marketing consultancies, and subliminal self-help tapes."

The Devil's in the Background Details

Some people believed rock music contained hidden Satanic messages put there by bands in league with the Church of Satan, or even Satan himself.

In 1978, Jack Chick, an evangelical Christian cartoonist infamous for comic book tracts that were morality plays against homosexuality, Catholicism, feminism, evolution, and Freemasons, released "Spellbound?" in volume 10 of his comic series, *Crusaders*.

Druids and witches working for Satan invade the music industry and use backmasking to add subliminal spells and ritual incantations to rock albums. The master tapes were "blessed" by an evil force during a full moon ceremony. (Nathan Dickey, *The Devil Has the Best Tunes: The Fundamentalist Crusade Against Rock Music*, 2015).

Chick's story may sound like what you'd expect from a religious propaganda comic book, but the belief that rock music was a tool for Satan spread into more mainstream outlets.

In 1982, the April, July, and August issues of *Contemporary Christian Magazine* featured articles about the use of backmasking by famous rock bands to hide satanic messages in their albums.

Discussion about satanic messages in rock music showed up on afternoon television talk shows and talk radio on the *Trinity Broadcasting Network*, "the world's largest Christian television network and America's most-watched faith-and-family channel" (per the TBN website).

In his book, *Satanism: A Social History* (2016), author Massimo Introvigne states that Baptist pastors Gary Greenwald and Jacob Aranza theorized that

Satanists were using backmasking to hide Satanic messages in the unused tracks of the stereophonic recordings, and the pastors traveled the evangelical lecture circuit to play records in reverse and expose the truth.

Aranza took the theory even further. In his book, *More Rock, Country and Backward Masking Unmasked* (1985), he proclaims that rock music specifically was invented by Lucifer before the creation of the earth. "Lucifer is the only angelic being mentioned in the Bible to possess a musical ministry," Aranza says. "At one point in time, he used his musical abilities for God's purposes, but now he uses them to exalt evil and draw men away from God."

Bob Larson, a former rock musician who became a radio evangelist, launched *Talk Back*, a two-hour call-in radio show out of Dallas, Texas, in 1982. Larson would encourage teenage rock fans and even Satanists to call in and debate him. Larson would attempt to convert them live on the air, even to the extreme of performing an exorcism. It seems music was a new method for possession. (Forrest Jackson, *Bedeviling Bob: Pranking "Talk Back with Bob Larson,"* essay from the book *Satanic Panic: Pop-Cultural Panic in the 1980s*, Kier-La Janisse and Paul Corupe [2015]).

These claims were about to reach a much larger audience when the flagship show on the world's largest Christian television network declared one of rock's most popular and enduring songs—"Stairway to Heaven"—to be Satanic, and attempted to prove it in front of a live audience.

On January 14, 1982, Paul and Jan Crouch, the hosts of the *Praise the Lord* show (and the founders of the *Trinity Broadcasting Network)*, interviewed guest William H. Yarroll of the Applied Potentials Institute in Aurora, Colorado.

Yarroll, a self-proclaimed "neuroscientist" and frequently cited scientific source within the evangelical community, claimed that rock groups had joined forces with the Church of Satan to add hidden messages to recordings so "the subconscious mind of listeners could grasp the 'secret' or subliminal communication." (R. Serge Denisoff, *Tarnished Gold: The Record Industry Revisted*, 1986).

While the studio audience absorbed Yarrow's statement, the couple's son, Paul Crouch, Jr. joined them on stage with a reel-to-reel tape player and a copy of Led Zeppelin's rock ballad "Stairway to Heaven." He alleged that the song contained multiple subliminal reversed messages that praised Satan, and he was going to demonstrate this to the audience.

There is seemingly endless fascination for this episode of the *Praise the Lord* show from those who have heard about it, yet it isn't easy to find. Even though the official *TBN* website has a section devoted to "classic episodes" that archives back to 1978, this episode is conspicuously missing (https://www.tbn.org/programs/praise-lord-classics/episodes). Video clips of this program constantly appear and disappear on the internet.

It is compelling viewing.

The Crouch family is quiet and polite. Paul Jr. even compliments the song by saying it's "very mellow, almost pretty."

As the exposé begins, Paul Jr. reminds the audience that "sometimes words have two meanings." He also prompts the audience on what words and phrases to listen for before he plays a passage in reverse. After a passage gets played over the studio speaker system, Crouch asks the audience if they heard the message. If only some did, Paul Jr. plays it again and more hands go up.

This is the message he alleges is embedded in the song lyrics about "a bustle in your hedgerow:"

> *"Oh, here's to my sweet Satan.*
> *The one whose little path would make me sad, whose power is Satan.*
> *He will give those with him 666.*
> *There was a little tool shed where he made us suffer, sad Satan."*

Look upon Satan's Little Toolshed and despair!

At the time, Swan Song, Led Zeppelin's label, responded to the accusations with, "Our turn-tables only play in one direction." (*Led Zeppelin's Led Zeppelin IV*, Erik Davis, 2005).

For Crouch's allegation against Led Zeppelin to be true, Robert Plant would have to sing 32 words in a way that would form reasonably clear sentences both in forward and in reverse. It's not plausible. Yet the legend and rumor about "Stairway to Heaven's" satanic verses persist to this day.

Any proof that Yarroll, Key, Aranza, or Crouch presented to show backmasking influenced the unconscious minds of listeners against their will, or even possessed them, was speculative at best. Studies by psychologists concluded that the biggest devil in the details was the power of suggestion from the evangelists, not the music.

A 1984 study for *The Journal of Psychology: Interdisciplinary and Applied*, asked 65 undergraduates from the University of Texas, El Paso, to listen to reversed music, with each student group getting different levels of detail on what they should listen for. The greater the detail of suggestion, including whether the message was satanic or not, the greater the proportion of students who heard messages. (Thorne/Himelstein, *The Role of Suggestion in the Perception of Satanic Messages in Rock-and-Roll Recordings*).

Another study in 1985 for *American Psychologist* concluded that "backward messages in popular music is more a function of active construction on the part of the perceiver than of the existence of the messages themselves." (Vokey, J. R., & Read, J. D., *Subliminal messages: Between the Devil and the Media*).

In other words, if a person believes there's a hidden message in the music, they're more likely to hear one.

Before metal legend Ronnie James Dio founded his own band, Dio, he was the lead singer for Black Sabbath on the studio albums *Heaven and Hell* (1980) and *Mob Rules* (1982). During a 1982 interview on WJBK-TV in Detroit, Dio was asked about backmasking. "It's the people that listen to them that makes us what we are. If that's what they want to believe, then I guess the devil gets his due..." said Dio, "but as far as backmasking, we haven't been involved in that at all, but now that you mention it, we'll do it on our next album." (Michael W. Walker, 1985, "Backward Messages in Commercially Available Recordings," *Popular Music & Society*, 10:1, 2-13, DOI: 10.1080/03007768508591233).

Dio may have made light of a tense situation, but things were getting serious. Despite the lack of any concrete proof of the existence of backmasked Satanic messages, or their effectiveness if they did exist, the impact of the *Praise the Lord* episode helped push the belief out from the fringes and into mainstream politics.

In March of 1982, California Assemblyman Phil Wyman proposed Assembly Bill 3741, which would require warning labels on any records "that contain discernable messages when played in reverse." Wyman appeared on the CBS Evening News where he warned that "young people" who had heard "Stairway to Heaven" upward of two or three hundred times were having "pro-Satanic messages or incantations" implanted in their subconscious mind. Soon after that, US Congressman Robert Dornan submitted a similar bill to Congress. They were soon followed by proposals from legislators in Arkansas and Colorado (*Turn Me On, Dead Media: A Backward Look at the Re-enchantment of an Old Medium*, Jacob Smith, 2011).

How did something as bizarre and as unsubstantiated as claims of hidden Satanic messages get taken so seriously?

There isn't a single factor that explains how the "Satanic Panic" phenomenon grew. It was a response to social, cultural, and spiritual anxieties at that time.

The same thing can be said for heavy metal.

Perhaps it was inevitable that these two very different responses to the tensions of the 1970s and 1980s would clash.

Satanic by Association

"I consider what we do art. Art can be a reflection of society. And we're picking up the dark reflections."—Tom Araya, bassist/vocalist for Slayer, quote from the documentary *Metal: A Headbanger's Journey* (2005).

Heavy metal was defiant and provocative from the beginning. The loud and aggressive sound came with the threat and danger of something forbidden. Back in 1980, when I was discovering heavy metal, there was a sense of something dark and taboo around it, even though there were very few bands who had anything overtly Satanic in their image or lyrics.

Judas Priest dressed in black leather and studs and sang about death, rebellion, Jack the Ripper, technology becoming our master, motorcycle gangs, and the outsider, but not Satan. Like the band's name, Judas Priest flirted with the blasphemous, but they didn't align themselves with it. The cover of their album, *Sad Wings of Destiny* (1976), doesn't have pentagrams or the devil; it has an angel, weeping, in what looks like hell. It's not a cuddly image, but it *could* be something you'd find painted on an old church ceiling.

The Satanic imagery depicted in metal was decidedly Christian. It catered to the Christian versions of good, evil, and the devil.

In the 2005 documentary, *Metal: A Headbanger's Journey,* sociology professor Deena Weinstein of DePaul University states, "If there wasn't Christianity, we wouldn't have metal as we know it. Religion is really crucial to it. Most of the creators of metal, at least in metal's first several eras, were raised religiously."

Even when bands claimed they espoused Satanism or quoted from Anton

LaVey's *The Satanic Bible* (1969), they did so with the Christian misconceptions of Satanism as a religion. Metal bands sang about Satan, but the Church of Satan, founded by occultist and novelist Anton La Vey, doesn't believe in supernatural beings, Satan included. As the official *Church of Satan* website states on their FAQ page, they are atheists who use Satan as "a symbol of pride, liberty, and individualism" and "an external metaphorical projection of our highest personal potential."

"That Satanism [in metal] that you see is not Satanism," says Alice Cooper, now a born-again Christian. "It's some kind of, you know, caricature of Satanism. If you're looking for Satanism, first off, don't look to rock and roll. A bunch of kids running around playing loud guitars and going like this (makes the "devil's horns" with his hand)…that's Halloween." (*Metal: A Headbanger's Journey,* 2005).

Like horror, metal was at its best when it pushed the limits of the status quo. When a band found something that scared the hell out of the previous generations, other bands followed suit.

Let Him Who Hath Reckoning…Realize It's Only a Gimmick

Iron Maiden epitomized the horror aspects of metal in the 1980s. The band had a corpse-like mascot named Eddie, who had long hair and wore a T-shirt, just like the fans who bought the albums. Eddie appeared on every album cover and even appeared on stage in concert.

Iron Maiden was inspired by horror movies such as *The Wicker Man* and *Children of the Damned*, as well as literature such as *Murders in the Rue Morgue* and *The Rime of the Ancient Mariner*.

The Number of the Beast (1982) put Iron Maiden on the map. It featured

Satan on the cover and the title track's chorus was "Six six six the number of the Beast." This was horror movie stuff.

Iron Maiden doesn't praise Satan in its songs, but he's the standard bad guy the songs' narrators fear. The morality and themes of "Number of the Beast" would fit perfectly within the Mystery Plays of the Gregorian Monks.

According to Mick Wall's *Iron Maiden: Run to the Hills, the Authorised Biography* (2004), when Iron Maiden toured America for *Number of the Beast*, religious groups burned the album at rallies outside of the concert sites and boycotted the tour. Band manager Robert Smallwood commented that the protestors initially burned the records, but later decided to destroy them with hammers for fear of breathing in the melting vinyl's fumes.

Tension escalated quickly. Somewhere between Ozzy Osbourne being crowned the "Prince of Darkness" after the release of his album *Blizzard of Oz* (1980) and Iron Maiden's *Number of the Beast*, conservative religious groups radicalized and mobilized their message. Churches held seminars on the influence of Satan and devil worship in rock music. Attendees like Art Diaz mobilized teenagers from the First Assembly of God Church in Des Moines, Iowa, to burn albums in effigy. This was followed by record burnings in Carroll and Keokuk, Iowa. (Steven Dougherty, "From 'Race Music' to Heavy Metal: A Fiery History of Protests," *People*, 16 Sep. 1985).

We metalheads ate it up.

I Was a Teenage Fundamentalist Satanist

When I heard about the evangelical rallies and the news reports, I thought two things. First, I felt relief, because I heard teenagers mock them and I knew I wasn't alone in the struggle. Second, I felt dread, because I personally knew the type of people who would burn albums and blame Satan for everything. Mockery was interpreted as persecution, which gave them resolve. They weren't going to go away.

Being a teenage metalhead living in a Fundamentalist Christian house had its challenges. I started openly rebelling against my parents after years of repression. I found heavy metal and my rebellion got a lot louder.

I fell in love with the horror overtones in heavy metal. It sounded like what horror movies felt like, and I wanted to be scared.

Even more importantly, this music was loud and brash, and outrageous enough to help me purge my constant rage. My family's church announced a very public end-of-world prophesy in 1975 that—obviously —didn't come true. I was already considered a weirdo at school, and this added unbearable humiliation. My parents divorced, and they both remarried church members and stayed devout. I was also expected to stay devout. As a teenager, the list of forbidden sins got longer and the restrictions tighter. These events upend-ed my life and my sense of worth, and I didn't have a say in any of it. I felt that the "big three"—Mom, Dad, and God—had betrayed me. My rage sat like a rock in my gut, but what I mostly felt was despair.

I was an outsider and a misfit both at home and at school, and this music described emotions I couldn't articulate. It felt like this music understood me. I heard Judas Priest's "Beyond the Realms of Death" and lead singer Rob Halford screamed these words:

> *Yeah! I've left the world behind*
> *I'm safe here in my mind*
> *I'm free to speak with my own kind*
> *This is my life, this is my life*
> *I'll decide not you*

The first time I heard that song, I wept. It wasn't sorrow; it was the joy of affirmation. It was the relief of finding my power.

I finally found my tribe—fellow metalheads—who actually understood me. They had the same pent-up rage and they felt the same release through music. We went to concerts to scream, shout, and sweat out our aggression. We found euphoria and peace.

The power of the music fueled us and exorcised our inner demons. It *didn't* give us new ones.

I also wanted bands to push the extremes, to upset the people who upset *me*: popular kids, religious leaders, teachers, and my parents. Now I was finally in control of the reason those people saw me as weird or pathetic, and *that* took away their power. It was a declaration of freedom. For that purpose, devil worshipping bands did not disappoint.

Did I think that there was real evil in the music? Hell, no. This was shock theater, and the obvious outrageousness was part of the fun.

For the most part.

Bands with a Touch of Evil to Them

Venom: Venom's *Welcome to Hell* (1981) scared me when I looked at the cover. It displayed a massive pentagram with the points forming a goat's head. Venom was the first band I knew of that claimed allegiance with the devil, with songs like, "Sons of Satan" and "In League with Satan." Band members Cronos (Conrad Thomas Lant), Abaddon (Anthony Bray), and Mantas (Jeffrey Dunn), had upped the ante.

It turns out they weren't devil worshipers. They were smart businessmen who felt they could sell records if they could "out-evil" Black Sabbath. In a 2015 interview with *Guitar World's* Jon Wiederhorn, Cronos said, "Since day one, we said, 'We are horror movies to music.' If Black Sabbath was *Frankenstein*, Venom is the *Evil Dead*…I used to listen to Sabbath, and Ozzy would be going off about all the fuckin' witches or elves. And then all of a sudden he would cry, 'Oh, God, help me!' And I would think, Oh no! You're supposed to be the evil bastard. Why are you asking God for help? So, I decided I would be the evil bastard." ("Venom's Cronos Reflects on the Band's Career and New Album," *From the Very Depths, Jun 16*).

The album recording is terrible, but that somehow enhanced the tone of evil, and Venom sold records, created the new metal subgenre Black Metal (the name of their 1982 album), and influenced later bands like Mayhem, Burzum, Immortal, and Emperor.

Mercyful Fate: Then came Denmark's Mercyful Fate, with their mysterious lead singer King Diamond. As opposed to Venom, Black Sabbath, and also his fellow band mates, King Diamond was a self-proclaimed Satanist. When I was a teenager, the legend among metalheads was that King sang with two voices—one a baritone, and one a high falsetto because he was possessed. Mercyful Fate's albums and lyrics dripped with horror elements and Satan.

In the 2012 "Shock Rock" episode of the TV series *Metal: Evolution* (2011-2014), King Diamond (Kim Bendix Petersen) discussed being an actual Satanist. "For me, Satanism isn't a religion. It's a life philosophy. It's never been just an image. King Diamond and Kim Petersen are absolutely one and the same." Yet, Mercyful Fate revels in the Christian views of Satan and evil. "We all like to get scared; it's just the way it is," says Diamond. "For me, it's not as much to put them in shock; it's to put them in a mood. The listener can make it much more scary than I can. He will pull from all the things that he feels most scared about."

At the time, I thought nothing was scarier than the songs "Corpse Without Soul" or "Melissa" from Mercyful Fate.

Things were about to get scarier in the real world.

Satanic Panic

The first time I remember seeing a large group of protestors with bullhorns and signs at a rock concert was March 23, 1984 at the Brendan Byrne Arena in East Rutherford, New Jersey. It was a Judas Priest concert for their *Defenders of the Faith* tour, and the arena, which had a concert capacity of nineteen thousand was sold out. The lines to get in the building snaked into the parking lot. The group of protestors found a bend in our line and camped uncomfortably close to us.

Their signs told us that we were going to hell, that we worshipped Satan, and that our music led us into drugs and sex. They shouted these sentiments to us as our line slowly moved. This upset many of my friends, who were practicing Catholics as well as metalheads. It didn't take long for someone in line to get fed up and flip off or argue with the protestors. When that happened, the outrage on both sides escalated. We were called trash and bums, and someone threw Jack Chick style religious comics at us. People from both sides had to be held back to stop fist fights.

Didn't these protestors realize this was all theater? Didn't they understand these were just horror movies set to music?

To be fair, the belief that heavy metal music was making us devil worshippers was just a part of the cultural phenomenon that became known as "Satanic Panic," and all that craziness didn't happen overnight.

In the book *Satanic Panic: Pop-Cultural Paranoia in the 1980s* (2015), co-editor Kier-La Janisse writes, "The Satanic Panic did not exist in a vacuum—its seeds were sown as far back as the late 1960s and percolated through the next decade before reaching a fever pitch in the Reagan era."

Janisse suggests that some of those seeds were dissent over Vietnam, disenchanted baby boomers searching for answers in unconventional religions (that included Jesus People, neo-Pagans, and Satanists), a "societal curiosity and acceptance of occultism," and a backlash against second-wave feminism that would focus on latchkey kids and working women.

"By the time the 1980s rolled around," says Janisse, "people had already been groomed to believe that there could be occultists living next door."

That belief was stoked by the book, *Michelle Remembers* (1980), the notorious memoir of Michelle Smith who, while under hypnosis by her psychiatrist (and co-author) Lawrence Pazder, had "recovered memories" of her abuse at the hands of her mother and the Church of Satan at the age of five. She was allegedly tortured, raped with snakes, forced to witness murders, and rubbed down with the blood of dismembered babies. Even though the story was later debunked as a hoax, "Satanic Ritual Abuse" and "recovered memories" became international buzzwords attached to any perceived threat to children, most tragically the 1983 accusations of rampant sexual and satanic abuse to children at the McMartin Preschool (*"The Only Word in the World is Mine: Remembering 'Michelle Remembers'"* essay by Alexandra Heller-Nicholas for the book *Satanic Panic: Pop-Cultural Paranoia in the 1980s).*

The hysteria around metal went into overdrive when fans of the music gave a horrible dose of reality to the discussion.

Say You Love Satan

On the night of June 16, 1984, in the town of Northport, Long Island, a 17-year-old self-proclaimed Satanist and local drug dealer named Richard "Ricky" Kasso went into the nearby Aztakea Woods with three high school acquaintances—Albert Quinones, James "Jimmy" Troiano, and Gary Lauwers. By the end of the night, Kasso had gouged out Lauwers' eyes and stabbed the boy 32 times. The two witnesses said that while Kasso stabbed Lauwers, he screamed, "Say you love Satan!"

The three teenagers left the body covered with leaves in a shallow grave. Gary

Lauwers wasn't missed within the circle of burnouts he hung out with, and his parents never filed a missing person report with the police. It was a certainty that some of the teenagers knew Lauwers was dead. Over a two-week period, Kasso took at least a dozen of them to view the body.

The murder was horrible. The apathy was terrifying. Then came the heavy metal and Satanism connection. Kasso, Troiano, and many of the teenagers were heavy metal fans. Kasso, nicknamed "The Acid King," was a big fan of Ozzy Osbourne and Judas Priest. His arrest photo shows him wearing an AC/DC concert shirt. (Breskin, David, "Kids in the Dark," *Rolling Stone,* November 22, 1984).

Suddenly, the motive behind any crime could be Satanism. In 1985, a baseball cap with the logo for the band AC/DC was found at one of the murder scenes of serial killer Richard Ramirez. The police had nicknamed the unknown killer "The Night Stalker," but once the baseball cap was found, the news reported on how AC/DC had a song called "Night Prowler" on their 1979 album *Highway to Hell.* Suddenly, AC/DC found themselves thrust into an uncomfortable spotlight as a killer's musical choices were suddenly important to the criminal investigation. Metal albums and T-shirts were entered as crime scene evidence like they were weapons. Judas Priest's 1978 album *Stained Class* was at the center of a trial where the band was accused of provoking two teenage friends, James Vance and Raymond Belknap, to shoot themselves in a 1985 suicide pact through the subliminal command of "do it" in the song "Better by You, Better Than Me." ("Judas Priest's Subliminal Message Trial: Rob Halford Looks Back" by Kory Grow, *Rolling Stone,* 2015).

Bands were also put on trial in the court of public opinion and had to appear on news broadcasts and talk shows to prove they weren't encouraging crime. The most famous of these was Geraldo Rivera's NBC live special, *Devil Worship: Exposing Satan's Underground,* on October 25, 1988. Ozzy Osbourne was live via satellite and was forced to defend all of heavy metal when Rivera said, "Every single kid that ever committed a violent act in Satan's name was also into heavy metal. What's your response to that, Oz?"

My Own Private Satanic Idaho

The rebellion between myself and my family intensified. The backward masking controversies were well documented in my church and now that the mainstream news was reporting a Satanic connection to metal, there were many long, angry arguments in my house over my music, my behavior, and my friends. Sometimes it got heated, and my dad and I got physical to the point of holes in walls. I never won.

The church elders came to my house. They'd corner me to tell me how I was selfishly risking the souls of my family by flirting with the devil. I was 16 and I was forced to go to church three times a week, and on more than one occasion the church elders called me out from the pulpit. To them this was a life or death battle. It pushed me farther away from the religion and from my family.

What kept me from losing my mind during that time?

Heavy metal.

Ironically, it was the elders who gave me the opportunity to find more heavy metal music. They made lists of forbidden bands and songs. They read specific lyrics during sermons to upset the congregation.

They did all my research for me.

The Satanic Panic caused a colossal uproar, but nothing concrete came out of the most sensational accusations. After seven long years and an expense of 15 million dollars, the McMartin Preschool trial ended with no convictions of any of the defendants. In 1990, Judas Priest was found not liable in the suicide pact between James Vance and Raymond Belknap. In *The Oxford*

Handbook of New Religious Movements (2004), Philip Jenkins states that "media coverage of Satanic Ritual Abuse began to turn negative by 1987, and the panic ended between 1992 and 1995."

The Dirty Handshake

In a way, the religious protests may have helped heavy metal continue as a genre. The music became more of an underground sensation and matured past exploiting the outrage around faux-Satanism.

Good horror focuses on what scares us. The horror stories metal now tells deal more with serial killers (Slayer's "Dead Skin Mask," Suffocation's "Bind, Torture, Kill"), nuclear annihilation (Dawn of Oblivion's "Nuclear Winter," System of a Down's "Boom!"), death (Autopsy's "Charred Remains," Ribspreader's "Dead Forever"), cannibalism (Bloodbath's "Eaten," Cannibal Corpse's "Submerged in Boiling Flesh"), and the End of Days (Black Label Society's "Tombstone Jesus," Six Feet Under's "Doomsday"). There are even activism metal bands, like France's Gojira and Britain's Architects (environmentalism) and Napalm Death (anti-capitalism).

Bands like Sweden's Ghost prove that Satan still has a seat at the table, but he's got a lot of company.

Heavy metal isn't the only place that horror and music thrive together. Punk bands like The Misfits and The Cramps created the "Horror Punk" subgenre. Their songs are influenced by horror films and old sci-fi B-movies, and their stage shows have the Gothic horror vibe reminiscent of Alice Cooper, with a little more violence thrown into the mix.

There's also the "Death Rock" subgenre, which pays homage to '50s songs about dead teenagers like "Leader of the Pack" and "Last Kiss," but with hypnotic guitar riffs.

Music has come a long way since the first time anyone heard the tritone. It's powerful magic that gets past the clutter in our minds and gives us release.

There will always be music that revels in the dark and scary side of life, and there will always be those who want to silence that music. But it never gets silenced for long because the dark and scary side of life exists.

Sometimes we need music that acknowledges our dark side and reminds us that the scary times are temporary.

Music not only allows us to confront our inner demons; it also supplies us with a backbeat and a groove that will enable us to dance with them too.

After all, the devil has the best tunes.

FIVE NOTABLE AND NOTORIOUS MURDER BALLADS

Murder Ballads are songs about apocryphal crimes, usually murders. Because this was a very popular oral tradition, actual dates and even locations of origin are not known. Here are some of the more notable Murder Ballads, listed by the multiple names some have.

1. *Pretty Polly/The Bloody Miller/The Berkshire Tragedy/The Knoxville Girl*: The story of a man who courts a woman and then brutally murders her and tries to escape justice. The song has many names, but they all share one detail: when someone notices blood on the killer's shirt, he uses a nosebleed as an excuse. The Byrds and Judy Collins have recorded versions of the song.

2. *The Twa Sisters:* Two sisters fall for the same man, so one sister drowns the other. The body is found by traveling musicians who cut her open and make a harp out of her breastplate. When the musicians stop at the homestead of the dead sister's family

and play a tune for food, the breastplate sings and accuses the sister of her murder. The parents boil her in lead and hang the musicians.

3. ***The Daemon Lover:*** The devil returns to an old flame to get back together with her, only to find out she now has a husband and a family. The devil seduces her until she leaves her new life for him. He takes her sailing on a ship and sinks it, so he can watch her drown.

4. ***Mack the Knife/Die Moritat von Mackie Messer (1928):*** Originally written for *The Threepenny Opera* by Berthold Brecht, the song tells the story of the robberies, murders, rapes, and arson of a real killer, Jack Sheppard. The killer became an anti-hero when Bobby Darin had a number one hit with the song.

5. ***Stagger Lee/Stagolee (1911):*** One of the most interesting modern Murder Ballads because it's based on an actual event is the cold-blooded murder of Billy Lyons by Stagger Lee Shelton over a Stetson hat. The view of Stagger Lee changes with the culture: in early versions the widow of Billy Lyons kills Lee, but in later versions he is a boogeyman the police are afraid of, and then in 1959 he becomes an anti-hero who escapes into the night. The song has been recorded over 400 times.

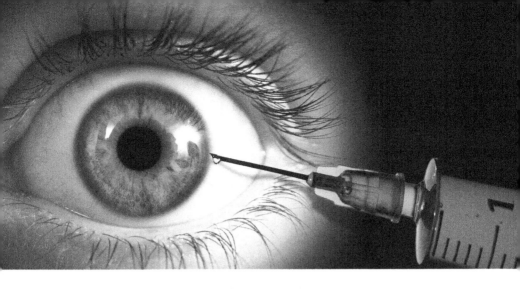

CHAPTER FIVE

MY OUTER DEMONS:

FIGHTING YOUR PHOBIAS WITH PHANTASMS

What scares you? What *really* scares you?

God, I hate that question.

Being a "horror guy," I get asked that question a lot. I'm afraid of the standard things like death, disfigurement, dying alone, horrible disease. Quicksand. Acid baths. My head exploding.

I'm just a regular guy.

But I really hate that question because it's the wrong question. People should ask, "What are you afraid of?"

That's more personal.

According to a 2017 report from the National Institute of Mental Health, nearly 10 percent, or 19.2 million Americans, have varying levels of phobias. Scientists and researchers aren't sure exactly what causes them, but it's thought that genetics, culture, and traumas play a part in their creation.

Watching Horror Movies is Not a Cure for Phobias or an Alternative to Medical Care

I am not a mental health professional, I'm not a sociologist, I'm not a doctor or a biologist. I'm a horror fan, obsessed and opinionated enough to write a book about the subject. This is not a medical text or a self-help book. I do not advocate self-medication for any ailments, physical or emotional, and I do not believe watching horror movies is an alternative to medical care of any kind. I strongly encourage anyone who needs medical attention of any kind to get it.

This is a book about horror, but it's not deadly serious. It's an extended barroom argument with additional research. Horror is about getting intense emotions like fear and dread firing in the viewer's mind. Its job is to make you uncomfortable and try to scare you. You go to horror willingly and with that knowledge. Horror is insensitive. At times, you may find this book insensitive, too.

Phobias on Film: Enter if You Dare

According to the National Institute of Mental Health, phobias are a type of anxiety disorder in which people experience a strong, irrational fear of something that poses little or no real danger.

There's a difference between fears and phobias. R. Reid Wilson, PhD, spokesman for the American Psychological Association, states that the key to distinguishing a fear from a phobia is that while most people get the jitters if a spider crawls up their arm, people suffering from arachnophobia (the fear of spiders) are physically and/or psychologically impaired by it.

Horror films have often exploited common phobias to crank up the anxiety of the audience. Many of these horror films promote the phobia-inducing element front and center, making it the selling point. That knowledge can make a viewer nervous before the movie starts. People who have a phobia or who want nothing to do with a movie that deals with that phobia wisely stay away.

Then there are people like me who get the jitters from whatever phobia is being paraded out, but are too curious to pass up a chance to get that extra chill up their spine. It's probably the same mentality that makes some people work their way up the Scoville scale eating hot peppers on a dare.

I know I'm in the minority, but I'm the kind of person who feels more relaxed after I've watched a scary movie. Scary movies put me in a better mood.

Nothing takes the edge off a stressful day better than watching someone getting decapitated by an ax murderer. When I'm feeling a little depressed, nothing blows away the blues like hearing the screams of an unlucky hunter while mutated bears shred him into mulch. Just the thought of someone unable to get their car engine to start while their undead relative smacks the windshield with a hammer drops my anxiety to a manageable level.

When it comes to watching movies that feature a phobia that I have, I find that cinematic versions of it can make my skin crawl, but it's manageable. It's fun. I can always turn off the movie.

So, for those of you who enjoy testing your "Scoville-for-scares scale" on things that creep you out on a personal level, I've made a list of horror films that revel in some of the most common phobias.

Arachnophobia (Fear of Spiders)

Let's start with the Big Kahuna, the most common phobia—the fear of spiders. It affects one in every three women and one in every four men, and that fact was never lost on Hollywood. There are a number of movies that play off that fear.

Tarantula! (1955)

If you need to start in the shallow end of the pool, I suggest the nuclear radiation giant spider movie, *Tarantula*. It's corny but still creepy because they use a real tarantula on miniature sets.

Arachnophobia (1990)

If you're ready for a more in-depth dive into eight-legged creepiness, I recommend the big-budget *Arachnophobia*, which has tons of special effect spiders as well as a bunch of real ones. The story is about a new species of Amazonian killer spider that mates with regular house spiders in rural California. The real spiders used in the movie are ugly, but they are actually harmless New Zealand crab-spiders. Try to keep that in mind; they're just actors. The movie also adds doses of comedy to the horror, so you have time to catch your breath.

Kingdom of the Spiders (1977)

If you're ready to confront your fear of spiders head on, try *Kingdom of the Spiders*. This low-budget horror film stars William Shatner, a veterinarian who realizes too late that his small Arizona town is on a new migration path for a horde of deadly tarantulas. Pesticides made the spiders into killers, and they will attack anything that gets in their way.

Director John "Bud" Cardos didn't have a lot of money, so he used what he had wisely. The movie boasts *five thousand live tarantulas*, and every one of them crawls all over the cast. Literally. In a 1998 interview for *Fangoria Magazine*, producer Igo Kantor explained that they paid Mexican wranglers

10 dollars for every tarantula they could find for the film. So, 50 thousand dollars of the 500 thousand dollar budget went to tarantulas. The production didn't have money for stand-ins, so when you see a little girl crying on a bed surrounded by tarantulas, it's probably not method acting. There are scenes where you may feel overwhelmed, and by the end, you might find yourself checking the cushions of your sofa for stowaways.

Claustrophobia (Fear of Enclosed Spaces)

Claustrophobia is the fear of enclosed spaces, but the space doesn't need to be physically small to make you feel like the walls are closing in on you. You just need to feel like you can't get out. Imprisoned.

Rosemary's Baby (1968)

An Upper East Side Manhattan apartment becomes a prison for a pregnant woman when "well-meaning" neighbors monitor her every move. As Rosemary Woodhouse's pregnancy advances, she is isolated by her neighbors, whom she doesn't really know. To them, the safety and health of the baby supersede anything else. She's an afterthought to the unborn child.

Rosemary is trapped in her womblike apartment. Not only is the world shrinking around her, but also something is growing inside of her that scares her more every day. Talk about the walls closing in.

The Descent (2005)

If you're looking for pure, primal claustrophobia that makes you stretch your toes inside your shoes while you watch, check out *The Descent.*

After mourning the loss of her husband and daughter in a car accident, Sarah reunites with her friends, a group of women outdoor adventurers, for a cave expedition. She hopes to reconnect with the outside world. Unfortunately, the leader of the group takes them to an unmapped cave system for confidence building.

What could possibly go wrong?

The cave collapses behind them. They are forced to move forward and downward, deeper into the earth. Lanterns are their only source of light. It's silent, except for their breath. And the passages get narrower. As they crawl on their bellies, single file, they realize they may not be alone.

I'm not usually claustrophobic, but there are sequences in *The Descent* that gave me an insight into that flash of terror. It's a brilliant horror film that is as much about the descent into madness as it is a descent into places one should not venture.

Agoraphobia (Fear of Open Spaces)

Let's go from the fear of enclosed spaces to the fear of open spaces. People who have agoraphobia fear being alone and helpless in a place that they feel is threatening and where there's no easy way to escape.

Let's talk about being lost at sea. The horrible infinity of the surface of the water is second in terror only to the horrific endlessness of the dark and hidden expanse underneath the surface. And the terror of what is there under the surface. What could be worse, right?

Now, imagine you don't even have a boat.

Open Water (2003)

This film is loosely based on a real incident that occurred on January 25, 1998, when an American couple, Tom and Eileen Lonergan, were left behind by their tour boat while on a scuba dive on Australia's Great Barrier

Reef. *Open Water* has a documentary feel. It was made on location, in open water. The two actors float in shark-infested waters without a cage. (Jason Daley, *Outside Magazine*, Oct.1, 2003).

That's right, all the sharks in *Open Water* are real. In Deborah Sontag's 2004 *New York Times* article on the making of the film, director Chris Kentis discussed how he jumped into the ocean with the two actors while a pro-fessional shark wrangler chummed the water off–camera. When a fin breaks the surface near the actors and they both let out high-pitched shrieks, it feels real.

By the nature of the production, the movie doesn't have the predictable post-*Jaws* suspense shots of a circling dorsal fin. Everything here feels authentic, and that includes the existential horror of two people trying to remain calm while they convince each other that the boat is on its way back for them. It's intense, and yet the situation is so horrible, it's almost absurdist in its tragedy. You could rename it *Bleeding for Godot*.

The Ritual (2017)

The dense forest of Northern Sweden takes the place of the ocean in *The Ritual*, where four friends hike to honor a dead friend. Even with maps and a compass, they get lost in the dense forest. They know they're only a few miles from their hotel resort, but every apex they climb only reveals another endless blanket of trees.

Then they see a disemboweled deer strung up high in the trees. They notice the ancient runes carved into all the trees nearby. They realize something is following them.

The Ritual does an exceptional job of capturing the helplessness of getting lost in the woods, the slow-motion race against the setting sun and uneven terrain. This movie realizes that a forest is scariest when it goes dead silent, those moments when it feels like the trees and the air are swallowing the sound. Because something out there made every living thing around you go quiet and freeze in place.

Pandorum (2009)

As vast as the ocean is, eventually there is a shoreline. Even the largest forest has an edge. Now imagine outer space. Deep space. You can't breathe out there. Anywhere. Your metal spaceship is the only thing standing between you and a horrible, lonely, silent death. It's a floating life-support system. Now imagine there's a malfunction.

In *Pandorum*, two astronauts are prematurely awakened from hypersleep to find that their ship, a huge vessel transporting the last five thousand humans to a new planet, is experiencing massive power failures due to malfunctions in the nuclear core. When they go to the bridge, they find out they are locked out of access. To make matters worse, their early emergence from hypersleep has physiological side effects. Both men have partial amnesia, and one of them is starting to show signs of "Orbital Dysfunction Syndrome," an illness that causes hallucinations. Just when it seems things can't get worse, they find evidence that someone, or something, dangerous is loose on the ship and stalking them.

Pandorum exploits the agoraphobic fear of feeling there is no escape by giving us multiple scenarios where the mental, existential, moral, and perhaps literal walls are closing in on us in the vacuum of eternal space.

Mysophobia (Fear of Germs)

The average person touches their face two thousand to three thousand times per day. Does that cross your mind when you're in a public restroom and you see someone who leaves without washing their hands? Do you think of that jerk in the bathroom the next time you're about to shake someone's hand?

If so, boy, do I have some horror movies for you.

Mysophobia is the fear of germs.

Cabin Fever (2002)

Five college friends rent a cabin in the woods for a week. Unbeknownst to them, a flesh-eating virus that attacks animals has just jumped to its first human. This movie is a laundry list of germophobic anxieties, from contaminated water supplies to diseased animals, to inappropriately sprayed bodily fluids, to unprotected sex. It also has a bathing sequence that hits at the most profound fear of germaphobes: no matter how much you scrub, you can't clean deep enough.

Contagion (2011)

Contagion is about a pandemic taking over the world, much like the 1918 Influenza pandemic which, according to a 2006 article in the medical journal *Emerging Infectious Diseases*, killed 50 million people, and infected 500 million—one third of the world population at the time.

In a 2011 interview for ComingSoon.net, screenwriter Scott Z. Burns noted that to make *Contagion* as realistic as possible, the filmmakers consulted virologist Dr. Ian Lipkin to create a realistic super-virus that could jump species, and also epidemiologist Lawrence Brilliant to help create an accurate depiction of a pandemic. Filmmakers consulted the Center for Disease Control and Prevention and the World Health Organization on how they would prepare for and combat this super-virus. The resultant chaos, terror, and decimation included in *Contagion* are based on their honest and unflinching answers.

Contagion has no opening credits, and there is little in the way of mood-setting music. The shooting style is straightforward like a documentary, and

there is no sense of security—any character can die at any time. That Oscar-winning actor or actress might not make it to the half-hour mark.

Trypanophobia (Fear of Needles)

Another widespread phobia is the fear of needles. Something is unsettling at
a primal level in the act of someone sticking a sharp object into your flesh.
They burrow deeper beneath the skin for the specific purpose of either shooting something foreign into you, or sucking something vital out of you.

Requiem for a Dream (2000)

Maybe that's why, out of all the drug abuses that exist, the one that creeps
us out the most is injecting heroin. *Requiem for a Dream* follows four people
who retreat from the world by using various types of drugs: prescription
drugs, methamphetamines, and heroin. Each story depicts a habit that ends
in enslavement. The filmmakers depict addiction as a possession, an invasion
that slowly transforms the host into a monster bent on its own destruction.
The effects of drug use are shown in horrifying detail. When we watch the
slow decline of Harry Goldfarb, the heroin addict, the camera forces us to
watch injections into infected wounds. We are so close to the devastation we
can almost smell the skin necrosis.

Audition (1999)

Audition is about a man who fakes being a movie producer so he can audition women for him to court and possibly marry. He meets a vengeful,
damaged psychotic and they start a relationship. The fake producer breaks
off the relationship and she exacts revenge.

The movie subjects us to everything you can think of that is unsettling about needles. Injections that paralyze without numbing the nerves. Injections into tongues so you can't cry out.

Oh, and it's not just hypodermic needles. Wait until the scorned psychopath breaks out the acupuncture needles.

Demonophobia (Fear of Demons)

Demonophobia is the extreme fear of demons or being possessed by demons. In the psychiatric community, it's called Dissociative Trance Disorder. A 1996 article for the *Journal of Personality Assessment* (Vol. 66) stated that although more data was needed, people claiming they are possessed by a demon or overwhelmed by paranormal experiences are more common than was previously thought.

Given the resurgence in movies that deal with demonic possession, like *The Conjuring* franchise, *The Exorcism of Emily Rose*, *The Rite*, *The Possession*, *The Last Exorcism* and its sequel, just to name a few, demons are in vogue again.

In my opinion, the scariest part of demonic possession films is the hunt, when the unseen force stalks the unsuspecting victim and toys with them by slowly making its presence known, with increasingly terrifying results. Here are some movies that relish the horror of predator and prey.

The Entity (1982)

This film declares that it's "based on true events." It's the story of Carla Moran, an unmarried mother of two who is attacked by an invisible entity. This entity, a demon, beats her and rapes her. Nobody believes her at first.

In one scene, Carla sits in front of her dresser mirror brushing her hair before heading to bed for the night. She hears a noise and stops combing. Suddenly her head snaps back violently, and her lip is bleeding. Something has hit her.

Before she can react, something invisible and powerful throws her onto the bed. The bedroom door closes. She doesn't even have time to scream.

In another scene, the family throws a birthday party for one of the sons. They're in the kitchen, and the mother puts a cake on the table. Carla goes to get plates. As she walks across the room, she collides with an invisible force. The demon stands there, unnoticed in the room, waiting for a moment to terrify her. Then it throws her to the ground.

The Entity does an excellent job of exploring the horror of total powerlessness and its comment on the mental torture that women endure at the hand of stalkers has the despair of reality.

Paranormal Activity (2007)

Another movie that really scared me when I first saw it at a midnight screening was the original *Paranormal Activity* (2007). I think the original's primal impact has been overshadowed by the many sequels and the "found-footage" phenomenon which it popularized. But *Paranormal Activity* had a sparseness and rawness that compelled audiences to watch closely and listen intently, as if they were in their own houses and heard a weird noise at night.

When I saw that film with a packed audience, you could sense their dread increasing as the movie progressed. The theater was silent except for the sound of gasps and breathless moans.

The entire movie is about a couple becoming prey to something that toys with them, just to watch them scream. There's no reason. The demon just chose this couple.

Katie and Micah move into a new suburban tract house in bright and sunny San Diego, and soon after, strange things start to happen. The happenings are subtle; at first, they seem insignificant. It starts with a door Katie knows she closed that is now open. And then personal items and books are found strewn on the floor or placed in the center of a hallway as if deliberately. Then there are noises downstairs while they're in bed. Was that the sound of footsteps? Small things pile up, and when there are enough of them, Katie questions their safety.

The husband sets up a static camera to record their bedroom at night, just like a security camera. This static shot at night has the audience scanning every corner of the frame and watching for any movement. We listen for any sound. We are on edge.

The footage shows the lights in the hallway turning on as the vulnerable couple sleeps. Heavy footsteps come up the staircase. The invisible force slowly pulls the covers away from them, exposing them both.

The documentary feel of *Paranormal Activity*, and the repetition of days turning into nights when they have to go to sleep, effectively amped up the dread, and this was not common when it premiered.

At the theater where I saw *Paranormal Activity*, there were no end credits. The movie cut straight to black. The entire audience sat there in the dark and we waited for the lights to come on. They did not. People started getting restless. Somebody finally yelled out, "Turn on the fucking lights!"

Some of the films I've mentioned, like *Paranormal Activity* and *Open Water*, freaked me out to the point where I had to turn on the lights in every room in my house. It wasn't because I thought something might be hiding. It was because I felt this horrible sense of being alone.

Even though I've met a few horror fans who didn't think those films were particularly scary, I got more than I bargained for. The way those movies scared me was...personal.

And, to me, that's the good news. I love when a movie gets under my skin. I want a movie to reach me personally. Sure, there's the potential of a sleepless night, but I find that I get a sense of relief afterwards. I get to laugh at myself, and when I laugh, I'm also consciously reminding myself that there's nothing to be afraid of. It's only a movie.

MORE PHOBIAS AND THEIR HORROR MOVIE COUNTERPARTS

1. **Aerophobia (Fear of Flying):** *Final Destination* (2000), *Twilight Zone: The Movie* (1983), *The Grey* (2011), *Alive* (1993)

2. **Herpetophobia (Fear of Reptiles):** *Spasms* (1983), *Stanley* (1972), *Venom* (1981), *Black Water* (2007), *Primeval* (2007), *Alligator* (1980)

3. **Agliophobia (Fear of Pain):** *The Marathon Man* (1976), *Hellraiser* (1987), *Hostel* (2005), *Burnt Offerings* (1976), *Martyrs* (2008)

4. **Anthrophobia (Fear of People):** *Invasion of the Body Snatchers* (1956), *Invasion of the Body Snatchers* (1978), *The Texas Chain Saw Massacre* (1974), *The Tenant* (1976), *The Crazies* (1973)

5. **Robophobia (Fear of Robots):** *Westworld* (1973), *Ex Machina* (2014), *The Terminator* (1984), *Hardware* (1990), *Blade Runner* (1982), *2001: A Space Odyssey* (1968)

CHAPTER SIX

KILLED BY DEATH:

FACING MORTALITY
THROUGH HORROR MOVIES

For the most part, the way dead bodies look in horror movies is bullshit.

There's almost always too much muscular tension in the face and neck. The expression on the face reflects the tragedy and violence. An *actual* dead body lets go of all of that.

There is no dignity and there is no grace to the way the body lies.

I was a firefighter in the military, so I've seen up close what bodies look like after a traumatic death. The closest I've ever seen a movie get was the opening sequence in *Henry: Portrait of a Serial Killer* (1986). There is a montage of the bodies of Henry's victims. When we see these bodies alone in their undiscovered crime scene, we hear an audio flashback to the murder in progress, like a ghost that haunts the moment.

There is one body within this montage that sticks with me. It's a girl lying in a ditch in a field. We start with an extreme close-up of her face. Her mascara is thick and messed. Her eyes are halfway closed. Blades of grass vibrate in the wind, close to those eyes. Her pupils are dilated and frozen, looking off to the side. Her naked and pale body is splayed awkwardly. She was disposed of without regard. It's a sunny day.

That image evokes the brief sorrow I allowed myself when I arrived at the scene of a fatality. I felt a sorrow for something that was no longer present. That which used to be but is no longer. And, if I were honest, I'd admit to a moment of terror as well. Inevitably, death comes for us all.

Death Pays an Early Visit

I was in kindergarten when I saw my first dead body.

My family lived in a brick double-residency home. We rented one side of the building, and our landlord lived on the other side.

It was summer, and my younger sister and I played in the house while my mother ironed clothes. The TV was tuned to my mom's soap operas.

Suddenly, we were startled by a series of frighteningly loud, violent bangs. The sound started at the ceiling, then it traveled down the length of one of the walls.

My mother ran out of the room and searched the house, floor by floor, but she couldn't find anything that could have caused the sound.

She went to the porch to check on the landlord's side of the house.

Then my mother runs back through the living room and into the kitchen and grabs the phone. She's a mess.

In an instant, our porch fills with our neighbors. A police car and an ambulance arrive. In all the chaos, my mother forgets about my sister and me.

I sneak up to the door.

My mother tells a neighbor that our landlord, who lived next door, had a massive heart attack, fell down the stairs and died instantly. I watch ambulance attendants remove his body from the house with an old-fashioned gurney. They don't cover his face with a sheet the way they do in movies.

I remember how wide open his mouth was. It was like he was frozen in a deep, silent moan. I realize now that they probably took his dentures out to try and resuscitate him. But as a kid, it looked like a big, dark hole. I remember how weird he looked without his glasses, how tiny his eyelids seemed. He just didn't look *real* anymore.

I couldn't take my eyes away from his face. It was unsettling, weird, and a little sad. But what terrified me was what was happening inside my house.

My dad was at work, so mom had to deal with the situation. She was emotionally fragile on good days. A neighbor noticed my mom edging towards hysterics and pulled her close. The woman told my mom to keep it together, "for the kids."

Suddenly I was scared. None of the adults knew what to do.

That death had a significant impact on my life. We were renters, so we had to find a new home. Overnight, I lost all my friends, and the comfort of my bedroom. I lost my sense of security. The landlord's death shook up my life, and I never even knew his name.

Death is our universal boogeyman, an object of morbid fascination, an endless inspiration for art.

Death is the Big Kahuna

Death may be a part of nature, but that doesn't make it any less terrifying. We all know that we will die. We know our loved ones will die. But we don't know when or how. It can come without warning and leave survivors devastated.

It's the Big Kahuna. Just the *threat* of death can freeze brave men in their tracks.

For as prominent and profound as it is, death itself is still a mystery. Even physicians find it a challenge to define death in a medical context. We can say that death occurs when there's no pulse, or heartbeat, or brain activity. But those are only a list of the symptoms of death.

To physicians, the thin line between life and death is still conceptual. (Henig, Robin Marantz, April 2016, "Crossing Over: How Science Is Redefining Life and Death," *National Geographic*). Medical advances have moved the line. People can be revived if their heart stops. There's even a medical term that expresses the mysteriousness of death. *Senescence* refers to when a person survives all the calamities that life throws at them, and they stay healthy and happy…and eventually die anyway.

The body begins to shut down on a genetic level.

In 2003, the International Longevity Centre reported that two-thirds of the deaths that occur daily across the world relate to senescence. Not disease. Not trauma. Old age.

Death happens 150 thousand times a day across the world.

One hundred twenty times every minute.

Two times every second.

Death is unknowable, and it's unstoppable, and it's coming for all of us. It's no wonder we think of death as a supernatural being. It's no wonder that we personify Death as something alive.

Laughing to Keep from Dying

Death is often personified as the Grim Reaper, a living skeleton in a cloak holding a scythe. It's one of the most instantly recognized archetypes, probably only second to how we personify the Red Devil with a pitchfork and a tail.

The devil usually represents evil. But Death? Death isn't evil. Death *just is*.

Even those of us who don't believe in an evil devil with a pitchfork fear the Grim Reaper. You might go your whole life and never come face-to-face with the devil. But Death knows all of our names.

Contemplating our mortality is uncomfortable. Maybe that's why so many movies and books show the Grim Reaper in a humorous or tongue-in-cheek manner. From *Death Takes a Holiday*, to *Monty Python's The Meaning of Life*, to *Bill and Ted's Bogus Journey*, to *The Last Action Hero*, Death seems like a cool dude you might meet at a bar after hours.

But even in those comedies, there's an element of horror. I think it's inevitable. No matter how you dress it, Death brings a horror story along with it.

Death Knows All the Chess Moves

Ingmar Bergman's vision of death in *The Seventh Seal* (1957) tells the story of a disillusioned knight who returns from the Crusades only to find out that the Black Plague has struck his homeland, Sweden.

On the beach, he meets Death, pale and dressed in black. The Reaper lets the knight know he's been waiting for him. The knight is a chess player. He tries to delay Death by challenging Death to a game.

Death agrees.

The match continues as the knight and his companions travel back to his castle. Nobody else can see Death, so his companions think he's playing alone.

During the journey, the knight meets people who call out to a god who doesn't answer. The plague kills with cruel equality, and God is silent. All the while, Death is there, moving the chess pieces.

Death says, "No one escapes me."

In *The Seventh Seal*, Death is like a boxer who cuts off parts of the ring from his opponent, biding his time. He is always moving forward, toward his final objective.

No one escapes him.

The title of the film comes from a passage in the Bible that says, "When the Lamb broke the Seventh Seal, there was silence in Heaven." When death is upon us, and we know it, we cry out in desperation for God. We cry out for mercy, and for more time.

But the only one there for us, the only one who hears us is Death.

And *that,* my friend, is the silence in heaven.

The Dead May Sleep, But Death Does Not

Not all movies and books use the traditional Grim Reaper. Sometimes Death is a beautiful woman, like in Jean Cocteau's *Orpheus* (1950) or Bob Fosse's *All That Jazz* (1979).

Sometimes, Death can hide in plain sight.

Phantasm (1979)

One of the more striking modern images of Death is The Tall Man, in Don Coscarelli's cult horror film *Phantasm*. The movie takes a surreal look at our fears around death.

We fear what happens to loved ones after they die, and we fear being left behind, helpless and alone. We fear that no matter what we do, none of us can outrun Death. Every time someone we know dies, it is a reminder that Death is getting closer to us.

Don Coscarelli has said that *Phantasm* explores the way we handle death in America. We hand our dead off to strangers, who cover the body with make-up and dress it up. These strangers make our loved ones look like they're sleeping.

Strangers hide the dead in caskets. Strangers put the casket in the back of a hearse.

Strangers drive the casket to a big marble mausoleum where they hide the dead underground.

Often cemeteries are out near the edge of town.

We try to distance ourselves from Death, but it's an illusion. A phantasm.

The emotional core of the film is the relationship between two brothers orphaned after the death of their parents. Mike, the narrator and the younger brother, believes Death isn't done with his family yet. He is terrified of losing his older brother.

In the film, Death owns the mortuary. He is known only as The Tall Man.

He dresses in a black suit, he rarely speaks, and he stares right through anyone who meets his gaze.

Once Mike gets The Tall Man's attention, he locks in on him.

The Tall Man follows Mike with purpose. He can be anywhere, he is relentless, and he is unstoppable. Like the chess board in *The Seventh Seal,* life is a game. You might play a good game.

But when the game is over, you go to The Tall Man.

Death Doesn't Scare Me, Dying Does

Both *Phantasm* and Dan Curtis' horror film *Burnt Offerings* (1976) share a location site, the Dunsmuir Mansion in Oakland, California.

I happen to live just a few miles from the Dunsmuir Mansion.

Both *Phantasm* and *Burnt Offerings* are essential movies in my life, but the reason *Burnt Offerings* resonates is much more personal.

A year or so after our Landlord died, my parents got divorced. My father and I lived at my grandparents' house for a while. My grandfather was dying—slowly and painfully.

He was a baker, and after years of working around loose flour, he had developed white lung. His lungs were hardening from the inside, and he was slowly suffocating.

My grandfather had the disease for many years. I only knew him sick. And he terrified me.

I remember watching a slide show of my parents' wedding day, and in one of the pictures was my grandfather, dressed smartly in a black tuxedo. He had a sturdy build, a powerful jaw, and steely eyes. The disease had changed that.

The man I knew was skin and bones, and his grey hair was slicked straight back with sweat. His bloodshot eyes were full of a mixture of fear and rage. He sat on the living room couch all day and slept there all night, coughing and cursing loudly. He would pound his fist on the coffee table when a cough doubled him over. He would glare at me when I walked in the room. I was afraid to look him in the eye.

But I *did* watch him. All the time.

I'd sneak down the stairs and spy on him from between the banister posts, kind of like how the narrator in "The Telltale Heart" watched the old man with the cloudy eye.

From my perch on the staircase, I also saw my grandfather when he was scared. Every few days, the doctor would make a house call and give my grandfather injections. He would moan and whimper and curse while the doctor looked for a suitable vein. Sometimes my grandmother would hold him down when he writhed in pain. Sometimes it was my father who held him down when he panicked.

Burnt Offerings (1976)

That's where *Burnt Offerings* comes in.

Burnt Offerings follows a family who rents an old, shabby, country mansion for the summer. But the dilapidated house is alive, and it feeds off the life force of its occupants. For instance, if someone cuts their hand, the dead flowers in a vase come back to life.

The house wants to regenerate, and it will slowly suck the life from all the occupants.

The idea is creepy, to be sure, but the reason *Burnt Offerings* haunted me for years came down to one scene.

Ben, the husband and father, has a recurring nightmare about his mother's funeral. He was a little boy when she died. He was terrified by the chauffeur of the hearse, who was dressed in an all-black uniform with a matching driver's cap and dark sunglasses that covered his eyes. The chauffeur stared at the boy all through the funeral and smiled at him menacingly.

The dream traumatized Ben as a child, and now he starts having it again.

He starts to imagine he sees the antique hearse on the country road. He believes the chauffeur looks out and gives him that horrible smile.

Then his elderly aunt, who is vacationing with the family, starts to die. Her health rapidly declines. In the morning she's a little tired and misses breakfast. But by nightfall, she writhes and screams in pain on her bed.

Her bones crack and her body twists up. She moans and pants like a sick dog. Her bloodshot eyes roll into the back of her head.

She is dying as my grandfather did. Ben holds her down like my father held down my grandfather.

As Ben holds his aunt down, he hears a car approach. He thinks it's the doctor, but when he looks out the window, he sees the hearse.

The Grim Reaper approaches. They both hear the front door open downstairs. They hear something heavy drag across the floor.

Ben and his aunt cry helplessly, desperately holding onto each other.

The heavy dragging sound is coming up the stairs.

Then it is outside the closed bedroom door.

The bedroom door crashes open, and there stands the chauffeur, with the horrible smile. He holds a casket on a gurney. He rolls it into the room as they scream.

The screen goes black.

I saw *Burnt Offerings* the same year my grandfather died. When I saw that scene, I remembered wishing my grandfather would die. Just so I wouldn't fear him anymore.

I was too young to know the selfishness of my thoughts. I felt the regret and I knew how cruel that was when he died.

Then I started having dreams with the chauffeur in them.

My grandfather died in his sleep. They said he died peacefully. Watching the last months of my grandfather's life, I started looking at death differently.

I don't fear Death. I fear dying.

I'm afraid of knowing what's happening and knowing it's out of my control. It's the horror of knowing.

The Horror of Knowing

That fear of dying fuels our love of horror films. We get to confront a fear based on primal emotion. Coming out on the other side is exhilarating. But when that "horror of knowing" is done well in a movie, the effect lingers long after the end credits.

It hits us.

You know when a movie is done well when there's no cheering or laughing in the audience. You can hear a pin drop in the theater. Those moments are rare.

The key ingredients are emotional connection and empathy. If we relate to the victim, we suspend disbelief. We become vulnerable. That moment of vulnerability can be cathartic and healing.

I was never a big fan of slasher films. For all the carnage and body count, there's very little emotional investment.

I respond to films that respect death and dying as they disturb the viewer. They are a meditation on the loss of life, and they are committed to making you feel that loss. They don't let you off easy. That can be cleansing.

Have you ever listened to a song and suddenly started crying? The music kindles a memory of unresolved grief. It gets past our defenses and gives us the healing we deny ourselves.

Movies can do that, too.

The Terror of the Normalcy of It All

In my opinion, the most disturbing, heartbreaking, and memorable death in cinema does not take place in a horror film. It happens in a gritty drama about a family.

Sometimes a Great Notion (1971)

Sometimes a Great Notion, directed by Paul Newman, tells the story of an iconoclastic logging family in Oregon and their fight to remain independent.

It's a rough and angry life cutting down trees, and danger is always near. Paul Newman plays Hank, the eldest son, and Richard Jaeckel plays Joe-Ben, his half-brother. Hank is prickly and feels the weight of the world. Joe-Ben is a dim-witted joker. Everything bounces off of him. He's a pure optimist.

One day, a tree breaks loose from its chains and rolls down the hillside. Hank's father's arm gets crushed.

The violent trajectory of the log knocks other logs free. They roll toward the river where Joe-Ben is cutting wood with his chainsaw.

Joe-Ben sees the logs rolling toward him. He dives to avoid getting crushed. He narrowly escapes death, and he's seemingly uninjured, but the log pins him to the shallow riverbed.

Hank stays behind to help get Joe-Ben free as the rest of the family rushes his father to the hospital.

The two men are entirely alone.

This scene plays out with long takes and very few cuts. There is no suspenseful music on the soundtrack. We hear the birds, the river water, and the wind in the tall, beautiful redwoods. It feels real.

It feels natural.

Even though he's pinned, Joe-Ben seems unconcerned. He's more embarrassed than anything.

Hank, on the other hand, is very concerned. He tries not to show it. He walks around the log, again and again, assessing the situation. Hank thinks about digging a hole, but Joe-Ben is on an underwater rock shelf.

As Hank does this, the camera watches. The birds sing.

Joe-Ben tells Hank to quit wasting his time. It's okay, because he's not in any pain, and the shallow water only comes up to his waist. Hank says he'll get a chainsaw and split the log and Joe-Ben argues that it's too big.

They have a sibling argument, with Joe-Ben wise-cracking his worry-wart brother. But we aren't laughing. The scene hasn't cut, and while Hank rushes for a chainsaw, we sit waiting with Joe-Ben.

The birds keep singing.

Hank returns with his chainsaw, and he starts cutting the log as close to his brother as he safely can. The sound of the saw struggling against the thickness of the wood is distressing.

The tide starts coming in, and the water begins to rise.

Hank keeps trying to cut the log, but it is too big. In his haste he gets the saw too close to the water, and he floods the engine. The chainsaw is frozen, deep in the tree.

Joe-Ben is optimistic. He thinks the water rising is a blessing. All they need to do is wait, and the water will lift the tree, and he can swim out.

The water does move the tree. But not straight up.

The tree, slowly, slowly...slowly starts to roll toward Joe-Ben. The tree turns just a little. It pushes Joe-Ben back just a little bit deeper into the water.

Just a little.

The first wave of panic hits Joe-Ben. "You're not gonna let this river drown me, are you, Hank?"

Hank shouts to the hills and the treetops for help. His words echo. The tree rolls just a little again.

This ordeal goes on for minutes. Joe-Ben babbles and laughs in panic. Hank tells him to shut up and calm down.

The tree rolls again.

Now only Joe-Ben's face is above the surface of the water. Hank tells him not to worry, that he will breathe for him when he goes under the water. He will blow air into his mouth every minute until the log floats away.

Joe-Ben goes under the water.

Hank keeps his promise and blows his own breath into his half-brother's lungs. They stare into each other's eyes. Every second is important.

Hank sees it happen. He screams, and cries, and begs.

Then it is all over. The birds still sing.

I don't fear Death. It's the dying that terrifies me.

A Compassionate Grim Reaper

Sometimes a Great Notion made me think back on the deaths of my landlord and my grandfather. I thought of the loneliness of their deaths and the indifference of the summer day, and the dark quiet of a sleeping household.

The normalcy of it all is terrifying.

Maybe we've got it all wrong. We fear the Grim Reaper, but perhaps he's the feeling of calm when death seems all but inevitable, like sliding off the edge of a pool into the water.

Maybe when Death says "no one escapes me," maybe he means "nobody enters alone."

I went to Ireland and visited an old cemetery in the South Country. I looked at the tombstones. They displayed a mixture of Catholic and Pagan faiths. Some had crucifixes on them, and some were adorned with spirals and runes.

I noticed that when I looked at the decidedly Christian stones, there was grief written all over them. How much the loved one was missed, and the words "beloved" and "sorrow" were chiseled in.

But on the Pagan ones, there were references to transformation and freedom. Inscriptions suggested that their loved ones were now "living in the wind." "As Above, So Below." They did not commemorate a loss, but a return.

I kind of like the Pagan sentiment. If Death is natural, perhaps the Reaper is nothing more than the wind. The wind doesn't judge, and it blows upon the just and the unjust equally. In the end, the fear gives way to the compassion of a gentle breeze. Wouldn't it be great if a compassionate Grim Reaper welcomes us to that new plane?

Of course, I'm in no hurry to find out.

A SPOILER-FILLED LOOK AT THE MOST RIDICULOUS HORROR MOVIE DEATH SCENES

After our discussion of seriously disturbing deaths, let's delve into death scenes that will make you laugh out loud.

1. *Deadly Friend* (1987): Not one of Wes Craven's best moments. An elderly woman suffers "death by basketball." A killer robot girl whips a basketball at the woman and her head explodes like a sledgehammered watermelon.

2. *Dawn of the Dead* (1978): This one is intentionally funny. A zombie with a weirdly elongated head—think Karloff's Frankenstein monster—sneaks up on a character who is refueling a helicopter while it's powered up and the blades are whirring. Zombie gets up on a crate to be scary, and…horror/comedy history.

3. *The Last Shark* (1981): More helicopter joy. Guy falls out of a helicopter into the ocean near an unconvincing mechanical shark. Helicopter lowers so the guy can grab onto the landing skid and he's raised out of the water. The unconvincing mechanical shark jumps out of the water unconvincingly and bites the legs off an unconvincing breakaway dummy hanging off the helicopter.

4. *Maximum Overdrive* (1986): Master horror author Stephen King himself made a horrible Stephen King movie adaptation. Many hilarious deaths, but the best is a man murdered by a soda machine that shoots high velocity cans of soda into his crotch until he falls to his knees and a jettisoned soda can pops his skull.

5. *Amok Train, aka Beyond the Door III* (1989): A demonically possessed steam locomotive slowly kills everyone aboard as Satanic sacrifices. There are several absurd deaths, but they pale in comparison to this one. Two people escape to a lake and get in a rowboat. As they paddle to freedom, the evil train jumps the tracks, hurtles through the lake, and runs them over. Severed heads fly in the air. I shit you not.

CHAPTER SEVEN
PICKING AT THE SCABS:
WHEN HORROR ECHOES REAL LIFE

An Executive Officer for a large financial company sits for a live televised press conference. He is the face of a corporation that was deeply involved in the largest economic meltdown in recent history.

He is a disgraced public figure, sent out there to take his 40 lashes from the reporters and to attempt to put a positive spin on this unprecedented shit show. He sits behind a desk, with the city his company bankrupted as his backdrop.

The Executive wears an awkward smile, but it cannot hide the fact that he is distracted and agitated, and nervous. As the grilling from the reporter gets more and more intense, the Executive abruptly stops smiling.

He decides to go off script.

"You want me to be honest?" the Executive asks. "You're right. The public should be worried. This will be impossible to fix."

Then he pulls out an old leather briefcase. He opens the latches, reaches in his hand, and pulls out a revolver. There is chaos off camera, and he calmly waves people to stay away.

He puts the barrel in his mouth and pulls the trigger. The Executive's brains splatter across the window behind him. Blood cascades out of his nose like a waterfall. The Executive's lifeless body stays propped for a moment in the chair, and the camera keeps rolling.

Are you Googling right now, to see if you missed something? Let me ease your mind.

I just described a controversial scene from the season one finale of the cable television show, *Mr. Robot* (2015). It didn't happen in real life. But it was created to remind you of something that did happen.

As I watched that scene, a person's name came into my mind: R. Budd Dwyer.

Truth Is Just as Insane as Fiction

On January 22, 1987, R. Budd Dwyer, the State Treasurer of Pennsylvania, called a press conference. A month earlier, the Federal District Court of Pennsylvania had found Dwyer guilty of 11 counts of conspiracy, mail fraud, perjury, and interstate transportation in aid of racketeering. Everyone assumed that the press conference would be for his resignation.

William K. Stevens of *The New York Times* reported that after about half an hour of professing his innocence, Dwyer pulled a .357 Magnum out of a large manila folder from his briefcase. Some reporters ducked, and others pleaded with him to not do anything rash. Dwyer warned everyone to stay away to avoid being hurt. Then he put the barrel of the gun in his mouth and pulled the trigger.

Dwyer died instantly, but his body slumped against an office table in a seated position, propped up in front of a television camera that did not cut away from the nightmare. The press conference hadn't been broadcast live, but many stations, including WPVI in Philadelphia, WPXI in Pittsburgh, and WHTM in Harrisburg, Pennsylvania, made the controversial decision to run the story with uncensored video of the suicide. ("Pictures Raise News Issue," *Associated Press*, *New York Times*, January 23, 1987).

One detail from the uncensored footage stood out in particular.

Blood poured from his nose like a waterfall. That eerily similar image and setup on *Mr. Robot* reminded me of that horrifying moment.

A Bucket of Fake Blood is Worth a Thousand Words

When a movie or a TV show recreates a visual image that is indelibly linked to a real event, I call it a "stinger." A good "stinger" elicits the visceral emotions the viewer would feel if they were watching the real event, and it can pack an unexpected wallop.

The "stinger" is another allegorical tool that horror can use to comment on a current event or a social issue, or to make comparisons between moments in history. When horror is at its best, it can challenge both sides of an issue without insulting or boring the audience. A bucket of fake blood is worth a thousand words.

Mr. Robot is the story of a cyber vigilante. He has the power to collapse the world economy by erasing the world's debt. But, even though *Mr. Robot* focuses on the angst of millennials who face massive debt, wealth inequality, technology overload, and a lack of security, we can all relate because there is real anxiety over our own lack of control in such an electronic world.

Why is there a "stinger" about R. Budd Dwyer's 1987 suicide in a show about a world mutated by the Great Recession of 2008? Only show creator Sam Esmail knows for sure, but when I saw it, I flashed back to when this lack of control had happened before—in the Crash of 1987—when the system failed and the sky fell because of an overreliance on "new and untested financial instruments deployed in the market by computer programs." (Christopher Matthews, "25 Years Later: In the Crash of 1987, the Seeds of the Great Recession," *Time Magazine*, October 22, 2012). I read it as a cautionary reminder that the same mistakes keep getting made, and they can happen again.

Or, maybe it's not. It's my interpretation, and I'm sticking to it.

When Horror Uses the Carrot Over the Stick

Since its beginning, the horror genre has commented on the social climate by focusing on what scares people in the moment.

Readers can interpret Mary Shelly's *Frankenstein* (1818) as a cautionary tale of the dangers of science overstepping its boundaries, or as a cautionary tale against the dehumanizing effect of the Industrial Revolution.

Or it could just be a story about a guy who makes a monster out of dead body parts, and the result wasn't what he planned.

Frankenstein's appeal is so universal that the story is still relevant today, and each generation can add a new analysis.

Expressionism: When Your Inner Voice Screams in Public

Horror movies have always picked at the scabs of what ails us, bringing attention to the wound that we want to pretend healed a long time ago. They find ways to express emotional tensions within us that we can't articulate.

That's what the artists in 1920s Germany were going for with the German Expressionism movement. It's broadly defined as the rejection of Western conventions and the depiction of reality that is widely distorted for emotional effect. The goal was to give expression to internal emotions that were beyond words and to bring those inner emotions into the external world by evoking them with images. (Alissa Darsa, "Art House: An Introduction to German Expressionist Films," *Artnet News*, December 26, 2013).

When Germany signed the Treaty of Versailles in 1919 to end World War I, the Allied Nations stripped Germany of its colonies, gave the Alsace-Lorraine region to France, placed restrictions on its military, and put stringent economic sanctions in effect to pay for a costly war. To make their first payment of 500 million dollars in 1921, Germany literally printed paper money, knowingly devaluing the currency. This led to massive inflation that made the price of food soar (Claire Suddath, "Why Did World War I Just End?", *Time*, Oct. 04, 2010).

That led to people starving: 700,000 Germans starved to death after the war was over.

The Cabinet of Dr. Caligari (1920)

The German people were beaten down from the rigors of war, depressed over losing it, and underneath it all, angry. Politically, the Nazis would exploit the shameful memories and rise to power. Artistically, out of that came the first expressionistic horror film, *The Cabinet of Dr. Caligari,* in 1920. (Anton Kaes, *Shell Shock Cinema: Weimar Culture and the Wounds of War*, 2011).

The story revolves around a hypnotist named Caligari who brings his traveling sideshow to town. The show features a somnambulist named Cesare, who answers audience questions while under hypnosis, like a fortune teller. Someone in the audience asks how long they will live.

"Until dawn," Cesare says.

That audience member is stabbed to death that night. Then other murders start happening.

Robert Wiene directed the film. He brought the look and feel of Expressionism to *Caligari*. Due to the high inflation rates, the Weimar Republic films were done on the cheap, so carefully painted abstract sets replaced expensive realistic ones.

In the movie, streets are twisted and crooked. There are no straight angles on the houses. They bend and distort as if they are staring down at the characters. Trees look like clutching hands. Rooms are black except for one slash of light.

The look and mood of the film registered strongly with the audience. This film visually captured the dark spirit of post-war Germany. Their ordinary world had distorted and become disorienting, and everything felt threatening. Expressionism brought that psychic scream to the real world.

Hans Janowitz and Carl Meyer wrote *Caligari*. Both were veterans of the war, and their experiences turned them both into pacifists. They wrote *Caligari* as a response to the unchecked tyrannical power of the government not only to start a war but also to have the authority to force men to become killers. Caligari represented the German government, and Cesare represented the "average German," trained and brainwashed to kill. (Kevin Kryah, "The Cabinet of Dr. Caligari: Dark Relationship with Postwar Germany," *The Artifice*, May 9, 2015).

That's straightforward symbolism and interpretation, but its twist ending makes *Caligari* interesting.

It reveals that the narrator is telling the story from an insane asylum. Every character from the story we've watched is in the asylum with our narrator. Dr. Caligari is a kindly doctor.

There have been varying interpretations of this ending. Is the narrator a metaphor for the collective German people, mad with guilt, blaming everyone except themselves for their fate? Or, is the kind Dr. Caligari just the duplicitous face of the government, never really stripped of any power, pretending to help while keeping the citizens enslaved?

Or is it just a fantastical story told by an unreliable narrator in an asylum to pass the years?

The writers had a specific meaning in mind, but the ambiguity allowed for different interpretations. That prompted people to think about things they typically wouldn't want to talk about.

Although talking about how the government fucked up was incendiary stuff, there were no civil wars caused by the varying interpretations of *Caligari*. It didn't incite violence and intimidation over clashing ideals. And yet, considering what happens in Germany the decade after *Caligari*, it's necessary to say that some interpretations can become dangerous. In his book, *From Caligari to Hitler: A Psychological History of the German Film*, Siegfried Kracauer proposed a controversial theory. He believed that motion pictures reflected "the unconscious motivations and desires of a nation." He also claimed that Caligari was a *premonition* of Hitler and the Nazi Party's rise to power, due to Germany's unwillingness to rebel against corrupt total authority. Both Hans Janowitz and Carl Meyer, the writers of Caligari, left Germany for the United States when the Nazis came to power in 1933.

A Highly Divisive Issue that Everybody Can Agree On

When horror movies use allegory and symbolism well, they leave room for ambiguity. That allows them to challenge people without insulting them.

Invasion of the Body Snatchers (1956)

An alien invasion started in a small Californian town in the form of plant spores rather than green men. These spores created pods that could replicate and assimilate human beings. These pod people looked the same, but they were devoid of human emotion.

How do the pods get you? They get you when you sleep, and everyone must sleep.

I can't think of another movie that has had as many different interpretations of its deeper meaning, and yet stands so perfectly on its story alone. It has been called a cautionary tale about the loss of individuality through the hyper-conformity of the 1950s. It has been called a cautionary tale about Americans' general decline of empathy after the Korean War.

What's great about *Invasion of the Body Snatchers* is that the two most popular readings of the movie, as an anti-Communism allegory or an anti-McCarthyism allegory, are in direct opposition to each other.

Both interpretations are correct. Because both anxieties were *real threats* at the time they made the movie.

No matter how people interpreted the movie, the simple story mirrored the fear of the audience and reflected it back to them. Even if you look to the creators of *Invasion of the Body Snatchers* for a definitive answer, you can't get it.

The screenwriter, Dan Mainwaring, was a front for blacklisted writers during the McCarthy Era (Frank Krutnik, *"Un-American," Hollywood: Politics and Film in the Blacklist Era*, 2007). The director, Don Siegel, was anti-communist, and had previously made the red scare propogandist film *No Time for Flowers* (1952), which "directed its virulence at America's new number one menace: communism" (Deborah Allison, "Great Directors: Don Siegel," *Senses of Cinema*, 2004). Author Jack Finney, who wrote the novel on which the movie was based, was just trying to come up with an original science fiction idea.

In his book, *Danse Macabre* (1981), Stephen King quotes Finney's thoughts on the "deeper message" of his story. "I've always been amused by the contentions of people connected with the picture that they had a message of some sort in mind. If so, it's a lot more than I ever did, and since they followed my story very closely, it's hard to see how this message crept in."

In a 1975 interview with Alan Lovel for BFI's *American Cinema* book series, director Don Siegel admitted that the movie was allegorical, but he intentionally shied away from any point of view that would be political. "I felt that this was a very important story. I think that the world is populated by pods and I wanted to show them. I think so many people have no feeling about cultural things, no feeling of pain, of sorrow.... The political reference to Senator McCarthy and totalitarianism was inescapable but I tried not to emphasize it because I feel that motion pictures are primarily to entertain, and I did not want to preach."

I think Siegel brings up an important point regarding film's role in culture. Movies are an entertainment. You don't have to see anything more than a movie about pod people taking over the world to enjoy *Invasion of the Body Snatchers*. The best horror movies keep the subtext *below* the text.

I also think that *Invasion of the Body Snatchers* proves that B-movie entertainment can make compelling observations on the cultural anxieties of the time.

Bomb Shelters and Bug Spray

That brings me to the trend that's probably most synonymous with the 1950s.

The Giant Bug movie.

These movies are remembered fondly by viewers. However, the event that gave birth to those movies is a terrifying moment in contemporary history.

On August 6 and August 9, 1945, the United States dropped two nuclear bombs on two Japanese cities, Hiroshima and Nagasaki. The combined bombings killed 262,020 people. Japan surrendered on September 2 and World War II was over. (Michelle Hall, "By the Numbers: World War II's Atomic Bombs", *CNN Library*, August 6, 2013).

We used a nuclear weapon on people. That was a hard truth to swallow.

Scientists, politicians, and regular Americans had divided opinions on whether the ends justified the means. There was doubt. It gave birth to new fear.

What if someone dropped the bomb on us?

Them! (1954)

If you watched the Giant Bug movies, they are full of "stingers" that remind you of the atom bomb. The movie *Them!* follows the discovery of giant, irradiated ants nesting in a desert in New Mexico. Americans were well acquainted with the New Mexico desert from watching newsreels of the early atomic bomb test in Los Alamos. The movie references the bomb regularly, and an old scientist even likens it to God's finger, and he proclaims that we've shattered Pandora's box.

Them! isn't going to land on too many scholarly lists. It's considered a B-movie, but I think it may have been the most successful interpretation of anxieties stoked by splitting the atom. Nobody knew what the long-term effects might be. The filmmakers hit the bullseye.

This simple premise gave birth to a flood of "Giant Bug" and "Nature Runs Amok" films, a subgenre that continues in one form or another to this day. One could argue that *Them!* helped create the "Ecological Horror Film."

The film *Annihilation* (2018), where a meteor strike creates a slowly growing area of rapid mutations that defy the laws of science and threaten all life forms, can be seen as a distant relative of *Them!* Even though the destructive forces in *Annihilation* come from outer space, the themes of ecological horror and self-destruction are a constant. The scientist in *Them!* proclaims that mankind broke open Pandora's box, and a psychologist in *Annihilation* says that self-destruction is coded into us, imprinted in every cell in our bodies.

All That Bad Karma Had to Go Somewhere

By the time the 1950s ended, we started to worry about what our neighbors might do to us. There was a new monster, the spree killer.

A teenager named Charles Starkweather and his 14-year-old girlfriend, Caril Ann Fugate, went on a killing spree across Nebraska and Wyoming and murdered 10 people (Charles Starkweather Biography, Biography.com website, January 14, 2016). In Kansas, two ex-cons, Richard "Dick" Hickock and Perry Smith, senselessly killed the Clutters, a family of farmers who were safely sleeping in their beds. ("Hickock, Smith Pay Extreme Penalty," *Garden City Telegram*, April 14, 1965).

These incidents happened in the middle of the country where nobody locked their doors at night. It seemed the country's moral center didn't hold anymore. The monster wasn't just out there somewhere. The beast might live next door.

In 1960, Alfred Hitchcock's *Psycho* directly tackled the fear of a motiveless killer who camouflaged himself within society. Norman Bates, the main character, symbolized that something inside the culture was broken.

Psycho was instrumental in helping create an era many critics and filmmakers refer to as "modern horror," where the emphasis was on realism over fantasy, increasingly graphic violence, a confrontational point of view, and a lack of resolution. (Jason Zinoman, *Shock Value: How a Few Eccentric Outsiders Gave Us Nightmares, Conquered Hollywood, and Invented Modern Horror*, 2011).

However, there was a film that I think made the point more boldly.

Targets (1968)

Peter Bogdanovich's first feature film is mostly forgotten (Matt Singer, "A New Kind of Monster," *The Dissolve*, August 21, 2013). But I think it's an essential bridge between what is considered modern horror and the horror of the 1950s. *Targets* uses the differences between horror movies that feature vampires in castles and real-life murderers as a metaphor for the differences in good and evil from one generation to the next.

The idea came out of necessity. Roger Corman, the King of the exploitation films, gave Bogdanovich money to direct his first movie, on two conditions: first, he had to use footage from a terrible, musty-castle Boris Karloff horror film called *The Terror* (1963), and second, Boris Karloff had to be in the movie. Karloff owed Corman two days of shooting, and dammit, he was going to get them (Jason Zinoman, *Shock Value,* 2011).

Bogdanovich used footage of *The Terror* as a counterpoint to the story of a murderer who ends up using a drive-in as a shooting gallery.

In the film, Bogdanovich recalled the real-life rampage of Charles Whitman, who shot and killed 15 people from the University of Texas Tower. (*Ibid.*)

Whitman had done this just one year earlier, and the images were still fresh in people's minds. The killer in the movie even *looked* like Whitman.

When the killer begins shooting at the audience from the top of the drive-in movie screen, people drag the wounded behind cars. Victims point toward the gunfire. These "stingers" mirror the news footage of the actual tragedy, replacing the observatory tower with a drive-in screen. (Public domain archival footage of the 1966 University of Texas sniper attack: https://www.youtube.com/watch?v=iyXLyERkZYE).

The film could be about a horror movie with a human monster, or it could be about the moral decline of a desensitized generation, or it could be a commentary about how the chaos of the real world was scarier than anything in a horror movie.

Targets is a lost horror gem.

Night of the Living Dead (1968)

So much has been written about the cultural significance of George A. Romero's game-changing masterpiece that I almost don't *want* to talk about it. But it's a good example of a horror movie with subtext and allegory *that doesn't* forget to be a horror movie.

The story revolves around Barbara, a woman who survives a violent attack from a ghoulish and crazed man when she and her brother Johnny are paying respects to their father's grave. Johnny is killed in the struggle and Barbara flees with the man slowly shambling after her. She hides out in a farmhouse where she finds several other people taking shelter there, including a man named Ben. They have had their own encounters with crazed people, and they barricade the windows and doors, and watch the news for answers. They gradually discover that the recently dead are reanimating and that they are attacking the living and eating their flesh.

Specific images in the film are so provocative that the social commentary can't be avoided entirely, even on an unconscious level. Seeing our hero, Ben, an African American man, shot and killed by a white man who mistakes him for a monster, still brings gasps. Though decades have passed, the movie is still relevant.

A lot of the social commentary derives from the lead character being African American, which wasn't originally planned. In Joe Kane's book, *Night of the Living Dead: Behind the Scenes of the Most Terrifying Zombie Movie Ever* (2011), Romero reveals that the part of Ben was originally written as a "resourceful, but rough and crude-talking trucker," until actor Duane Jones auditioned for the role.

"Duane Jones was the best actor we met to play Ben," said Romero. "If there was a film with a black actor in it, it usually had a racial theme, like *The Defiant Ones*. Consciously I resisted writing new dialogue 'cause he happened to be black. We just shot the script."

Not changing the script based on race ended up being a stroke of genius, especially in 1968. Duane Jones on screen would be a strong enough statement. As producer Russ Streiner admits, "We knew that there would probably be a bit of controversy, just from the fact that an African American man and a white woman are holed up in a farmhouse." Nothing speaks to the disparity that existed between the races than how nervous everyone got on the set when Ben had to slap a white woman, and punch and shoot a white man.

That's some innocuous shit to see in a movie if he's a white guy.

There was even talk of changing the ending of the film to a version where Ben survives, but Jones fought to keep the original. "I convinced George that the black community would rather see me dead than saved, after all that had gone on, in a corny and symbolically confusing way." (Joe Kane, *Night of the Living Dead: Behind the Scenes of the Most Terrifying Zombie Movie Ever*, 2011).

Romero had one highly original and influential idea from the beginning. He reinvented the zombie and, in the process, created one of horror's most enduring metaphors.

Traditionally, the zombie was an undead slave in Haitian folklore, the recently dead resurrected by a sorcerer's potion and no longer in control of its own body. In the documentary, *The American Nightmare* (2000), Romero elaborates, "I remembered being frightened by the old zombie films, but it [the zombie] was always the guy out doing the work while Lugosi was up in the castle…. What scared me was the idea of someone dead walking around. The zombie was the blue-collar monster. He was us."

Romero made the zombie into a flesh-eater, a ghoul, and he introduced the idea that if you get bitten by a zombie, you die and become a zombie. "I thought of it as a revolution, or something devouring…a new society devouring the old, completely, and just changing everything."

It's about the change you can't stop, and his movies are about how people deal with the problem of change.

Romero used that central metaphor of "zombies as revolution" again and again to comment on different decades in his sequels. I think he was most successful with the idea in the original *Night of the Living Dead* because it was *his* generation that he was commenting on; it was *his* revolution.

"You know, we were Sixties guys and, thinking in those terms, we were sort of pissed off that the revolution didn't work. Peace and love didn't solve anything in the end. In fact, shit was looking worse," said Romero in the documentary *Nightmares in Red, White and Blue* (2009). "In my mind, most of the power that it has relates to the time it was made. And the anger of that time, and the disappointment of that time."

Night of the Living Dead doesn't end happily. There is no resolution.

And that's why it works so well.

Times Change, and So Do Allegories

When a horror film uses allegory and subtext with skill, the audience can interpret the film to find their own deeper meaning. If a horror film uses allegory and metaphor to reflect the anxieties of one generation, a new generation can see something else.

They Live (1988)

In John Carpenter's *They Live,* John Nada, one of the working homeless, discovers that the wealthy ruling class is comprised of aliens who conceal their appearance to control the human race. Nada finds a special pair of sunglasses that removes the alien camouflage and reveals subliminal messages in mass media, in advertising, and even on the money, to make humans a bunch of unquestioning slaves to their status quo.

They Live came out in 1988 when the boom of Reaganomics was torpedoed by the aforementioned Crash of 1987 and the first reverberations of the "Savings and Loans bank scandal" in America, where greedy banks ran out of money and covered it up by selling risky "junk bonds" to investors until it created a financial catastrophe that left millions homeless. It was the '80s version of the 2008 bank failure and, just like in 2008, the government used taxpayer money to bail out the banks. (Sean Wilentz, *The Age of Reagan: A History, 1974-2008 [American History]*).

"I had a deal with Universal [Studios] to make some movies where I would write the scripts and I'd have complete creative control," said Carpenter in the documentary *Nightmares in Red, White and Blue* (2009). "I wanted to do something about Reaganism, because it pissed me off so much."

Carpenter never uses 1980s terms like yuppies or Reaganomics in the film. It just tells a story about the rich, the poor, and the police.

But if you saw it as I did on opening weekend in 1988, you knew what the movie was talking about. When you deal with allegory, context weighs significantly on interpretation.

They Live wasn't a hit when it came out, only making 13 million dollars (Box Office Mojo), but it found a large cult following in the last decade. Its iconic visual style of posters with the word "OBEY" on a blank background has become a street art staple.

I was happy to see it get its due. I looked forward to talking to a new generation of fans at horror conventions, and I started conversations every time I saw a *They Live* T-shirt on someone.

When I talked with a younger fan, I was surprised by his interpretation. He believed the aliens represented liberals.

I was stunned.

The younger fan gave me his context. He interpreted the subliminal messages in the film as political correctness that was proliferated by the liberal media through the news and commercials to force conformity with messages like "OBEY." He saw the aliens as the rich liberal "cultural elite," who abandoned the working class and were taking over neighborhoods with gentrification.

There have been more extreme interpretations. Neo-Nazis and white supremacists had long co-opted *They Live* and claimed that it was in fact a metaphor for Jewish control of the world, with a white hero unearthing "the truth." "*They Live* is, by far, the best pro-white movie ever," read a 2008 post on the neo-Nazi internet forum *Stormfront*.

On January 3, 2017, John Carpenter took to Twitter to denounce these theories. "*They Live* is about yuppies and unrestrained capitalism. It has nothing to do with Jewish control of the world, which is slander and a lie." Carpenter was immediately bombarded with memes and illustrations from the alt-right to prove that he was wrong about the movie he wrote and directed. (Adam White, "John Carpenter condemns neo-Nazis who have co-opted his cult 1988 satire *They Live*," *The Telegraph*, January 5, 2017).

A good allegory reflects the anxieties of the times.

All You Zombies

Perhaps one of the best examples of a metaphor changing in meaning over time comes from George Romero's invention, the zombie. It's hard to remember a time when zombies weren't part of popular culture. AMC's series *The Walking Dead* (2010) which, as of 2018, has the highest total viewership of any series in cable history, helped make zombies a cultural phenomenon. There are Zombie Fun Runs worldwide, where runners dodge volunteers made up as the living dead during a 5K race.

But for decades, zombie movies were in short supply. They appealed to a small cult following.

That changed at the turn of the century. On September 11, 2001, terrorist attacks brought down the Twin Towers of the World Trade Center and partially collapsed the Pentagon building. Many of us watched it live.

Nameless phantoms caused this living hell. Even when we were able to put names on these boogeymen, the anxiety remained. The boogeymen could be anywhere, and they could strike at any time.

28 Days Later (2002)

Director Danny Boyle's *28 Days Later* gave the zombie metaphor new life. Technically it's not a "zombie film"; it's about people getting infected with a disease. The infected people look a lot like zombies, but they are not the reanimated dead. They are living, virulent, insane people with a high pain threshold who sprint after their prey with alarming speed. They spread the disease to healthy people by way of blood, saliva, or bites. However, the disease itself is a *psychological* virus. The virus is *rage*.

In *28 Days Later*, animal activists infiltrate a research lab in London that experiments on monkeys. They unwittingly release the "rage virus" when one of them is attacked and bitten by a monkey. The infection jumps from one person to the other rapidly and violently. Within 28 days, London, and perhaps all the UK, has been overrun by the infected and left desolate. We follow the story of Jim, who has woken from a coma to find the hospital abandoned. He's naked, dehydrated, weak, and he has no idea what has happened, or what might be out there waiting for him.

In a 2003 interview with *Filmmaker Magazine's* Kim Newman, Director Danny Boyle and writer Alex Garland talked about how *28 Days Later* was "a paranoid story coming out of a paranoid time," where the social rage in England could be the subtext for a horror film. Garland, a fan of Romero's zombie films, wrote a story that commented on the government's inability to deal with real diseases like mad cow and foot-and-mouth disease.

Danny Boyle also sprinkled the film liberally with "stingers" to heighten the realism. "We deliberately referenced images from news footage throughout the film," says Boyle. "So, the church [full of bodies] is from a photograph of Rwanda, and there was a shot in the petrol station that's from a bomb going off in Northern Ireland. And when [the characters are] being led out to the execution ground, that was referenced from a photograph from Bosnia. There's one point when [the protagonist] picks up all the money on the steps outside Buckingham Palace, and that's from a very famous photograph taken after the Khmer Rouge abandoned Phnom Penh. The streets of this deserted city were literally covered in money."

Horrible fate would add another layer of "stingers" to the movie. Although the film was written and nearly completed before September 11, 2001, *28 Days Later* would unintentionally mirror back to the audience the chaotic days right after the attacks.

There's a scene early in the film where Jim wanders through an abandoned downtown London. It is eerily silent. One of the terrifying details I remember about the day after the attack in the United States was the silence. All air flight was grounded, the work day was canceled, and government buildings were abandoned.

During that sequence, Jim discovers a long chain-link fence covered with photos of lost loved ones, leaflets pleading for information, and phone numbers for survivors—which was painfully evocative of news footage of the photo-covered barriers around Ground Zero, where the World Trade Center once stood in New York City.

28 Days Later struck a cultural nerve just like *Them!* did 50 years earlier. The zombie apocalypse became a catch-all metaphor for serious, satirical, and comical purposes. Since 2002, there have been more than *250* zombie films made.

Dawn of the Dead (2004)

Zack Snyder's remake of Romero's *Dawn of the Dead* has an opening credit sequence that is a masterpiece of visual "stingers" reflecting our post-9/11 anxieties. Snyder immediately taps into primal dread with a shot of a mosque full of hundreds of worshippers bowing simultaneously, their prayers echoing loudly. Then he cuts quickly to a close-up of a zombie, mouth open, ready to bite. It provokes a visceral response. We then see a faux news conference from the Center for Disease Prevention, and a beleaguered official takes questions from the press.

"Is it a virus?" asks a reporter.

"We don't know," replies the official.

"How does it spread? Is it airborne?" asks another.

The official answers, "It's a possibility. We don't know."

"Are these people alive or dead?" asks a reporter. There is silence for a moment. The official looks truly lost.

"We don't know," replies the official, and pandemonium breaks out in the room.

When I saw that moment, the "stinger" took me back to 9/11, specifically to one of the first news conferences after the attacks, before any organization took responsibility for 9/11. The nation wasn't sure the attacks were over yet. Rudolph Giuliani, the Mayor of New York City, held a press conference three hours after the towers fell. Giuliani was stunned, and he had little information that he could impart. His answer, again and again, was "We don't know."

When a reporter asked him, "How many are lost?"

Giuliani answered, "The number of casualties will be more than any of us can bear ultimately." (*New York Times*, September 21, 2007, Michael Powell).

In *Dawn of the Dead*, the credit sequence continues with stock news footage of riots and chaos intermixed with images of blood cells and zombie faces. Then Snyder shows faux live news reports that mimic the unstable CNN satellite reports from Baghdad during the 2003 invasion of Iraq as retaliation for 9/11. Communications break down in every news report. The credits end with a reporting crew in a building that overlooks the Umm al-Qura Mosque in Baghdad. Suddenly, their room is attacked by zombies. The armed guards are quickly overtaken, and a disfigured zombie smashes face-first into the camera. This sequence evokes the dread we felt around Al-Qaeda, a real-life swarm of monsters who couldn't be reasoned with.

The original *Dawn* was legendary for its biting social commentary and satire about consumerism. The best part is, it didn't have to try. In the original, our heroes make a fortress inside a mall, which gives them most of the amenities they could want and need. Soon they become disillusioned with the creature comforts; they want a full life.

The remake sets us up from the beginning to equate a zombie apocalypse with terrorism. Initially, various groups of survivors converge upon the mall and form a very uneasy alliance. They watch the news, hopeful they will see order restored. Instead, they watch as all the television channels stop broadcasting. For all they know, this means the end of civilization as they know it. Things will never be like they used to be again.

But, hey, life does need to go on.

So, the group creates a "new normal." They try to live with the problem. This is where I think the movie makes a subversive, and very cynical, comment about how no matter how much we try to act like everything is normal, ignoring the problem doesn't make it go away.

The movie has a deadpan sense of humor. Right after the zombie apocalypse hits, the group is focused on survival. But soon after that, they start to adapt to a life where the zombies are just another inconvenience. Such is life in the new normal.

There's a clever visual joke where a gun shop owner named Andy is stranded in his store across the street from the mall. He communicates with Kenneth, a police officer, by way of standing on the roof writing messages on a large dry erase board. They start a friendship and we see the two of them playing chess with separate boards on their respective roofs, writing out their moves to each other. Below them is a mass of zombies that fill the street. No rescue attempt is made, and none is asked for. They just keep playing the game as if everything is normal.

Life inside the mall falls into routine. The group assembles daily at the mall's coffee bar as if it were just another day. Members of the team pick stores to make into their homes. They even decorate them. We even see two people having a conversation as they walk down the hallways as if they were in the old neighborhood. Fluorescent lights substitute for the sun. Music pipes through the loudspeakers.

Each character indulges in the mall as their new gated community to find their own escapism. A couple have a date night watching *Animal House* on a plasma TV. A teenage girl spray paints graffiti art. Others have sex. Some treat themselves to expensive lingerie that makes them feel sexy. Andy and Kenneth give up on chess and play a new game where they shoot zombies that look like celebrities. This musical montage is accompanied by comedy band Richard Cheese and Lounge Against the Machine singing a swing version of Disturbed's "Down with the Sickness," by Dan Donegan, David Draiman, Michael Wengren, Mike Wengren, and Steve Kmak:

> *I can see inside you the sickness is rising,*
> *It seems that all that was good has died,*
> *Oh no, the world is a scary place,*
> *Now that you've woken up the demon in me.*
> *Get up, come on get down with the sickness!*

No matter how much the group tries to normalize their situation, the problem won't be ignored. Someone hides a bite from everyone and becomes a zombie. The generator fails and some of the group gets eaten by zombies hiding in the dark corners. Isolation isn't working. They can't find a new normal because there is nothing normal about what has happened.

By the time they decide to act, the mass of zombies has multiplied into an ocean that surrounds the mall and they find their sanctuary is now a prison.

The terrifying thing about zombie apocalypse films is that they are nihilistic by nature. There is no happy ending. Once the dead start killing the living, there is no going back, and there is no conflict resolution on the horizon. There is no end to the war. If *Dawn of the Dead* asks us to equate the zombie apocalypse to the global war on terrorism, where do we go from here?

Are you down with *that* sickness?

Heal the Nation, Watch a Horror Movie

Great horror can have universal cultural appeal and still cultivate meaning for the individual. One doesn't cancel out the other. And nothing says you can't see a good movie just for entertainment; subtext be damned.

But if you do step into the world of subtext, you'll find that horror can start some enriching and exciting conversations.

A horror movie can challenge people without insulting them. The stakes aren't as high. Even if you're discussing provocative topics, it's hard to get overheated when you're talking about giant ants, or zombies, or pod people from outer space.

When uncomfortable and divisive issues are dealt with in the abstract, both sides relax, and when we relax we begin to listen to each other. We are open to persuasive arguments.

Which is exactly what allegory is meant to do.

WHY ELI ROTH'S *HOSTEL* ISN'T XENOPHOBIC: MY HIGHLY UNPOPULAR OPINION

Eli Roth's *Hostel* (2005) is not a xenophobic piece of trash. It's a brilliant allegorical piece of trash. Xenophobia is an irrational fear of people from other countries. *Hostel* taps into the growing xenophobia in our culture, but it also comments on a more widespread cultural rot.

1. The Americans are rude, loud boors who mock the culture and the poverty of Slovakia, where they go to get cheap sex. These aren't blameless, sympathetic victims. You'd think a movie that wanted to paint foreigners as evil would make the Americans likable.

2. The victims aren't picked because they're American. They're picked because they're poor students traveling under the radar and they won't be considered missing for weeks.

3. Americans aren't the only victims. There are students from multiple nationalities and speaking different languages, who are paraded out for torture.

4. The torturers are not Slovakians; they are from other countries. There are men from Japan and Amsterdam, and even an American. The members of this elite club don't have nationality or heritage in common.

5. What the members of this elite club (the torturers) have in common is that they are rich industrialists. What their victims have in common is that they are poor.

6. These obscenely rich industrialists pay huge sums of money to fly into Slovakia, murder someone, and then fly home for their next board meeting.

7. Why the villains being rich foreign businessmen who aren't from Slovakia matters: when Czechoslovakia broke from the former USSR, the country was left destitute. To try to revive the economy, the government of the new country of Slovakia sold

off their state-owned companies and created a flat tax to entice foreign business. The businessmen brought manufacturing but didn't invest in Slovakia itself. All the revenue and profits went back overseas with the businessmen. Slovakia is the second-poorest nation in the EU, and the working poor are below the poverty level.

8. When one of our Americans escapes, he's rescued by a homeless gang of Slovakian kids, a real-life gang to whom Roth gave acting jobs. Not very xenophobic of him.

9. The allegory: The Bad Guys in *Hostel* are rich overseas businessmen who come in to feed off what's left of a struggling nation. They see poor people as playthings, regardless of their nation of birth. The Bad Guy is an institution that profits off others' misfortune. You can hate *Hostel*; just hate it for the right reasons.

CHAPTER EIGHT

YOU WILL DENY HORROR THREE TIMES BEFORE THE DAWN:
MY HORROR MANIFESTO

In a recent Oscar year, the Academy of Motion Pictures and Sciences did something that had never happened before. Two horror films, Jordan Peele's *Get Out* (2017), and Guillermo del Toro's *The Shape of Water* (2017) were both nominated for Best Picture. Together, both films amassed 17 Oscar Nominations.

Right on cue, Hollywood gave both movies an "Extreme Makeover," just in time for their close-ups. They were going to be magically transformed from horror films into something else. Because horror is an embarrassing undesirable when it comes to the Oscars.

It's the age-old culture war immortalized by *National Lampoon's Animal House* (1978). It's the slobs versus the snobs. The Deltas versus the Omegas. To keep the *Animal House* analogy going, whenever I see such a sense of privilege, I think the situation absolutely requires that someone comes up with a really futile and stupid gesture. Someone should cause an embarrassing ruckus at the Oscars akin to driving a float that has "Eat Me" written on it through the homecoming parade.

The Time-Honored Tradition of Backtracking Initial Praise for Horror

When *Get Out* first premiered, it was lauded by critics everywhere as a brilliant horror film. I remember an article written about the movie that was entitled, "Horror Gets Smart," which is a left-handed compliment if ever there was one. But after receiving *four* Oscar Nominations, and then winning the Best Original Screenplay Oscar, *Get Out* is now referred to as a "Social Justice Thriller."

"Social Justice Thriller." Just rolls off the tongue, doesn't it?

How about the movie directed by the most critically-acclaimed and highly-regarded horror director in recent memory? Guillermo del Toro's *The Shape of Water* scored an incredible 13 Oscar Nominations, and won four, including Best Director for del Toro. But the most amazing thing was that *The Shape of Water*, a monster movie about different types of monsters, won **Best Picture**.

That in and of itself is an astonishing accomplishment for an independent film that had such a limited initial release that Guillermo del Toro himself was announcing where the movie was playing *on his Twitter page*. It was *not* a long list.

Yeah, that's how much faith the studios initially had in his horror movie.

Del Toro is a well-known director and is respected in certain circles. A year before *The Shape of Water* was released, del Toro had a very popular art museum tour that was called, "At Home with Monsters." It showcased props from his films like *Pan's Labyrinth* (2006), *Cronos* (1993), and *Hellboy* (2003), as well as his notebooks of artwork and his personal movie memorabilia, and it also chronicled his perspective on "the art of the horror film." The press had acknowledged for some time that he was an artist who made poetic and beautiful horror movies. Del Toro was even given a generous profile write-up in the prestigious and art-conscious *New Yorker* magazine in their February 7, 2011 issue by the magazine's feature director, Daniel Zalewski.

Zalewski's respected profiles include art luminaries like Werner Herzog and author Ian McEwan. In his piece on del Toro, "Show the Monster," Zalewski writes, "The vicious incisors of 'tooth fairies' were offset by wings resembling oak leaves; the feathers of a skeletal Angel of Death were embedded with blinking eyes that uncannily echoed the markings on a peacock. A del Toro monster is as connected to a succubus in a Fuseli painting as it is to the beast in 'Predator.' His films remind you that looking at monsters is a centuries-old ritual—a way of understanding our own bodies through gorgeous images of deformation."

Del Toro was the King of the Monsters.

Four Oscar statuettes later, the monster movie, the *horror movie*, is discussed as a "Fantasy Romance that happens to have a creature in it."

The Dirty Shame

Why is it so hard to just say "horror?" Why do people equate horror with cheapness? Why is the phrase "horror genre" considered synonymous with "bad movie?"

Let's get down to it. People who are dismissive of horror will say it's because the movies are low-quality, vulgar, unrealistic, and amateurish. But that's not true. If it came down to technical storytelling issues, there wouldn't have been any praise for the movies of Amos Poe (*The Blank Generation*), No

Wave Cinema, Derek Jarman (*The Last of England*), or the Kuchar Brothers (*Sins of the Fleshapoids*).

The truth is they think horror is simple. As in stupid. Uneducated. Lacking social or cultural sophistication. Dim-witted. Movies made for dimwits by either fellow dimwits or sleazy hucksters ready to make a quick buck off the dim-witted. They believe it's too shallow and simplistic to concern itself with social issues, or politics, or the human condition. The impression is that horror caters to the basest human emotions and does so as a cheap thrill. It is undignified entertainment of the lowest common denominator.

I'm not saying that there aren't horror movies that earn that condescension, but this judgment of worthlessness, this dismissal of value, is presumed across the entire genre. It's proliferated in coded messages like "a thinking person's horror film," and "surprisingly smart," which subtly imply that horror movies are fundamentally dumb. If a horror movie impresses, it's an anomaly; if it's an anomaly, perhaps it's not really a horror film. This prejudice perpetuates itself.

The Name Game

This trend isn't new. The movie *Misery* (1990) became a "thriller," *Silence of the Lambs* (1991) became a "psychological thriller," and No *Country for Old Men* (2007) became a "gothic western." The closer a horror movie gets to those golden statues, the symbols of respectability, the further away everyone involved gets from acknowledging it as a horror movie.

As I said, it's nothing new.

I'm very passionate about the subject of horror, especially about how I believe that horror is an art form. Hollywood has always been in horror *denial*, using artificial genre labels to hide their secret dependence on horror movies and tropes.

Horror fans, and even the horror artists themselves, often feed into this. As I see it, the first step to "recovery" is admitting there's a problem. Consider this my Horror Manifesto...

Grand Theft Oscars

Horror fans I meet often call it the "Oscar Snub."

But it is not actually a Snub; it's flat-out stealing.

I call it stealing because it's stealing the best ideas from a group and then mocking that group for never having any good ideas.

It's stealing, and it's mocking, and it's throwing a big dinner party that occasionally invites the mocked group for a meal so they can be the brunt of the dinner table jokes.

It teaches that mockery to generation after generation, so the genre is continually suffering from a lack of respect. Respect is denied.

And this also means that horror fans are marginalized.

Hollywood loves horror, but it wouldn't be caught dead admitting it. Horror is like Hollywood's prostitute, hidden away at the edge of town, used as a muse until Hollywood gets what it wants, and leaves a few bucks on the dresser.

It's Time for a Really Futile and Stupid Gesture to Be Done on Somebody's Part

Quite frankly, I don't care about the Academy Awards, and it's not just about how they treat horror films. As a movie lover, I've seen so many brilliant, original movies lose to cookie-cutter films. And it's futile to protest. The self-congratulatory shit-show will go on as it always has, whether I complain or not.

So, why say anything, right?

If it makes no difference what happens if you say something or you don't, why the hell would you pick staying quiet? Me, if I'm outnumbered, I prefer to at least put up a fight. Why make it easy for them?

It's during moments like this that I like to quote from the movie *Animal House*, **"This situation absolutely requires that a really futile and stupid gesture be done on somebody's part!"**

You know those unscripted moments during the Oscar show where someone says something shocking and people boo from the audience?

I love those moments.

I want someone to demand that Hollywood acknowledge their horror hypocrisy.

It's Not a Makeover, It's Camouflage

Let's talk about the Extreme Makeovers for *Get Out* and *The Shape of Water*. First off, "Social Justice Thriller" isn't a genre, it's a label. It does exactly what most labels do: it separates and excludes. The genre is still horror, so why can't they just say "horror?"

As for *The Shape of Water* being a Fantasy Romance with a creature in it, I have a question. Why can't it be a horror movie that centers around a fantasy romance? Horror movies can have, and certainly have had, the emotional depth to include love stories as central to the plot. *The Phantom of the Opera* (1925), *King Kong* (1933), and *The Hunchback of Notre Dame* (1939) spring to mind.

I've also had people say, "It's more of a monster movie than a horror movie." Well a monster movie is a type of horror movie. It's a subgenre. That's like saying you're a resident of Kansas, but not a citizen of the United States. The genre is still horror, so why can't you say the word?

Because to use its name is to own it, right? Because the stigma that horror is undignified entertainment is real. How can something that traffics in the basest human emotions for the lowest common denominator audience be enlightened enough to be art?

That stigma makes even the creators distance themselves from using the word once the Oscar race heats up.

In the February 16, 2017 edition of *The New York Times*, film critic Jason Zinoman interviewed Jordan Peele about *Get Out*, which was the secret screening at that year's Sundance Film Festival. In the article, Peele said the movies on which he modeled the paranoia of *Get Out* were *Rosemary's Baby*, *The Stepford Wives*, and *Night of the Living Dead*. Both Peele and Zinoman refer to *Get Out* as a horror film. "A really good horror movie has like three good scares these days," said Peele. "I started off with 20. The first thing I did was make a list of my favorite types of scares in movies, and I said, if I can get 20, I'll have a classic."

Less than a year after his interview with Jordan Peele, Zinoman wrote another article for *The New York Times* entitled, "Why Are We Ashamed to Call 'Get Out' and 'The Shape of Water' Horror Films?" (January 18, 2018). *Get Out* had recently been nominated for a Golden Globe in the Comedy and Musical category. "Mr. Peele weighed into the ensuing controversy with concerns that the comedy label trivialized the subject matter. At the same time," writes Zinoman, "Mr. Peele didn't insist on it being labeled horror, either. He said *Get Out* doesn't fit into a genre, and he described it as a 'social thriller.'"

Jaws was nominated for Best Picture in 1976, and critic Roger Ebert called it "an adventure film." Director William Friedkin rejected the horror label for *The Exorcist* when it was nominated for Best Picture in 1974. (Ibid.)

It's sad, because the *poetry* in horror was the reason the movies were nominated. These artists did it so well that they overcame the bias. They did the hard work. They beat the odds and got to go to the party.

But when these artists distance themselves from the source of their poetry, it does nothing but reinforce that bias against horror. The bias says that if horror creates true poetry and art, it's no longer horror. Something this good must be something else. There is no way that such a good film could have horror as its pedigree.

And that's when the re-labeling begins.

What's in a Name? A Lot, It Seems

Re-labeling doesn't sound like much, but think about it. The stigma isn't about the movie; it's the baggage that comes with the name. That baggage is other horror movies. They are like the nominated movie's embarrassing relatives. The smart kid can come to the party but don't invite his obnoxious parents; they'll steal the silverware.

Horror gets judged based on its lowest common denominator. Whatever movie that person hated, that's what the word "horror" means to them. Consequently, when a horror movie shows greatness that even people who hate horror can't deny, the answer is to re-label the film as another genre.

If you change the name of the genre every time there's an exceptional horror film, then there are never any exceptional horror films.

Horror Does Not Have a Velvet Rope

It's not just Hollywood. Horror fans also refuse to acknowledge *Get Out* and *The Shape of Water* as horror movies.

What's crazy is that those two Oscar winners aren't the only two contemporary horror movies being dismissed by a lot of horror fans. This phenomenon is something new that's been building over the last few years. Movies like *The Witch* (2015), *It Follows* (2014), and *The Babadook* (2014) have been dismissed as not being horror movies by *fans*.

Perhaps it's an embarrassment of riches. There is a horror resurgence spawning a fantastic number of good movies, with an amazing diversity of styles and storytelling. To prove that, the two Oscar-winning horror films of 2017 were wildly different from each other.

Where I've championed the expansion of the horror universe, others have not. Horror has always been open to experimentation, transgression, and symbolism. It has always pushed conventional limits. One of the great things about horror is that it refuses to abide by rules and by definitions for very long. Trends happen, but trends burn out. Horror evolves; it grows another head.

You don't have to like these horror movies; just don't decree that they aren't part of the horror genre. The horror genre isn't an exclusive club; there is no velvet rope keeping out the experimenters, the inventors, the new geniuses….

Horror Is an Emotion First and a Setting Later

Horror is so adaptable and universal because it connects with you, the moviegoer, on a personal and emotional level. It goes directly to our primal fears and anxieties, and that's an area where we are all created equal.

Once that's happening, horror is free to work in any setting. It can be supernatural, but it doesn't have to be. Hockey masks, knives, and zombies can come in handy, but they aren't required. That allows movies as different as *Hellraiser* (1987) and Robert Wise's *The Haunting* (1963) to be horror films.

Horror movies can fluctuate wildly in emotional tone. George Romero's *Dawn of the Dead* (1978) and John Landis' *An American Werewolf in London* (1981) balance comedy with the scares and the gore, as do *Evil Dead 2: Dead by Dawn* (1987) and *Return of the Living Dead* (1985).

And *Dawn of the Dead* not only mixes horror and comedy, it even throws in social commentary, so does *Get Out*.

Yet fans will say that *Get Out* is a comedy, or a social satire. The movie is intentionally funny, and it certainly has social satire. But the film is about a secret society that kidnaps people and cuts open their skulls to perform a radical brain surgery where another person's consciousness controls the body. The original person is still trapped inside their body, profoundly aware of how their lives and bodies have been stolen, but they're unable to say or do anything about it.

Sounds like a horror story to me.

Get Out uses comedy and satire to tell its horror story, and that brings me to my next point.

Horror Needs Hybrid Vigor

Hybrid Vigor means cross-breeding. Combining the genes of two very different parents makes for a stronger and healthier baby. Some people pay top dollar to own purebred dogs with papers, yet they know they are inheriting hip dysplasia, heart problems, or a high-strung temperament from the inbreeding. Sure, you know exactly what you're going to get and there are no surprises.

But you are slowly killing the gene pool.

On the other hand, a mutt at the pound can give you the best of every breed it's made up of, and provide you with something great.

Horror is the perfect, magnificent mutt.

I welcome all the crossbreeding of horror with other genres that is happening right now (and has been for some time) in the movie-making world. Maybe it doesn't *all* work perfectly, but some of it works magnificently. Horror purists might grumble about this and talk about how "real horror" or "pure horror" is a dying breed. Well, I have news for them. Unless they are talking about the silent films of Lon Chaney and F.W. Murnau, and *The Cabinet of Doctor Caligari* (1920), they're talking out of their ass. Because every horror fan alive now is a beneficiary of Hybrid Vigor.

And here's another thought....Do we insist that a movie be "pure romance," or "pure adventure," or "pure historical"? Of course not!

Horror has been trading genetic material with other genres from the very beginning. Mary Shelley's *Frankenstein, or The Modern Prometheus* (1818) was a hybrid of horror and science fiction. Scary stories like *The Golem* existed before *Frankenstein*, but those stories used magic to bring the monsters to life. Mary Shelley replaced magic with science and that brought the creature into a more contemporary reality.

Hybrid Vigor is essential because the world changes. What was scary around the first campfire might not be scary now. Of course, on a fundamental level, we are still scared of the same things that we were scared of back then. We are still afraid of dying, losing our loved ones, and disfigurement. We still fear The Other.

But as our culture, technology, and civilization change, so does who The

Other is, and where The Other hides. Even what is considered "out there" changes.

Hybrid Vigor helped move horror from the era of the Universal Monster to the Giant Bug movies, and to the Alien Invasion films after World War II when we became paranoid about science and the skies. Then horror was crossbred with another genre, this time the true crime movie, and we got Norman Bates and serial killers.

Horror doesn't throw anything away; it collects all the hybrids and expands its universe. Today directors are using old combinations to present new perspectives and update anxieties. More movies are pushing horror into unexpected territory by taking old concepts and modifying them to show how a different generation and a different demographic looks at the world.

More women and more minority directors are making horror movies, so we get a new perspective on standard horror tropes that catch us by surprise.

It's what John Carpenter did when he remade *The Thing* (1982), and what David Cronenberg did with *The Fly* (1986). The reality is that most of the horror movies we revere are hybrids of either ideas or genres.

People who hate horror as a genre tend to judge the genre by the horror movie they hated. People who love the horror genre tend to judge them by the horror movie they loved. Our strongest connections are to the horror movies of our youth, when we got our "First Kiss." And that brings me to the next point.

Stop Judging Modern Horror Films by Standards That Are Older Than Everybody's Parents.

George Romero gave birth to modern horror with *Night of the Living Dead* in 1968. That was 50 years ago, which makes modern horror eligible for AARP.

I love the films that created the modern horror movie. They're the movies of my youth, and they revolutionized the way horror films felt and looked.

Did anybody really think that was the last time horror would ever need to change?

Cinema, and definitely horror cinema, evolves and changes right along with the culture. Horror fans, on the other hand, *do not*. We tend to fall in love with the era that spoke to us, and that period informs how we look at everything that comes after it. A lot of time has gone by since the movies of the 1970s and 1980s were cutting edge.

The movies are still great. But it's important to acknowledge that films change in meaning and importance, even while they influence newer films. Even a highly original idea like *The Exorcist* (1973) isn't immune to the passage of time, or how religion's role in society changes.

If today's audience doesn't connect with a movie anymore because they don't have the same social context that the film initially addressed, it's not their fault.

It just means times change. How we tell stories changes too.

The directors making movies today aren't only influenced by older films and television and books. There's a whole world of technology that has changed the visual language of film as well. It's unrealistic to think that these things wouldn't influence the style or pacing in horror films. And technology opens a whole new avenue to tweak our collective anxieties. I consider the BBC anthology series *Black Mirror* (2011), which tells nightmarish stories about how technology unleashes people's inner monsters in unintended ways, to be one of the best horror anthology series since *The Twilight Zone.*

Yes, that's right; I call both *Black Mirror* and *The Twilight Zone* horror. Hybrid Vigor!

As a veteran horror fan, I want to keep myself immersed in *the evolution of horror*. It allows me to connect with younger fans, and that will enable me to be an ambassador for the movies I grew up with.

If you can't enjoy new horror films because you willfully dismiss the context in which they are made, you've got nobody to blame but yourself.

There's a trend by some new fans, and even some new filmmakers, to distance themselves from the horror title. And that brings me to my next point.

Horror Does Not Deserve Your Shame

Some horror movies *might* deserve your shame. Every genre has movies like that. But you don't hear critics abandoning drama because of *Gigli* or *Bonfire of the Vanities*.

Yet there's a new subgenre called "post-horror" that gives a new name to an old insult. Steve Rose, film critic for *The Guardian*, coined the term in his July 6, 2017 article, "How Post-Horror Movies are Taking Over Cinema," to describe a new batch of movies that break from the "strict rules and codes" of the horror genre, to tell more profound stories than horror's "rigidity" allows. The examples of the "strict rules and codes" Rose gave were, "… vampires don't have reflections; the 'final girl' will prevail; the warnings of the gas station attendant/mystical Native American/creepy old woman will go unheeded; the evil will ultimately be defeated, or at least explained, but not in a way that closes off the possibility of a sequel."

Rose's list of strict rules is confounding. Horror films like *Martin* (1977), *Near Dark* (1987), *Habit* (1995), and *Let the Right One In* (2008) all feature unconventional vampires who cast reflections and break several other "vampire rules."

Not every horror film has a "Final Girl," and if they do, they don't always survive: *Black Christmas* (1975), *The Blair Witch Project* (1999), *Open Water* (2003), *Rec* (2007), *The Ruins* (2008), *Inside* (2007).

Horror has a long history of not explaining, or not defeating, the evil at the end of the movie: *The Birds* (1963), *Night of the Living Dead* (1968), and just about the entire zombie subgenre, as well as *The Texas Chainsaw Massacre* (1974), *Picnic at Hanging Rock* (1975), *Henry, Portrait of a Serial Killer* (1986), *Jeepers Creepers* (2001), *The Mist* (2007), *Absentia* (2011).

Rose states that "post horror" films showcase *dread* over shock and gore. Some of the films he gives as examples, like *The Witch* and *The Neon Demon*, are movies I praise in this book, and paradoxically, he also lists horror movies like *Don't Look Now, Rosemary's Baby, Repulsion, The Tenant*, and *The Shining* as influences on "post horror." I would like to add *The Innocents, The Others, The Changeling, Session 9,* and *Deliverance* to his list.

Rose is confusing "strict rules" with *clichés*, which run rampant in every genre. You don't abandon a genre because of its clichés; you invent new, original ideas to avoid using them. Every cliché was an original idea once upon a time.

It's frustrating because these movies that are being earmarked as "post horror" are the descendants of a proud facet of horror's broad storytelling style. They are great horror movies, and they are what horror has been working up to for all these years. But suddenly, they're not horror films.

I discuss "post horror" with a level of weariness because critics and fans who use this term are just doing The Academy's job for them. It's saying that because a particular horror movie is experimental and smart, it's no longer horror.

If you change the name of the genre every time there's an exceptional horror film, then there are never any exceptional horror films.

I expect that disregard from critics. But it's the audience and fan support that bothers me.

And this is what bothers me most about "post horror" as a description of a type of horror film. If you use the term "post horror," you're not describing what the movie is; you're only telling me what the movie is *not*.

You're also telling me what you *really* think of horror movies.

It's that slip of the lip that reveals that you're condescending, that there's a limit to how much association you want with horror. Or, to be accurate, what other people will think of you when they hear you mention the word "horror."

For some, there is shame around loving horror movies.

It's as if there's something wrong with a person admitting they like horror. I have watched cineastes, lovers of film who pride themselves on seeing every type of film, apologize for liking a horror movie. You can hear their tone of voice waver. They act embarrassed when they admit to liking a horror movie, and film lovers feel the need to clarify that they aren't talking about some of the more sordid films.

They need to *justify* why they like a horror movie instead of just liking it. It's an embarrassment that is reserved for when we feel we don't match up to the cool kids.

Why are so many people so ashamed of liking horror movies that they feel the need to go to the extent of creating a new subgenre to feel okay about it? The answer might be included in the first point of this manifesto: "Horror Is an Emotion First, and a Setting Later."

In our culture, we judge certain emotions to be "good" and others to be "bad." Some emotions are considered socially acceptable, and others are not.

Some people don't want to deal with those "bad" emotions, and so they look down upon them, and anything that has to do with them.

The Academy re-labels a horror movie because they don't want to be associated with the "obnoxious parents," the undesirable horror films of ill-repute. But when fans re-label, they do it because they're *ashamed* of those obnoxious parents. They pretend that those parents don't exist when they're around their cool friends.

These fans love the excitement and the emotional rush they get from horror, but they don't want to be seen with it. They don't want to deal with the shame of liking what they like. Horror is linked with the ugly parts of us, those emotions that are not socially acceptable. By liking horror, you might find yourself also socially unacceptable.

Of course, none of that is real. It's someone else's opinion. Emotions are just emotions; they don't align with good or bad. It's what you do with those feelings that fall into good or bad.

Horror does not deserve your shame.

Just because you don't like horror movies that use shock and scares doesn't mean the film that you want, one that uses *chills* instead of scares, isn't a horror film

Just Because a Movie Doesn't Scare You Doesn't Mean It's Not a Horror Movie

There are horror fans on the other side of this issue who don't consider these dread-infused horror films as horror because the movies didn't *scare* them.

We may all fear the same general things, but how those things get represented in stories and how our fears are explored is what makes horror so diverse.

It's not like they've stopped making horror movies that are easily defined as horror movies, so what's the issue?

We are living in a time when there's no one trend that rules horror. Without one dominant pattern, the critics and detractors can't generalize all of horror with one movie title. They don't get to use *Saw* (2004) as a one-syllable put-down.

So why are we horror fans bellyaching and trying to force one trend to define what is and isn't horror? It's not like horror movies that are more *chilling* than they are scary is anything new. Do we have to go back and remove all the Val Lewton films, like *Cat People* (1942), from the horror catalog?

You don't have to like these movies, but declaring that they are not horror movies because they don't fit your preference is problematic.

It's also counterproductive. Critics and horror detractors are more than happy to take excellent movies like *Get Out, It Follows,* and *The Witch* off your hands if you're throwing them away. You might grumble about how the Academy keeps horror in the slum, but you're helping them build the wall.

Stop being a horror elitist; you're just playing their game.

We've seen Hollywood re-classify movies repeatedly over the decades when awards season starts. But there is a positive side to this, and it's something I'm sure Hollywood hopes nobody gets wise to.

The re-labeling has happened enough to be a trend. People talk about it more now.

Two horror movies received Best Picture Nominations in 2017: *Get Out* and *The Shape of Water.* That proves horror can meet the requirements with more success than some of the other tailor-made Oscar movies out there.

Horror Films Reflect the Culture, Where Dramas Preach to the Converted.

I think we've all been subjected to a "message movie." It's a film where it's almost all message and very little movie. That can be detrimental to both the message and the movie. The filmmaker's intentions might be sincere, but they are as subtle as a tire-fire. Horror movies aren't immune to that problem, but when filmmakers lean into the fantastical and the allegoric, they can talk about the same subjects and not feel like a polemic.

Let's look at the example of two films released in 2017 that dealt with racism. One film was made by a creative team whose last two collaborations garnered Oscar nominations and a Best Picture win, and generated buzz before they even opened in theaters. The other movie was most certainly *not* being considered for the Oscars before it came out. Those movies were Kathryn Bigelow's *Detroit* (2017) and Jordan Peele's *Get Out*.

Detroit was directed by an Oscar-winning director. It was based on an actual incident in Detroit in 1967, where a botched police raid on a night club sparked one of the largest and most destructive race riots in American history. This led to a deadly incident at the Algiers Motel, where police and the National Guard raided the building and left three unarmed black men shot dead, their white girlfriends stripped naked and terrorized, witnesses lined up for mock executions, and a conspiracy among law enforcement. The movie's release even coincided with the fiftieth anniversary of the Detroit riots.

Get Out discussed racial tensions, the fallacy of a post-racial America, the betrayal of the black community by the liberal elite, and how white people still build culture and communities on the backs of black people. Jordan Peele tackled these divisive topics using the allegory of a black man who visits his white girlfriends' parents for a weekend, only to find out they are mad scientists who are body snatchers.

What happened? *Detroit* was a victim of the volatile politics of 2017 on both sides of the race issue, and nobody went to see it. The movie was made for 34 million dollars and made a record-low seven million dollars, and it only reached number eight at the box office on its opening weekend, which was the worst opening of the year.

Despite a lowly January opening, the Gulag of movie release months, the low-budget *Get Out* made 33 million dollars on its opening weekend. It has gone on to become a cultural phenomenon. This horror film also started a YouTube video trend of people doing the "*Get Out* Run," a fan–re-creation of a crazy moment from the film.

Guess which of those movies generated more discussion about race this year? That's because audiences like being told a story, not being talked at. At a time when public discourse can get inflammatory in seconds, talking about a touchy issue through an allegorical horror movie can diffuse the tension.

When uncomfortable and divisive issues are dealt with in the abstract, both sides relax, because the stakes don't feel so high.

One Futile and Stupid Gesture Deserves Another

Now that *The Shape of Water* won the 2017 Oscar for Best Picture, do I think it will make a difference in how horror is regarded?

Fuck, no!

It didn't change after *Silence of the Lambs* won, a movie that featured cannibalism, severed heads, evisceration, and two characters that were serial killers.

But it might make a difference the same way dripping water affects a stone. The first drop doesn't erode the surface, but there would never be any erosion if there weren't that first drop of water.

A horror-loving teenager might see a horror movie win Best Picture and decide that they can take the crazy story that they have in their brain and make it into a film as well. Maybe, decades from now, the stigma might erode away too.

Perhaps Guillermo del Toro said it best while accepting the Best Picture Oscar for *The Shape of Water*. "I want to tell you, everyone that is dreaming of a parable, of using genre and fantasy to tell the stories about the things that are real in the world today, you can do it. This is a door. Kick it open and come in."

He couldn't have said it any better…unless he said the word "horror."

#SayHorror!

MAINSTREAM MOVIES THAT ARE REALLY HORROR FILMS IN DISGUISE

I have two criteria that movies need to pass to be *horror* films: Does the film evoke horror through the feelings of dread, fear or shock? And why does the movie want to evoke horror using dread, fear or shock? They may be called action films, suspense films or Westerns, but these films use the techniques and imagery of *horror* films and evoke a sense of *horror* in their audience.

1. *Mullholland Drive* (2001): David Lynch may be the greatest practitioner of Antonin Artaud's *Theatre of Cruelty*, where powerful and strange images and sounds create a sensory world of emotional storytelling over narrative. Lynch's films carry the subconscious dissonance of horror, and *Mullholland Drive* is his best. He takes a film noir story of attempted murder, amnesia, conspiracies, and Hollywood, and then, at a crucial moment, splinters the narrative, the characters, perhaps even the timelines. There are no dream sequences; this is all dream. Lynch doesn't explain anything. The mood shifts in mid-scene, characters blend into each other, and hypnotic shots linger until you feel you might scream. You don't watch *Mulholland Drive;* you surrender control to it.

2. *The Revenant* (2015): The legend of Hugh Glass, a real fur trapper who was left for dead in the frontier of the 1820s, gets turned into haunted history. A revenant is a person who has returned from the dead, and Glass is the specter of vengeance. After he is buried alive by his own party after a brutal bear attack, Glass returns to kill the man who murdered his son and left him for dead. Death and dying is in every frame of *The Revenant*, and the constant violence is intense. But the scariest monster is the frontier itself, nature that is equally beautiful and deadly. It's a character, a living entity, and its ruthlessness possesses every man who struggles to survive. It not only rips the flesh, it tears the souls from the men and leaves them little more than animals. Or ghosts.

3. ***No Country for Old Men* (2007):** The only difference between killer Anton Chigurh and The Terminator is a coin and a Prince Valiant haircut. He is the embodiment of the unavoidable fate of bad choices, and the movie uses darkness, shadows, and sound (and the lack of sound) to tell a story with symbolic imagery over dialogue. The mood is dread from the first minute to the last.

4. ***Dirty Harry* (1971):** From the first shot, where a sniper rifle is pointed right at the viewer, with no explanation, the movie wants to instill fear in you. *Dirty Harry* creates a mad world where nothing works; all systems fail, because that's the only world where you can justify Dirty Harry. If you don't agree, watch the movie again and answer the questions that I'm posing: Why does 75 percent of the film take place at night? In the daylight, Harry is shown in a traditional hero pose, but as the movie goes into darkness, why is he photographed from menacing low angles? Why is he mistaken for a criminal by civilians? Why is he a voyeur? If we're supposed to cheer for Harry, why is there horrifying music when he shoots the killer in the leg, and why do we hear the wounded man's screams as the camera pulls away? If this is a story of good versus evil, which side moves the line between the two?

CHAPTER NINE
WELCOME TO THE NEW TENSION:
WOMEN HORROR DIRECTORS

Women in the horror genre aren't a new concept. One of the single most important influences on the horror genre is Mary Shelley's *Frankenstein, or the Modern Prometheus* (1818). Shelley also wrote *The Last Man* (1826), an early post-apocalyptic science fiction novel about the fate of what's left of civilization after a devastating plague.

Marjorie Bowen (a pseudonym of Gabrielle Margaret Vere Campbell Long) was a prolific writer of supernatural stories, including *The Viper of Milan* (1906) and *Black Magic: A Tale of The Rise and Fall of the Antichrist* (1909). Bowen published over 150 volumes in her career.

Daphne du Maurier was one of the most popular novelists of the twentieth century, and several of her books and short stories were made into films, including *Rebecca* (1938), *The Birds* (1952), and *Not After Midnight* (1971) which became the film *Don't Look Now*.

Although there have been many women authors throughout history, the list of women film directors is much smaller. How much smaller? Dorothy Arzner was the *only* woman film director during Hollywood's Golden Age. She directed movies for Paramount, RKO, Columbia, and United Artists from 1927 to 1943 (Field, Allyson Nadia, "Dorothy Arzner," *Women Film Pioneers Project,* September 27, 2013).

When it came to directing horror and exploitation films, genres that often center around female characters, it took until the mid-1960s for Stephanie Rothman to direct the films *Blood Bath* (1966), *The Student Nurses* (1970), and *The Velvet Vampire* (1971) for Roger Corman's New World Pictures.

Corman was well-known for giving filmmakers Martin Scorsese, Francis Ford Coppola, and Jonathan Demme their start. Even though Rothman had a cult hit with *The Velvet Vampire,* her career was halted. In Colleen Kelsey's 2016 article, "The Cult of Stephanie Rothman" for *Interview Magazine,* Rothman talked about her inability to find work.

"No one would even meet me, and I had very good agents," said Rothman. "When it came to feature films, I was once invited by an executive at MGM to go and meet her…and she said to me, "We're getting a new script ready for a first-time director who we want to use and we were talking about the fact that we would like it to be a vampire film. Something, you know, like *The Velvet Vampire* that Stephanie Rothman made." My response when I heard that was, "Well, if you want a vampire film like Stephanie Rothman made, why don't you get Stephanie Rothman?"

The struggle for women film directors is still ongoing. Even though there has been more visibility given to women in creative leadership roles, the reality is that progress is slow. In January of 2018, *The Hollywood Reporter* divulged the results of a 2017 study done by the University of Southern California showing that out of the 1,100 films released between 2007 and 2017, the percentage of female directors was **four percent**.

However, there is an encouraging wave in horror films that's getting noticed.

Women directors are working in horror in unprecedented numbers and, as Phoebe Reilly wrote in her 2016 article for *Rolling Stone*, "movies like Jennifer Kent's *The Babadook* or Karyn Kusama's *The Invitation* have helped elevate the genre by opening it up to stories that unsettle audiences in new, different, and unexpected ways."

Jovanka Vuckovic, an award-winning writer and director, who also held the position of editor-in-chief of *Rue Morgue Magazine* for six and a half years, weighed in on this. "Those films are evidence of something we already knew…that even the smallest shift in perspective results in new storytelling possibilities and fresh ideas. And that the horror genre is badly in need of new perspectives. Because women are not historically depicted as actual human beings much of the time, it feels totally novel, authentic, and satisfying when they are!"

It's not an easy road for women to work in a genre that is often dominated by sexualization, gore, and violence. Women aren't encouraged to make horror films. There is still a mindset that believes horror isn't the way women are supposed to express themselves.

"The first time I really realized it was after I made *American Mary*," director Sylvia Soska said in a 2014 interview. "The reviews weren't as much a commentary on the film, but very hateful, bigoted language against women. Saying things like, 'There isn't a rape culture,' or 'Women don't do this. Men don't treat women like this.' I was getting very upset by it.

"I was talking to my dad, and I said, 'I don't understand. These are things that I've gone through.' And my dad looked at me and he was like, 'A misogynist is never going to like your work. They're never going to like when you put a flashlight on those kinds of issues. Because they don't want to talk about it. They don't want to accept it. And they like being that way.'" (Hayley Krischer, "A Battle to the Grave: An Interview with the Soska Sisters," *The Hairpin*, October 30, 2014).

Women Bring the Pain

Determined filmmakers have long known that low budget horror and exploitation is a financially viable doorway into a male-dominated industry. In the competitive 1980s, Kathryn Bigelow's vampire film, *Near Dark* (1987), Mary Lambert's adaptation of Stephen King's *Pet Sematary* (1989), Amy Holden Jones' feminist slasher-satire *The Slumber Party Massacre* (1982), and Mary Harron's *American Psycho* (2000) were springboards for these rising stars. (Mark Kermode, "The Female Directors Bringing New Blood to Horror Films," *The Observer*, March 19, 2017).

Those movies proved that women could bring the grit, and the blood, and the controversy that male directors could, during a time in the industry when that wasn't the prevailing sentiment.

In an interview with Samantha Kolesnik, independent filmmaker and co-director of the Women in Horror Film Festival, I asked her why she thought it was important for women to prove themselves in the genre that way….

"I don't think it's important that women 'prove themselves' in the genre by seeking to deliver 'grit and blood.' I think it's important that women tell their stories, whatever they may be, and that they have the freedom to do so without being measured against a yardstick of male expectations," said Kolesnik. "I think it's important that women in horror are allowed to succeed (and fail) just like men are allowed to—and in equal measure, with equal access to resources and opportunities."

And yet, women filmmakers still need to struggle against the belief that women can't address the horror genre because it's too messy or bloody.

"There's a question I'm commonly asked, which is, 'Do you think women can be as *hardcore* in horror as men can be?' says Kolesnik. 'Of course they can! But, why is that the benchmark for making good horror anyhow? I'd argue that the best horror films prioritize story first, with the violence therein necessitated by the story and not the primary objective of the film.'"

The increased presence of women writing and directing horror films is rejuvenating old templates. As more women occupy the key creative positions, we get to see stories that have the power to unsettle audiences in different ways than we've come to expect. Women writers and directors are offering us a view of horror through underused lenses.

It is a new perspective.

It is a new tension.

What do I mean when I say a new perspective and a new tension? Let me give an example.

Wretched (2007)

The film takes place in a family-style restaurant, and we eavesdrop on a conversation between a husband and wife. It's the kind of discussion you wish you didn't overhear. It starts with the husband expressing disgust at how she eats.

She eats without looking at him. She devours her food. It's one constant motion from plate to mouth. Her focus is entirely on the meal in front of her, and she is oblivious to his stares.

The husband says, "Jesus, you sure can put it away, I'm surprised you're not huge and fat."

"What, you think I'm a pig?" she says.

"No," he says. He's glad she's not like other girls, who are afraid to eat.

She says, "I *am* afraid of food, I'm getting fat." As she says this, she continues to eat. The way she's holding herself, you get the feeling she's swallowing more than food.

From there, the conversation only gets worse. He demeans her with every comment. The dynamics change from husband and wife to parent chastising a lazy child.

The wife continues to eat, but the action takes on an air of violence. She rips at the food with her teeth. She barely makes eye contact with him, but in the rare moment she does…those eyes.

Those eyes.

They show hurt, pleading, like a younger version of her is trapped behind them. The rest of her body moves insect-like to attack the food.

She asks to be excused, and she heads to the bathroom.

As she enters the ladies room, we hear her narration, "I always go into a handicapped stall. It's the only way nobody can see what you're doing if someone walks in. The other stalls are too small, and they show your legs when you're kneeling."

She enters a handicapped stall, locks the door, and kneels in front of the toilet. "It's harder when someone else is in the room with you, but it can be done. It's better when you're alone."

And then, while we watch her stick her fingers into her throat, we hear her calmly say, "It's important to have a system."

I, as a viewer, realize that I am in uncharted territory. I am surprised, I am uncomfortable, and I'm weirdly vulnerable as I watch this woman violently vomit out her food. Her narration is calm and steady as she describes the need to drink a lot of water to make the vomiting less painful.

And to layer the food.

She even eats in order of color: you start with the green food, then water to make a layer. Then the brown foods. As you purge yourself, you watch for the color change.

"You stop at the green food. It's good for you," she says. "You need to maintain control."

But this experience is far from over. The wife goes back to the table, and her husband insults her. She begins to eat again.

We are repeating a walk within these circles of hell, and I feel the dread and tension build. In a horror movie, even the best systems fail. Horror can strike anywhere, even in the banal surroundings of a family restaurant. Right after dessert.

The wife is back in the accessible stall, but the narration has lost its cool detachment. She messed up the system and had French fries and dessert, and now she can feel the fat growing on her.

We watch helplessly as remnants of the chocolate cake fill the bowl. We brace ourselves for the color change. And we get a color change. But it's not the brown.

It is red.

Something inside has snapped. She vomits blood, uncontrollably, and she is frozen into that position by the involuntary muscle spasms.

And as gouts of blood still course from her, she screams. But no one hears her because she's alone. Because this works best if you're alone. Blood covers the tiles of the bathroom floor. She drags herself through puddles of it and slides under the stall to get help.

She looks toward the bathroom door. She sees it open. Instead of screaming for help, she recoils in horror. It's another woman who has come in to use the bathroom. That woman is confused and asks if the wife is okay.

We see there is no blood on the floor. It's just the wife lying there, looking confused, embarrassed, and scared.

When she returns to the table, she tells her husband she's sick and needs help. For real. And this is where the real horror kicks in.

Her husband has spent the entire film telling her how broken she is, but when she says that she *is* sick, he gets reticent. He blames what she's feeling on the stomach flu that's going around.

He says, "You know I love you, right?"

We realize she won't be leaving these rings of hell for some time. If ever.

Heidi Honeycutt produced, wrote and co-directed the short film. This movie was an original vision that made me think about the different levels of domestic abuse, and how verbal sadism can go undetected. But it also made me see bulimia as a physical defense to verbal abuse, a purging of more than food. *Wretched* showed me anxiety that was simultaneously foreign and very familiar, and I discussed that with Heidi.

S.A. Bradley: What did you want the audience to feel or think about with the story as you told it?

Heidi Honeycutt: I wanted the audience to be absolutely horrified. I wanted them to look at this relationship between this man and this woman and say, "Hey, why the fuck are these people together? Why do people stay in fucked up relationships when neither person is happy?" I want them to understand that we hide our problems inside when the people we love won't allow us to share our pain.

SB: I found *Wretched* uniquely disturbing, long before the horror payoff at the end. What do you feel your film says differently than other movies that focus on eating disorders and bad marriages?

HH: *Wretched* looks at eating disorders as the anxiety coping and control mechanisms that they are instead of beauty-standard issues. It's not a societal problem. I know many people disagree with me. Women don't throw up their food because they think they're fat when they see skinny women in magazines; they throw up their food because they are self-harming in order to feel like they have some semblance of control over their own lives. If your life feels out of control, you pick something you CAN control, and you control the fuck out of it because it makes you feel better.

SB: So, what looks like a loss of self-control is really a dangerously high level of self-control?

HH: That's what eating disorders are. Your mind decides on staying thin and being afraid of fat and the physical relief that vomiting brings, but on a deeper level bulimia is no different than cutting, or excessive drug or alcohol use, or any activity that one engages in to actively, knowingly harm one's self. It is a pathology and it needs to be treated. Removing hot chicks from magazines isn't going to do anything to help that. People will just fixate on some other form of torturing themselves if you don't fix the root problem. Unfortunately, the root problem is usually other people.

SB: The point of view you showed made familiar setups feel unfamiliar. Like how she reacts to her husband's badgering by digging into the food. Normally, I'd assume she's using the food to ignore him, but the way you shot and edited it, I felt she was attacking the food instead of him.

HH: *Wretched* is extremely autobiographical. I think the only part I didn't plagiarize directly from my own life is the blood hallucination in the bathroom stall. I don't think it is necessarily men that don't understand women's experiences, but that people don't connect with or understand each other.

Whenever you have an unequal relationship, the dynamic of the relationship is unhealthy. You don't have two people able to engage in a fair exchange of any kind. One person has control over the other person, and therefore will treat them with less kindness and fairness than they do with other people. Most spouses, and parents and siblings will say things to their close ones that they would NEVER say to anyone on the street because they'd get punched or worse. When you have power over someone and you know they can't run away, most people will take advantage of that situation to be abusive to a lesser or greater degree. The situation in *Wretched* seems familiar because it is, and it's very uncomfortable.

SB: *Wretched* is a very accessible and engaging film because it deals with the universal theme of unhealthy human relations. Yet, it's a psychological story told from a woman's point of view about a very difficult and intimate subject. Do you think horror and its fans have progressed enough to sustain more diverse perspectives than they did in the past?

HH: Horror fans definitely have a capacity to appreciate any horrific event as "horror;" horror fans are usually very sophisticated cinephiles, despite stereotypes to the contrary. Some of the best horror films are some of the most thought-provoking, artistic, and intellectually challenging films ever made. Of course, there are shit horror films. But the films we remember and are discussing today, and in this book, are not those. They are the films that stay with anyone that watches them, not just horror fans. *Alien, The Shining, Halloween, Suspiria*...these are films that are more like abstract paintings. Narrative structure doesn't even come close to having the systematic impact that the art direction, music, pacing, cinematography, and complete artistic expression have on the audience in horror films.

Breaking the Waves

Over the last decade, there has been a wave of horror films written and directed by women that colored outside the lines of the familiar horror tropes and, at times, reveled in the abstract. These perspectives give new takes on familiar anxieties. I found that these movies got under my skin, made me pay attention, and most of all surprised me.

And they didn't forget to be damn good horror movies.

The Babadook (2014)

Sometimes a movie comes along with a monster that we're not comfortable looking at. What if a film makes us face a monster we were trying to ignore? What if the movie subverts our comfort zones altogether?

It's that constant subversion of the audience's comfort zone that makes Jennifer Kent's *The Babadook* so hard to forget. It's also why I consider it one of the most profound horror films I've ever seen.

The story follows Amelia, a widow, and her troubled son, Samuel, as his seventh birthday approaches. Samuel's birthday is also the anniversary of her husband's death. Her husband died violently in a car accident while he drove Amelia to the hospital to deliver their son.

Her son is a fucking nightmare. Samuel is hyper and out of control. He screams for attention, he is destructive, and he is disturbingly clingy. He's the kind of kid that, if you saw him acting out in a store, you'd judge the parent immediately. Amelia knows she's being judged, not only by strangers but also by her sister.

And even herself.

She takes care of Samuel because it's her job. It's her duty. But she finds him impossible to love. The young boy suffers from bad dreams about a monster coming to kill them both. She is isolated, and grief-stricken, and exhausted as Samuel's behavior gets worse.

Samuel has a hard time distinguishing fantasy from reality. He brings weapons to school to fight the monster he's imagined. The school finds the weapons and he gets expelled. Now they are both trapped in the house with each other.

One night, Samuel pulls a pop-up book called *Mr. Babadook* off the shelf for a bedtime story. Amelia has never seen it before. On the first page, a shadowy figure with a top hat appears mysterious but friendly, and he speaks in Dr. Seuss-like poetry.

As Amelia turns the page, the tone of the poem becomes threatening. "*If it's in a word, or in a look, you can't get rid of the Babadook.*" With the turn of every page, Mr. Babadook becomes more and more menacing. He becomes a huge, shadowy beast with sharp teeth.

Samuel is sure that the Babadook is the monster from his dreams. He starts to hallucinate. The young boy becomes even more unpredictable. He also becomes violent. Amelia realizes this book has worked her son up, so she tears up the pages and throws it out.

And the book comes back.

But now, when Amelia picks up the book and opens it, the drawings and the poem have changed. "*You start to change when I get in, The Babadook growing right under your skin.*" It is at that moment Amelia realizes that the Babadook isn't coming for her son.

It's coming for her. It was always coming for her.

The Babadook is about the ugly side of grief. Anyone who's ever mourned the loss of a loved one knows that there's a "socially acceptable" part of grief. There's a "socially acceptable" timeframe to grieve. It's some mysterious line, and when it's crossed, friends and polite society tell you it's "time to move on." It's usually when your grief makes *them* uncomfortable.

The Babadook examines grief, and we are forced to sit in it until we see it as a monster that devours the one it possesses. It is fucking inescapable.

The Babadook himself represents the ugly thought. He's that horrible, irrational, selfish, and vengeful thought that lives deep in all of us. He's the personification of that thought which shames us for just having it. We might be ashamed of that thought, but that doesn't mean it goes away.

Amelia harbors resentment toward her son for the death of her husband. In a way, she hates him.

A mother hating their child is still a taboo. If we see it in a movie, we instinctively see the mother as the villain. Jennifer Kent dives directly into the emotions around this ugly thought.

Kent uses Samuel's unlovable behavior, again and again, to give us a taste of our own inner Babadook. If there's ever a complaint about the movie, it's never about the visuals or the mood. It's always about how much of Samuel's behavior we are subjected to. "Yeah, there's too much of that kid. I mean, jeez, I get it, I get it already. It's too much."

But that's the point, right? Amelia can't get away from Samuel. Ever.

There's another standard horror trope that gets subverted by the perspective that Jennifer Kent uses, and it makes for a true one-of-a-kind climax to the movie. I've never seen the conclusion this movie comes to in any other horror film.

We as viewers have been trained to look at the monster as a problem that needs to be solved. We want a resolution, even if it ends in tragedy. But that's not how life works. Jennifer Kent breaks from expectations and comes up with a decision perfect for this story.

Because we never really stop grieving. But if we acknowledge it and confront it, it becomes manageable.

The Invitation (2015)

The next film also deals with grief, but in a different way, and with terrifying results. Karyn Kusama's *The Invitation* is all about transformation, and how tragedy can transform you and your loved ones into something you don't recognize anymore.

The tragedy at the center of *The Invitation* is one of the worst ones possible. The main characters, Will and Eden, watched their child die in front of them in an accident during a picnic at their home in the Hollywood Hills. They divorced, and Eden disappeared out of everyone's lives.

Two years later, out of nowhere, Will gets an invitation to a reunion party thrown by Eden and her new husband. All their old friends, who drifted away from both Will and Eden, are also invited. This party is held at the old Hollywood Hills house that Eden still owns. The house where their son died.

Yes, that's some heavy shit.

Even though Will has a new woman in his life, he has not "moved on." Will is a haunted man, and he is compelled to go back to the house to see Eden. Maybe he needs to go to see how Eden is. Perhaps it's to finally get closure. Maybe it's to feel the pain.

We meet Eden and her new husband. As soon as we see her, we know something is off. Her smile is too broad, her welcomes are too big, and she's too *happy* about this reunion.

Will notices the strange behavior. He's concerned. The friends notice, too, but they're happy for her, and they want to make this night work. As one of the friends says to Will, "We're all trying to figure out how to go on."

We find out that Eden met her new husband in Mexico at a New Age commune for people who have suffered traumatic loss. They have just returned to LA after doing a lot of work on themselves, and their lives are changed.

They keep saying that. A lot.

The legendary writer Shirley Jackson said that houses, homes, are the manifestations of the family that live in them, and the house in *The Invitation* is clearly haunted. It is stuck in time. It holds ghosts, grief, and memories for Will. He also notices things that don't add up. Will begins to suspect that something weird is going on at the party. They're hiding something from the guests.

This starts an exploration of paranoia and grief that evokes the quiet dread of *Rosemary's Baby* (1968), which dealt with a pregnant woman who suspects that the doting attention of the friendly neighbors in her posh Manhattan apartment building has a sinister ulterior motive. Kusama takes 12 characters and sits them around tables and couches, and makes this setting intense.

The story is told from Will's point of view, and his point of view is full of half-heard conversations and secret glances. Will notices that the new man of the house keeps the doors and windows locked.

Is being in this house too much for Will, to the point where he's growing more paranoid by the minute? Is grief sending him into a nervous breakdown? Or is there something else going on here?

Grief and loss permeate *The Invitation*. We are not spared the flashbacks that Will has every time he opens a door in this haunted house, or his gut-wrenching responses. All this emotion leaves us raw and vulnerable.

That's precisely where we should be when the shit hits the fan. And boy, does the shit hit the fan.

The Invitation works so well because it fills us with empathy for *everyone*, even the people we might think are villains. We feel everyone's tragedy before one drop of blood falls.

In My Skin (2002)

Carl Jung defined the *persona* as the social face we present to the world. It's a mask we wear to impress, but also to conceal our true nature. Jung also says there's the danger of a person disconnecting from their true self if they try too hard to conform and to belong. They lose any concept of who they are outside of what society expects of them.

I wonder what Carl Jung would think of the modern corporate world.

The main character in writer, director, and lead actress Marina de Van's *In My Skin* goes to extreme measures to reconnect with her true, inner self.

Esther is a beautiful woman working in the corporate world as an International Jewelry Marketer in Paris, and she has to wear many personas. Esther's looks got her in the door. But she needs to be aggressive to counter the beauty. She must show humility with her boss and show tact and gratitude with the other women on the team.

Esther got the job through her friend Sandrine, and Sandrine takes Esther to an exclusive company party at the house of one of the executives.

For a moment, we see the real Esther. She is socially awkward. She dodges Sandrine's attempts to introduce her to people. She finds sanctuary in the dark backyard and walks out there alone. However, she stumbles into a work site in the dark and falls into a junk pile. She seems unhurt and goes back into the party.

It isn't until Esther is upstairs in the private bathroom that she realizes she has cut her leg deeply and trailed blood through the house. Even though this wound will require stitches, she realizes that she doesn't feel any pain. She feels so good she decides to dress the wound with a bathroom washcloth and then go out for drinks with Sandrine before heading to the hospital.

When Esther goes to the hospital, the doctor is surprised that she didn't feel a lot of pain or seem concerned about any cosmetic damage that a wound like this would cause.

"Are you sure this is your leg?" jokes the doctor.

She is fascinated by her mutilated flesh and the stitched gash. It is a crack in her outermost persona.

The next day at work, Esther can't focus. She sneaks off into a utility room. She finds a piece of metal on the floor and cuts a new wound into her leg.

She looks euphoric while she does it.

About now, you should have an idea of what you're in for. It is a testament to Marina de Van's acting and direction that you will still watch this movie holding your breath.

Throughout the movie, there is a recurring motif of numbness. At one point, Esther wakes up and her arm is asleep, and she examines it like it is a specimen in a dissection tray. She continues to insist that the cutting doesn't hurt, and that she's careful not to do any permanent damage.

So, you can read *In My Skin* as Esther's desperate attempt to feel something real, anything really, in a fake world that leaves her numb. And that would make sense…if all she was doing was cutting herself. But it doesn't explain the looks of ecstasy she has as she *watches* her flesh rip open. She *must* watch, and that means *we* must watch. If we can.

Women and men cutting themselves is not an uncommon phenomenon. So, what makes this a horror film? There are a few reasons, in my opinion. There is a pervasive sense of dread in the film that's created with dark colors, shadows, and many shots of distorted images in mirrors. It's expressionistic as opposed to realistic. We don't see the world objectively; we see it subjectively, through the emotional state of Esther.

There's a scene where Esther is in a fancy restaurant with important clients. She looks down to see that her arm has been bloodlessly severed from her body at the elbow and is lying on the table. Nobody else notices. She grabs the arm, reattaches it, and then she slides it under the table and begins to dig into it with a fork while she half-listens to the conversation around her. She draws blood.

There's an ambiguity to how we're supposed to feel about what Esther does to herself. The only time she seems to experience pleasure in her life is when she's cutting herself. We see her stiff and uncomfortable in the life she lives, but she is confident and relaxed after she cuts.

This ambiguity doesn't change as her cutting and self-mutilation get more extreme.

At one point, she props her leg over her face to let the blood drip on her as she stares into the wound.

And then she pulls off some flesh and puts it in her mouth.

She chews away at herself in a state of euphoria. She bites into her forearm and makes a new wound. While she eats the flesh, Esther watches herself in a mirror. She stares as lovingly at her injuries as others would gaze longingly at the beautiful flesh everywhere else on her body. She is enraptured by what's beneath the skin, on the other side of the hole in her persona. She's slashing away at the façade she's built in response to the world around her, desperately looking for her true self.

After all, it's what's on the inside that counts.

American Mary (2012)

The Soska Sisters' *American Mary* is a top-notch horror film. I think it's a wildly original take on the Frankenstein story, where the monster is a career (a film career, perhaps?) and the villagers are the patriarchal system that sees everything as currency, including flesh. And this system wants all the currency for itself.

The story follows Mary Mason, a struggling medical student practicing to become a surgeon. As money runs low, Mary interviews at a strip club to make some cash. Circumstances find her in the basement of the club trying to save the life of a mob snitch.

She saves his life, and the club owner pays her five thousand dollars. Once word gets around the strip club that she's a surgeon-in-training, she discovers the lucrative black-market world of body modification.

In *American Mary*, body and money are connected as symbols of worth. Surgeons, strippers, and body modification artists are occupations whose economies are inexorably tethered and dependent on the human body, and Mary's career decisions are driven by lack of money and her limited opportunities. She's a college student with heavy debt and she takes a questionable job purely for the money. Then that job sucks her in and she can't leave. It sounds like the economic realities after the 2008 Great Recession.

It's Mary's adventures in body modification that gives *American Mary* it's subversive and brilliant power. In most films, the body-mod crowd would be looked at as freaks or used as horror fodder. This movie reminds us that body modification is a choice, that people do this to reclaim ownership of their body. It is open defiance against molds that they've been forced into by others.

They turn self-loathing into self-actualization.

In a 2013 interview with Steve Rose for *The Guardian*, Jen and Sylvia Soska discussed their thoughts on bod-mod. "I personally don't see a difference between cosmetic surgery and body modification," said Sylvia. "Except with cosmetic surgery, more often than not, someone is trying to feed into an overall ideal, usually an American ideal, of what is beautiful—and that I can't support."

Jen adds, "With someone who's put horns on their forehead, forked their tongue, and filed their teeth, you can't say, 'Oh that person's just trying to fit in, the poseur.'" ("The Soska Sisters are the New Faces of Horror," *The Guardian*, 2013).

This subversive notion of body modification as a form of revolt allows the Soska Sisters to add biting social satire about the objectification of women, how women are seen and judged based on their bodies, and how some people use women's bodies against them. These points are driven home by the introduction of some fascinating and heartbreaking characters.

There's Beatrice Johnson, a stripper at the club. Beatrice has her body altered so she looks like a flesh-and-blood Betty Boop. She's a cartoon of sexiness that comments on how the men at the club see her, and how they make her feel about herself. With her surgeries, she empowers herself by claiming ownership of her sexuality and taking the power away from those that objectify her. "I'm lucky enough to be able to afford to make myself look on the outside the way I feel on the inside," says Beatrice. "Fourteen different surgeries to make me look like this."

And there's Ruby Realgirl, a clothing designer who has been sexualized and objectified so much in her life that she wants to be turned into a living doll…by having any physical details of her sex, like her nipples and her labia, surgically removed. "I've never had any of these surgeries to become a sexual object," Ruby tells Mary. "No one looks at dolls in a sexual manner. A doll can be naked and never feel shy or sexualized or degraded, and that's what I want."

Both of these women are responding to being sexually objectified. These characters wear their internal pain on the outside. The Soska Sisters' perspective gives the viewer a glimpse into how many women feel they are perceived and marginalized in society, and they do it through brilliant characters that breathe life into the metaphor.

Mary just wants a career, and she works within the rules of the system. She leaves her family, struggles on her own, and takes the bruises to earn her place in the establishment. The surgeons know she has the mind and the guts for a seat at the table, but they use her body against her, to crush her. They invite her to an elite party, drug her, videotape her, and rape her. We find out that the surgeons have these parties all the time, and many women have suffered Mary's fate.

However, Mary doesn't quit. If the system is rigged and the gatekeepers are amoral swine, she'll make her own path and she'll create her own system. Success might be the best revenge in business, but Mary wants some of the personal, old-fashioned stuff too.

Several times in the film, Mary is referred to as an artist, and I think *American Mary* can be read as a parable about another industry that sees flesh as currency: motion pictures. The difference between the respected and envied world of the surgeon, and the barely legal and nomadic world of body modification feels like a knowing parallel to the differences between Hollywood and Independent cinema. The surgeons are jaded, cynical, and do their work on auto-pilot. Everyone in the bod-mod world is flawed and damaged, but they are passionate.

As a character, Mary Mason is smart, resourceful, selfish, tragic, fearless, destructive, tenacious, and melancholy. She's flawed. She participates in her own destruction. In other words, she's very human.

I had a conversation with a horror fan about *American Mary*, and he said he couldn't get into it because he didn't find Mary's character likable. I asked if he thought Dr. Frankenstein was likable. The answer was no, so I asked why the mad scientist in *this* movie needed to be likable. The answer eluded him, but I'll bet the Soska Sisters have a good idea. *American Mary* has bite.

The Box (2017), from the anthology film XX

XX is the first horror anthology film in which all four of the segments are directed by women. The segment I want to discuss is *The Box*, directed by Jovanka Vuckovic, and it's based on the award-winning short story of the same name by Jack Ketchum. I'm a fan of the short story, and the movie is a very faithful adaptation.

Except for one change.

That change brings a whole new reading to the story, and it made me stop and think about how I reacted to it.

In the original story written by Jack Ketchum, the father, Robert, narrates. The story starts with him and his children, his twin girls Clarissa and Jenny, and his son Danny, riding in a train after a day of Christmas shopping in Manhattan. A man holding a box sits next to them. The box is decorated with red wrapping paper.

Danny asks the man what's in the box. The father apologizes, but the man says it's okay. He opens the box just a crack, just enough for the boy to peek in. Danny's smile slowly fades, and he sits back, deep in thought. The man with the box gets off at the next stop.

That night Danny announces he's not hungry. He doesn't eat. He's not troubled, or upset, or sick. He's just not hungry. The father explained to us that this happened every so often, so he wasn't worried.

Danny doesn't eat the next day either.

On the third day, Susan, his mother, makes roast leg of lamb, his favorite dish, and bargains with him to eat it. He still isn't hungry. The father loses his temper and the boy cries. Yet he will not eat.

By day five, they take Danny to the doctor, who finds nothing wrong with him, other than the fact that he has lost five pounds since his last visit. The doctor tells Danny he must eat, or he'll die. The boy says, "So?"

He's not confrontational; it's as if the boy isn't concerned about dying.

That night the father hears Danny whispering to the twins. The next morning the twins are not hungry either.

Then, two nights later, while sitting over the baked lasagna she has worked all day to make, Susan asks her husband how in the world he expects her to eat while all of her children are starving. With that, she stops eating.

While Robert sadly watches his emaciated family genuinely celebrating what will certainly be their last Christmas morning, he narrates his inner thoughts, his confession. He talks about how he carries loneliness in him, a distance, a detachment from even his own family. He says he always expects tragedy. He thinks that's the reason he wasn't affected like his wife, and why he doesn't join the rest of his family in starving to death. It's the reason he's still hungry, and he still eats.

Jovanka Vuckovic's film version is faithful to the text of the story. In fact, it is a scene-by-scene rendition, and even most of the dialogue from the book is intact. There's only one change.

Director Jovanka Vuckovic made the mother the narrator. The dialogue doesn't change, nor does the way the lead character responds emotionally to the situation.

Yet, I find I'm upset when she seems unconcerned for her children. Why does Susan dismiss the husband when he says that they should take Danny to the hospital? Why is she so cold and so distant?

When her children stop eating, her husband is appalled to find her eating in the kitchen. Her husband asks her how she can still eat when her babies are starving. She answers, "Because I'm hungry. I've got to eat."

I'm angry at how selfish she is. When she visits her son in the hospital, why doesn't she cry?

Then it dawned on me that I'd been unconsciously reading the characters' motivations differently based solely on their gender. I hadn't realized it until I saw the roles flip.

"It's amazing how a tiny shift in perspective can result in a totally fresh-feeling story," says Vuckovic. "By casting a woman as the parent who worked and was unable to make meaningful connections with her family—all these new storytelling possibilities emerged; it became about ambivalent mothers, about how not all women are meant to be mothers. And it became an exploration of the 'negative' associations around motherhood. We've all seen plenty of doting mothers portrayed onscreen. This one is about the flawed, insecure, imperfect mothers out there who resent their kids. Yeah, they exist."

When I read Ketchum's original short story, I felt terrible for the father as he ate alone at the kitchen table. But when the mother did the same thing in the film, I thought she was callous and selfish. When I read the story, I empathized with the father when he confessed his loneliness. I never thought poorly of him because he wasn't as close to the kids as his wife. But when the mother made the same confession in the movie, I was angry with her.

The whole tone of the story changed because my expectations of gender behavior got tweaked, and Jovanka Vuckovic knew that would happen. I was caught completely by surprise.

Women are bringing the pain to horror, big time. Is there something uniquely horrific about the female experience? Jovanka Vuckovic reflected upon that question.

"I've been quoting Bela Lugosi a lot because he made some valid observations about women and horror back in his day—that were mordantly funny. He said, "Women have a predestination to suffering. It is women who bear the race in bloody agony. Suffering is a kind of horror. Blood is a kind of horror. Therefore, women are born with a predestination to horror in their very blood. It is a biological thing." This statement is bolstered by the fact that early readers of the gothic romance, the French Decadents and later the pulps, were primarily women. It seems lots of gals love a good horror story.

"And nothing has really changed in the intervening years," remarks Vuckovic, "as today more than fifty percent of all horror film ticket buyers are women. Lugosi also said, "Women gloat over death. Avidly. Morbidly." This would absolutely be true of the five women involved in [the anthology film] *XX*! But to answer your question, I don't believe the stories themselves are inherently different; it's the perspective that shifts when women are doing the telling. And since ninety percent of all films in the last century have been made by men, most horror films have been told from their point of view. I've heard people say that women are the next frontier in horror cinema—and I think Bela Lugosi would agree."

Welcome to a new kind of tension.

WOMEN IN HORROR: WATCH THEIR WORK AND THANK ME LATER

Karyn Kusama – *The Invitation* (2015)

Jennifer Kent – *The Babadook* (2014)

Kathryn Bigelow – *Near Dark* (1987)

Mary Harron – *American Psycho* (2000)

Mary Lambert – *Pet Sematary* (1989)

Jen and Sylvia Soska – *American Mary* (2012)

Jennifer Lynch – *Chained* (2012)

Roxanne Benjamin – *Southbound* (2015)

Leigh Janiak – *Honeymoon* (2014)

Alice Lowe – *Prevenge* (2016)

Heidi Honeycutt – *Wretched* (2007)

Axelle Carolyn – *Tales of Halloween* (2015)
(segment "Grim Grinning Ghost")

Stephanie Rothman – *The Velvet Vampire* (1971)

Anna Biller – *The Love Witch* (2016)

Julia Ducournau – *Raw* (2016)

Marina de Van – *In My Skin* (2002)

Kei Fujiwara – *Organ* (1996)

Amy Lynn Best – *Splatter Movie* (2008)

Ana Lily Amirpour – *A Girl Walks Home Alone at Night* (2014)

CHAPTER TEN

THINGS THAT GO
BUMP AND GRIND IN THE NIGHT:
SEX AND HORROR

You know you should look away, but you don't.

You're witnessing something horrible and indecent. Something you'd never want to happen to another person and certainly not to yourself. Yet you don't look away. What you see goes against your moral code, but you continue to watch.

What you see makes you uncomfortable. But it also excites you.

You can't stop watching.

Shame can keep that forbidden fantasy in a shadowy corner, but it can't prevent it from existing.

You are repulsed by what you see. But you realize that you are also attracted to it.

You may say to yourself, "What's a nice person like me doing watching a movie like this?"

Horror explores our primal anxieties around forbidden fantasies. A good horror movie should remind you where your boundaries are and your responsibility for them.

I'll cover films that explore the sexual nature of horror violence, and the risky business of indulging in taboos for entertainment.

Sex and Violence: When Horror Films Get Personal

With horror movies, we get to flirt with the forbidden, even with the stuff that we have forbidden ourselves to think about.

So, what better way to do that than with a movie that mixes sex and violence?

Sex. And violence.

Sex. And violence.

Just reading those words together can be hypnotic. And erotic. Half of you reading this just got a little uncomfortable, and the other half of you are *leaning in* to learn more.

Those are both understandable reactions because human beings have a complicated relationship with both sex and violence. When you put the two together, the result is both provocative and controversial for most people.

It may be even more controversial for horror movie creators and their fans, because when most people think of sex and violence in movies, they think of horror movies first.

Horror explores our primal anxieties. Sex and violence are about as primal as you can get. The combination of sex and violence can be seen so often in horror films that it might be considered a staple of the genre. However, even though the reputation is rightfully earned, most horror films merely dabble in this mixture. Many titillate with a nude scene or a sex scene, but they shy away from any real risk.

Only a few films dig deep enough into the complicated emotions around sexual violence to strike a nerve. Those movies go beyond titillation to revel in our discomfort as they deliver us into dark and uncomfortable places. Shameful places.

Only a few horror films dare to get *personal*.

The Science of Sex and Violence

Horror's function is to surprise us, to disarm us, and to make us vulnerable. I'm fascinated by horror films that dare to go right to where we are the most exposed.

So, *why* sex and violence? Who was the morally bankrupt lout who put this chocolate with this peanut butter? Sorry to put it to you like this, but there's no single amoral swine we can blame for making the unholy connection.

It's always been with us.

Sex and violence are linked in our brains. It's the dark side of our biology. Scientists discovered that even though these two behaviors seem like they are opposites, they both share the same part of the brain—the hypothalamic attack region. That means they share the same neural circuits and the same intense arousal hormones. (Nelson, R. J. and Chiavegatto, S. "Molecular basis of aggression," *Trends in Neurosciences*, Vol. 24, December 2001: 713-19).

To make it even more complicated for the zealous to take the moral high ground, both behaviors release shots of dopamine and serotonin, the body's pleasure and reward drugs. (R. Douglas Fields Ph.D., "The Explosive Mix of Sex and Violence," *Psychology Today*, January 26, 2016).

I think it helps explain and normalize why we sometimes get excited when sex and violence are combined in an image. They pluck at those subconscious connections deep in the brain, and you may find yourself emotionally confused when a repugnant image turns you on. When that happens, even for just a moment, we experience conflicting emotions, like anger or shame.

With that said, it's profoundly important to state that a biological imperative doesn't give us a license to go around punching and fucking each other. There's another part of the brain that stops that from happening. If a person *can't* self-regulate, and resorts to violence and rape, society regulates that person by locking them away.

It's also prudent and responsible to note that there are studies that link watching violent porn to an increased likelihood of perpetrating sexual violence. (Jessica Sciaraffa, "The Relationship Between Violent Media, Pornography, and Cyber Dating Abuse Among Adolescents", The University of Western Ontario, 2015).

We are still ultimately responsible for the actions we choose.

Shock, Dread, and Your Inner Pervert

Conflicting emotions are the secret weapon of the horror film. A horror movie is working well if it can make you feel like *you're* doing something you shouldn't be doing just by watching it.

Psycho (1960)

A great example is the shower scene in Alfred Hitchcock's *Psycho*.

The scene starts with straight-up titillation, with Janet Leigh in the shower. There is the sensual *hiss* of the water spray hitting tile and porcelain, and we watch as she soaps her soft skin.

Except for that hiss of the water, it is silent. We experience this quiet for an unusual amount of time while we secretly view this naked woman. The longer we stare at her without her knowledge, the more anxious we become, even though there is no hint of danger.

Is this arousal? Is this dread? Why are we already scared before anything happens?

Whatever the emotional stew is, all our receptors are wide open by the time we see the bathroom door slowly open. When we notice a shadowy figure enter the room.

Slowly.

Everything changes when the shadowy figure pulls the shower curtain open violently. We are then treated to the most brutal forty-five seconds that any movie had ever shown.

I think that moment where the shower curtain is pulled open and we see the silhouette of what looks like an old lady, is the payoff to the fear we've felt. We were voyeurs; we got off on something naughty and shameful. When we hear the screech of violins as that curtain pulls open, it's like we tripped an alarm.

We are caught in the act! Not only that, we were caught by *Mom*!

It was Mother Bates, but I think we register it as our own scolding matriarch.

Double shot of dopamine, coming right up.

I confess that there is one shot in *Psycho's* world-famous knife murder montage that I've always found erotic. It's a close-up of Marion Crane's belly. You can see the knife come in from the side angle. The shot shows you the size, the danger, and the power of the knife up against that vulnerable belly.

There's something so sexy about how Marion Crane gasps and yelps in that shot, and how her hand comes in to protect herself from the knife.

Did Hitchcock intend to get a sexual rise out of the audience with that shot, or was it an accident of editing? Am I perverted because I saw that moment as erotic?

Well, perhaps.

The question of whether the person next to you is going to think you're a pervert makes people jumpy around sex and violence. Sex is where we are all the most self-conscious, and the most vulnerable, and where we are most likely to feel shame.

In other words, it's a perfect breeding ground for horror!

The Dangerous Business of the Fine Line

Alfred Hitchcock might be the kinkiest director who somehow convinced mainstream audiences that he wasn't kinky at all. Most of the main characters in his films are voyeurs, or they lead secret lives, or they're compulsive liars, but Hitchcock painted them as innocent folks whose curiosity just got the best of them. Hitchcock empathized with the voyeur so well that he made the kinkiness acceptable to a relatively conservative audience.

However, there's a fine line between kinkiness and perversion, and accentuating the sexual nature of horror violence is always a risky proposition.

Just ask director Michael Powell.

Peeping Tom (1960)

Alfred Hitchcock teased the audience about being voyeurs. Michael Powell, on the other hand, went right for the jugular. In his movie, *Peeping Tom*, everyone is a voyeur, and the sexual component is out in the open. He makes no bones about telling the audience they're voyeurs too.

And it cost him his career.

Most people don't know the name Michael Powell today, but before the release of *Peeping Tom*, Powell was the jewel of the British film industry. It's hard to believe this exploitive film was made by the same guy who was nominated for *three* Oscars.

Made the same year as *Psycho*, *Peeping Tom* also has a lead character driven to madness by a domineering parent, but that's where the similarities end. From the first shot in the movie, Powell tells the audience that watching sex and violence is a turn-on and he continually reminds them that's what they're watching.

Powell introduces a blind woman as a key figure. She can't see anything, but she learns intimate facts about the main character by listening to him through the apartment walls.

This blind woman knows the main character is dangerous and that he hides a horrible secret, and yet she enters his lair anyway. There is a moment when she's trapped in the corner of his apartment. Her life is in danger. She's frightened. But she is also turned on.

By introducing the blind woman into the mix, Michael Powell made the attraction to sex and violence more than just a visual thing. It was an emotional response, an attraction to physical danger.

The critical response in Britain was colorfully over-the-top. In his book, *Million-Dollar Movie* (1995), Powell reprinted the critical reviews of the time to show the level of disgust expressed by English critics. Derek Hill of *The Tribune* wrote, "The only really satisfactory way to dispose of *Peeping Tom* would be to shovel it up and flush it swiftly down the nearest sewer." In the movie, to have a woman turned on by her own peril was considered obscene, and Michael Powell's career was essentially over. (Essay "Peeping Tom: Shudder Bug" by Peter Keogh, in *The X-List: The National Society of Film Critics Guide to the Movies that Turn Us On*, Jami Bernard, 2005).

The Double Standard of a Sexual Revolution

People remember *Psycho* as a rule-breaking and boundary-breaking movie, and rightfully so. But there's a strong moral code at the center of *Psycho* that kept Hitchcock from getting crucified the way Michael Powell did. The shower scene in Psycho is a shocker, but it is still steeped in the morality of the old-guard generation from which Hitchcock came.

Marion Crane has sex with her boyfriend, and then steals money at work, and then skips town. Her "fallen woman" lifestyle catches up with her in a motel bathroom. Her demise is essentially *retribution for a sinner*.

Filmmakers and critics in the '60s removed some of the moral stigma when they introduced casual sex into movies like *Deep Throat* (1972) which showed explicit sex and nudity. The sexual revolution embraced and idealized that which used to be shameful.

Movies like *Bonnie and Clyde* (1967) pushed the envelope of onscreen violence as a comment on the grim reality of an increasingly brutal society.

Yet, this is the era when horror films first get labeled misogynistic and irredeemable garbage. This revolution prided itself on challenging how sex and violence were represented in the old regime. But in this revolution where nothing was cleaner than sex, nothing was dirtier than sex and violence together.

There was good reason for the scrutiny. There was a cultural shift happening around violence to women that was a direct result of 1970s grassroots feminist activism, known as the Battered Women's Movement. During the early 1970s, domestic violence remained largely unrecognized and virtually ignored in the legal, medical, and social spheres. Culturally, woman battering was deemed a "private matter" and one did not intervene. Police and medical practitioners alike were reluctant to intervene into "private affairs," or what was then deemed "matters between a husband and his wife." In the span of less than a decade, however, significant gains were made. (Catherine Jacquet, "Domestic Violence in the 1970s", *NIH, US National Library of Medicine*, October 15, 2015).

Horror films, always indulging in the outrageous and mirroring the anxieties of the culture at the time, were bound to take some collateral damage.

Brian DePalma, a provocative director who was one of the filmmakers who spearheaded the "New Hollywood" of the 1970s, along with Martin Scorsese, Francis Ford Coppola, and Robert Altman, relished piling on sex and violence. With his movies like *Carrie* (1976) and *Home Movies* (1980), he exploited how audiences got turned on by the dangerous and the forbidden by making his characters turned on by the deadly and the forbidden. And he continued to do it, even after he was called a pervert for it.

Dressed to Kill (1980)

His film, *Dressed to Kill*, is his overt retelling of Hitchcock's *Psycho*. At the very beginning of *Dressed to Kill*, DePalma gives us an eroticized shower sequence. A beautiful nude woman showers alone, and we are aroused while she turns herself on with a bar of soap.

Suddenly, a hand covers her mouth as she is attacked from behind. Or so we think. It's her lover giving her one more sensuous poke of casual, anonymous sex.

The gag works because anyone who's seen *Psycho* knows what happens in a shower in movies. We are surprised when it doesn't happen. In that one scene, DePalma tells us that demonizing casual sex is bullshit.

In *Dressed to Kill*, the woman continues to have dangerous sex with strangers because it turns her on. Every time she does, we're sure the stranger will murder her, but it doesn't happen. It must be so frustrating for audience members who believe horror films are only reactionary morality tales.

Where's the retribution?

In *Dressed to Kill*, it's not sinning that singles you out for retribution. The movie doesn't blame the sexually promiscuous woman for her own demise. It blames the sick creep who kills her because he can't deal with his sexual issues. Right where the blame should be.

Slasher Films: How to Make Sex and Violence Boring

I think it's also significant that *Dressed to Kill* came out in 1980, at the height of the slasher films.

Slasher films piss everybody off. Some say slashers are puritanical morality tales that say casual sex will be punished. Others say they undermine the puritanical morals of society, and others say they promote violence against women.

Me? I hate them because they're lazy-ass excuses for horror movies.

The entire subgenre was based on an idea that was made to provoke. When the first few movies got a strong response and made money, a lot of talentless hacks followed the early films verbatim.

The 2006 documentary, *Going to Pieces: The Rise and Fall of the Slasher Film*, chronicles how Hollywood and independents took notice of the considerable profits made by *Halloween* (1978), *Friday the 13ᵗʰ* (1980), and *Prom Night* (1980), and then a slew of slasher films were released in 1981. "Anybody that gets in at the beginning of the cycle with a good film," said John Dunning, producer of the slasher *My Bloody Valentine* (1981), "has a good chance of succeeding."

This led to producers (mostly investors with no film experience) making movies for little money and pushing them onto as many movie screens as possible. A blueprint was quickly established: teenagers, a masked killer, a variety of weapons, and murders. And a little titillation.

Rabbi Herb Freed, the producer and director of *Graduation Day* (1981), described how he came up with his film's structure. "We went to see *Halloween* and *Friday the 13ᵗʰ*, and we saw how these things were constructed. If you watched carefully, and watched them several times, you could see that you have to have your buildup to a horror activity…some kind of massacre, and then it continues. They all fit that pattern. We did take a stopwatch and realized that every couple of minutes you gotta have some [killing] to fit in that genre."

That template was so by-the-numbers, it got boring very quickly. If you can make sex and violence boring, you've got a big problem.

The truth is that even though they seemed disturbing and offensive, slashers played it safe. They pushed the envelope with gore, but when it came to sex, they stopped at titillation. I think slasher films should be called "nudity and violence" films. You could cut out all the sexuality, and it wouldn't harm the movie at all, and it might change the running time by two minutes, tops.

On the other hand, if you took out the violence, you'd have a dull 30-minute short film. Why is there such a disparity between sex and violence in these films?

They were afraid to offend the audience.

There is nothing safer than showing nudity and straight sex to an audience made up of teenagers. These movies never challenge the comfort zone of the audience. The fans were much more comfortable with transgressive violence in these movies than with transgressive sex, so the filmmakers catered to what made the audience comfortable.

What the hell is the point of a horror film that does that?

Laughing in the Face of Misogyny

Slasher films were easy targets for advocacy groups, but they were equally easy targets for satire. Tobe Hooper's *The Texas Chainsaw Massacre 2* (1986) is a wonderfully subversive and gory satire of horror movie excess and the movie industry's lack of originality. Unfortunately, nobody realized it was a satire when it was released during the slasher glut, and it tanked.

The irony is that a horror movie that satirized and parodied the sex and violence template of the slasher films was more effective and erotically charged than the slasher films ever were.

TTCM2 contains a scene that overtly mocks the trope of a weapon portrayed as a phallic symbol, and I don't think it's ever been topped.

The scene involves a claustrophobic chase within a small college radio station. The lead character's name is Stretch. She's a long-legged woman in Daisy Dukes and cowboy boots, and she is being pursued by the legendary Leatherface, armed with his chainsaw.

It's not the chainsaw from the original film, which was a normal-sized chainsaw. Since this is a sequel as well as a satire, the chainsaw blade is at least twice the size of the first one.

After a short chase, Stretch is trapped inside a converted meat locker with reinforced walls. The only exit is the way she came in, through a heavy sliding door. Of course, Leatherface is in the doorway and has cut off her only escape route.

Stretch climbs up on top of a large steel tub full of ice and beers, and she's forced to stay in a squat as Leatherface enters the room with his chainsaw. He revs his chainsaw, with the big blade aimed between her spread legs.

She screams and begs and pleads while Leatherface continues to wave the whirling blade in her direction as a perverse threat. The more she cries and pleads, the more agitated and, um, excited Leatherface gets. He holds the body of the saw at crotch level, and he dips the whirling blade into the ice and beer.

Now Stretch is sprayed with a mixture of water and beer foam while she screams for mercy. It is patently absurd. However, the scene goes on so long that the absurdity turns into eroticism, and then it turns into something unsettling, and then it careens back to absurdity.

In a movie that's a satire of mindless horror movies, Tobe Hooper pushed the male domination sexual fantasy so far that he revealed it as silly. And rightfully so.

Because most fantasies are silly in the light of day.

Raising Sadism to High Art

The Texas Chainsaw Massacre 2 was a satirical look at sex and violence in horror movies, but the film still struck a nerve by sexualizing the domination a sadist has over his victim. It showed one person with power getting an erotic high over whether another person lives or dies.

Of course, there are horror films that take this idea very seriously.

The Italian *Giallo* film both stylizes and fetishizes the sexual nature of sadistic violence. These movies elevate the combination of sex and violence to the level of an art form.

Most Gialli are highly cinematic and made with considerable technical skill. They are gorgeous to look at, with dazzling photography and lavish use of color, and they are populated by stunningly beautiful actresses.

At the same time, they focus on brutal and sadistic violence against women, who are strangled, or stabbed, or drowned by a killer who in these films almost always wears leather gloves. There's a uniformity to how the killers look in these films that make the killer character an iconic image. It also makes them interchangeable. The killer is more of a symbol of violence than a distinct character.

The killer mentally tortures his victims, deliberately dragging out the inevitable until the victim is on the edge of madness, and the killer relishes every moment of terror he inflicts on his victims.

It's murder foreplay, and it's done with high-fashion artistry.

If someone were to accuse the entire subgenre of misogyny, I couldn't argue with them. And yet, many *Giallo* fans are women.

"Gialli are my favorite," says artist Chelsea Fetherlin, a graduate of Edinboro University. "One thing I like about Gialli is that the violence is an art form. Each death, male or female, has a macabre beauty that is not really biased towards a specific gender other than the fact that there is more female nudity. But even that is more to add to the poetry of a murder, than it is pornography or exploitation."

Dr. Rhonda Baughman, author and editor of *Grindhouse Purgatory* magazine and *Medium Chill*, agrees. "Do I enjoy them? Very much so. It's an *Adult Slumber Party* movie for refined tastes, I think. Do I try to internally reconcile the violence toward women? No. It's a film and I enjoy it on its own merits as I would a book: plot, characters, scene, themes, setting, symbolism...and then as film for music and set design, fashion, and cinematography. Violence is a fact—and we're a violent species. It doesn't mean I agree or disagree, or need to reconcile it, although a *Giallo* without violence would be like...chips without salt! Confusing."

One of the most wildly artistic, and insane, Italian movie directors is Dario Argento. Before he created legendary supernatural horror films like *Suspiria* (1977), Argento infused the *Giallo* film with his unique brand of hypnotic camerawork and nightmarish violence.

Argento uses blood spatter like a deranged Jackson Pollock, and the result is horrible/beautiful. When there's murder in his films, the gloved hands on the screen belong to Argento. Literally. The director stands in for murder close-ups in all his movies. Not creepy at all.

Opera (1987)

His film *Opera* showcases a perverse twist on brutal sadism. The killer forces his victim to watch him slaughter other people in front of her. He ties her up and tapes a row of sewing needles beneath her eyes.

When she shuts her eyes, she shreds her eyeballs with the needles. She's forced to watch the gruesome deaths while she stabs her eyelids with inevitable blinking.

Argento sexualizes the sadism; he turns the eyeball into an erogenous zone.

Too Real to Be Entertainment

It's hard for many to reconcile Argento's sexualization of sadistic violence toward women. But I think the carnage is so stylized, and often so surreal, that it would be hard to mistake the violence as realistic.

Rape-revenge films, on the other hand, are too real.

It's a complicated and a hotly debated topic that is all too relevant. In 2010, the CDC released the *National Intimate Partner and Sexual Violence Survey*, which found that one in five women had been raped. Yet filmmakers have been using rape to titillate since silent films like *Birth of a Nation* (1915) and *Intolerance* (1916).

Society's view on rape has changed considerably over the past few decades. It may be hard to understand just how rampant rape scenes used to be in movies.

It was even common in mainstream films. The PG-rated Western, *The Outlaw Josey Wales* (1976) included a rape scene, which did nothing to further the movie's plot. It was used as a cheap shock.

The subject of the validity of rape-revenge horror is complicated because you can't say that horror allows us to confront our darkest thoughts and then exclude some of our darkest thoughts from the list. And since people have rape fantasies, it's problematic to discredit a scene for titillation without sex shaming people.

Hey, I'm a pragmatist, not a moralist.

I look at horror movies with rape in them the same way I do slasher films. A lot of these movies follow a lazy template. If rape is in a horror film and it doesn't scare you, or challenge you, and it plays it safe by being mere titillation, what's the point?

A rape scene should make you uncomfortable; it should punch you right in the gut. You should feel the threat escalate like a bad dream becoming real. You should feel the loneliness and the terror of being helpless to stop your own violation.

Even if you're excited by rape fantasies, a horror movie should make you feel the pure brutality beneath the fantasy. Good horror should remind you of where your boundaries are. You can still have conflicting emotions watching these films, but you'll know that you've come to your darkest thoughts honestly, not through fake romanticizing.

The irony is that when a horror movie does its job and does it well with the brutality of rape, it gets punished for it. John Boorman's *Deliverance* (1972) is given lip service as a great film about the inherent violence of human nature, but it is mostly remembered as the punchline to jokes about male-on-male rape. Gaspar Noe's *Irreversible* (2002) tells the story of a loving couple destroyed by a violent rape in *reverse chronology*, so we are faced with the horrible emptiness of revenge before we see any cause, and we endure an endless graphic rape without any titillation. Audiences claimed it was exploitive trash. *The BBC News World Edition* of Sunday, May 26, 2002, ran the headline, "Cannes Film Sickens Audience." The article chronicled how *Irreversible* "proved so shocking that 250 people walked out, some needing medical attention." Fire wardens had to administer oxygen to 20 people who fainted during the film.

I Spit on Your Grave (1978)

However, times have changed. Women now embrace certain rape-revenge films that were once considered repugnant as being feminist films. Probably the most surprising reassessment must be for the original *I Spit on Your Grave* (1978). It was famously called "a vile bag of garbage" by film critic Roger Ebert, and it only played the exploitation grindhouse circuit.

The film centers around a tremendously brutal gang rape that lasts nearly 30 minutes, long past any chance of titillation. The next 60 minutes has the woman finding the men who did it and mutilating and torturing them, including a castration in a bathtub.

Professor Carol Clover supports *I Spit on Your Grave* as a feminist film. In her influential book *Men, Women and Chainsaws: Gender in the Modern Horror Film* (1992), Clover argues that even though the film seems to give sadistic pleasure to the viewer, the movie always sympathizes with the victim, not the tormentor, and the victim metes out justice on her attackers in the end.

Why does this level of violence appeal to feminists? "I think a lot of women are just fed up with the hypocrisy of the patriarchal and judicial systems, their molasses pacing and archaic notions," says Dr. Rhonda Baughman. "While most women aren't going to go out and slaughter a whole bunch of assholes, that doesn't mean they haven't embraced it as a valid form of entertainment."

Body Horror Goes Deep Inside Sex and Violence

Body horror is a subgenre obsessed with the anxiety and dread caused by the transformation of the human body. The change can be natural, like disease or decay, or it can be unnatural, like grotesque mutation or surgical disfigurement. It fetishizes the human form.

Up until now, I've discussed movies that brought sexual eroticism to their violent stories. But two influential body horror films added a little violence to the sexual eroticism.

The movies are Clive Barker's *Hellraiser* (1987) and David Cronenberg's *Videodrome* (1983), and no discussion of the volatile mixture of sex and violence would be complete without them. These two movies are openly about sex and sexual obsession. In the process, they altered and expanded the boundaries of horror and welcomed in new fans.

When I go to horror conventions, I meet a lot of people who are fans of both horror and heavy metal. I see as many metal T-shirts as I do horror T-shirts. I also see a lot of tattoos. Most of them are horror movie and heavy metal related.

Sometimes I catch a glimpse of a Bondage Duck tattoo.

It's a rubber duckie with a leather harness, or a ball gag, or a blindfold on it.

I've met people who have a heart with a keyhole in the center tattooed to their chests, and people with triskelion tattoos made up of three connected spirals.

Those tattoos are subtle declarations that the person is into BDSM, or bondage and discipline, or domination and submission, or sadism and masochism. There are no absolutes, of course, but often when I ask those people what their favorite horror film is, chances are good they say *Hellraiser* or *Videodrome*.

Hellraiser (1987)

Horror, heavy metal, and BDSM are different avenues that allow us to release our dark side and test our boundaries in a safe environment. But until Clive Barker's *Hellraiser*, I never would have seen a connection.

Hellraiser isn't a movie about BDSM, and you don't need to be into BDSM to love it. *Hellraiser* focuses on our anxieties around sex. The visual imagery the movie uses suggests a horror movie version of BDSM imagery, where leather-clad creatures take sexual practices like needle play, body suspension, body modification and cutting to the extreme level of torture, dismemberment, and death.

"I thought there was a strong fashion link to kink in *Hellraiser*, no doubt," says Leona Joy, BDSM enthusiast and dungeon designer in the San Francisco Bay Area. "The visual styling of the film leaned heavily into expressions of what some might rightly think of as edge play. Some of the interactions between Frank and Julie smack of D/s (dominant/submissive) Power Dynamics. Neither Frank's general sexual predilections nor his states of decomposition seem to be much of a deterrent to the connection between him and Julie. Indeed, those things are integral to their mutual frisson."

Hellraiser was the first major horror film to prominently feature "alternative sex" and still become a box office success. It brought to light provocative sexual ideals outside of the safe confines of the comic book sex of slasher films. *Hellraiser* took the chance of using sexuality to make audiences uncomfortable.

Horror audiences embraced it.

Leona Joy adds that the kink community embraced it, too. "Does the kink flavor enhance the film? For some of us, most certainly. It surely did make it something to talk about over a cup of coffee with other BDSM enthusiasts."

She also adds some clarification around the intersection of horror and BDSM. "The danger in depicting BDSM with horror is that going 'all the way' with depictions of what is clearly malice, bad intentions, mental and physical cruelty, and…well, death…conveys a lack of safe boundaries and a lack of adequate informed consent, both of which are prized precepts in the kink community at large. While those who engage in BDSM activities may enjoy horror film depictions of ritualized or sexualized gore, violence, and mayhem, it's not what they do in real life. This is an important distinction to make. Given that, it can be hot to watch scenes of torture or power dynamics that one would never actually do, or even come close to doing."

It took a chance, but it didn't go too far. At its center, *Hellraiser* is a cautionary tale that says if we chase the darkness and the forbidden, we may find the consequences to be more than we bargained for. The visual metaphor that propels that theme is an ornate black and gold Chinese puzzle box, and that choice is genius in simplicity. Who hasn't been tempted to try to solve a puzzle box?

Frank, the owner of the box, wants to solve the puzzle to open the lock mechanism because it holds the secrets of the darkest and most forbidden pleasures. He has no idea what's waiting if he solves the puzzle. Frank experiments, and experiments, trying different combinations. The longer it takes to solve, the more obsessed he becomes. Every time he fails to solve the puzzle, it's his chance to walk away.

But he chooses to continue.

The box is an entry gate into our world for the Cenobites, beings from another dimension who are devoted to pain as pleasure. And Frank just called them over to play with him.

Visually, the Cenobites are a nightmare version of body modification taken to impossible extremes. Pinhead, the chief Cenobite, has a grid of deeply carved scars that cover his entire head. Long metal pins have been hammered into the junction points of the grid of scars and his skull, so he looks like a demonic metal porcupine. He is the embodiment of pleasure and pain, and attraction and repulsion.

The horror of *Hellraiser* is that when the owner of the box finally solves it, and it opens a portal that will lead them to their destruction, they realize too late that they did it to themselves.

For those of us who are attracted to the dark side of everything in life, this idea at the center of *Hellraiser* was powerful and resonant.

Videodrome (1983)

Speaking of the dark side of everything in life, David Cronenberg's *Videodrome* gives us a society that feels like it's trapped inside a giant, invisible Chinese puzzle box, and nobody realizes it yet.

Director David Cronenberg has been making movies about body horror his entire career. All his films deal with how your body is in a constant state of revolt against you, staging mini-revolutions that will bring your downfall.

Cronenberg sees sex as a revolutionary act. "The sixties were unprecedented in terms of sexual openness and experimentation. And always, it was political. The sex that you were engaging in had strong political overtones. You were always aware that it had political meaning. So, sex had meaning beyond sex, beyond the physical," says Cronenberg in the documentary, *The American Nightmare* (2000).

He considers aging and decay as subversive acts. "To me, biology is destiny...from beginning to end, biology is destiny. But it's a very human thing to want to derail destiny, and therefore it's a very human thing for us to want to derail biology. And many of my characters are trying to derail biology to derail their own destiny as well."

He sees entropy and death as revolutionary acts. When the sexually-transmitted parasite from his early film *Shivers* (1975) finally takes over the body of the hero, Cronenberg considers that a happy ending.

"Right from the beginning, I felt that I would not strain out any of my own ambivalent thoughts about things...I could deliver to you, quite directly... that things might be dangerous and wonderful at the same time. On a very basic level, I'm afraid of revolution. I don't want to have to experience it. And yet I recognize that there are times when those things are absolutely necessary, because there's no other way to change things."

Cronenberg's movies often fetishize the body and comment on sex, but I consider *Videodrome* to be his most subversive revolutionary act. The film is about overstimulation, addictions to sensation, and addictions to the forbidden.

Videodrome asks the question, "Why do you watch?"

The story revolves around Max Renn, the owner of a cable company who specializes in "subterranean" video—soft-core porn and anything that can be pirated off the airwaves. His business meetings take place in fleabag hotel rooms where men sell him videotapes in hand-drawn boxes.

Max longs to find something "harder" to show on his network. You get the feeling he wants it more for himself than for his viewers. He is numbed by overstimulation.

One day, his pirate satellite technician intercepts the broadcast of a feed that shows a woman in chains strapped to an electrified clay wall. It looks like she's slowly tortured to death. There is no plot to this broadcast, just extreme violence. The subterranean show is called *Videodrome*, and there are rumors it is a live snuff show disguised as S&M.

After Max watches *Videodrome*, he starts to have violent sexual hallucinations, and he can't tell the difference between what is real and what is a hallucination caused by watching the broadcast.

Cronenberg immerses us in a world of violence and sexual deviance. But he also makes a harsh comment about the debate around whether sex and violence in the media affect the real world. In *Videodrome*, that ship has already sailed, and reality has been abandoned for the new hyperreality of the video world.

In 1982, Cronenberg envisioned a world where people would immerse themselves in a video world of pure sensation rather than live in the world outside their door. In this video world, you can have the excitement of murder without doing it yourself.

It's only a movie, right?

It's Okay, We All Have an Inner Pervert

Sometimes a horror film goes to extremes that get under our skin and make us reassess our boundaries. Maybe they can even shock us into examining our conscious thinking as well as our darkest thoughts.

Since we delved into some taboo subjects in this chapter, you might feel some conflicting emotions about what you read. If you do, that's okay. The conflicting feelings of repulsion and attraction are valid and legitimate.

And they don't make you a freak…

Unless you proudly identify that way.

FIVE MORE HORROR FILMS
THAT PUSHED THE ENVELOPE
WITH SEX AND VIOLENCE

1. *Trouble Every Day* (**2001**): An American couple travel to Paris to save their marriage only to have the husband run into a mysterious woman…who is a cannibal when sexually aroused. And she is aroused a lot. Claire Denis' horror film shocks because it shows cannibalism as a reverent sex act, full of play and joy and…gristle.

2. *Teeth* (**2007**): After an introverted virgin is sexually assaulted, she develops an unsettling gynecological anomaly. Her vagina grows sharp teeth. The fierceness of the primal fear this movie exudes when you realize her plans for revenge make this a jaw-dropper.

3. *Antichrist* (**2009**): A searing examination of grief and blame. A couple grieves the accidental death of their infant who they left unattended while they had sex. They retreat to a cabin in the woods, where they take out their mental pain on each other in very physical ways. The sexual violence is extreme.

4. *Hard Candy* (**2005**): The premise is disturbing enough: a 14-year-old girl insinuates herself into the home of a man she suspects to be a pedophile. She's a vigilante, and she's out to exact revenge. The possibility that she might be wrong makes the shame, denial, and fear of the man palpable, especially when her aim is to castrate him while he's still conscious.

5. *It Follows* (**2014**): A powerful, creepy, and emotionally draining film about a teenage girl who has sex and is told by the boy that he's passed a curse onto her. A demon will be coming to kill her, and it can look like anyone. It can be a stranger, or someone you trust. What at first sounds like a film about STDs reveals itself to be a horrifying allegory about rape culture, violation, victim blaming, and what life is like as a rape survivor.

CHAPTER ELEVEN

SHUT UP AND WATCH THE MOVIE:
TIME FOR YOUR HORROR THERAPY

If you're someone who hasn't watched a horror movie in years and you've made it this far into the book, I think it's safe to say your curiosity has been piqued. Perhaps you're ready for a horror restorative, a heady brew of great movies that will bring the color back to your cheeks.

Ironically, I know it can be hard to get good recommendations from most of us horror fans. We tend to champion the movies of our youth, or we promote the most revered horror films. We keep recommending the same 20 films that are 30 years old.

If we only talk about the movies of the past, we aren't representing the vitality and diversity of the modern horror film.

That's a problem I'm going to rectify here. I've made a list of horror movies that were released within the last five years of the writing of this book, 2013 to 2017, that I think are worth watching.

These movies make my list because they either surprised me, or were imaginative, or gave me a good scare. I also made this list with the diversity of styles of horror in mind, so whether you like slow-burn films, or gore fests, or subtle ghost stories, there's something on this list for you.

Some may not be to your liking, but I encourage you to get out of your comfort zone and take a chance on a movie that made you nervous just from the description. Give yourself the opportunity to be pleasantly surprised.

I want to start with one that you most likely already know.

Get Out (2017)

Get Out follows Chris Washington, a black man, who travels with his white girlfriend, Rose Armitage, to visit her parents at their family estate in the country. Chris is used to the city, so going to the country, and possibly being the only black person out there, has him understandably nervous.

Especially since Rose admits she hasn't told her parents that Chris is black.

Rose explains that her parents are very progressive, and even though they will probably say stupid and embarrassing things, her "parents aren't racist."

It's worth noting that this doesn't make Chris relax.

When Chris meets Rose's parents, they are just as advertised. Dad is a neurosurgeon and Mom is a psychotherapist/hypnotherapist, and they are cloyingly supportive and uncomfortably personable. Their vast estate rests inside a private community of like-minded people.

They have Walter, a black groundskeeper, and Georgina, a black housekeeper, to help maintain their home. The Armitages refer to the two employees as "family."

Chris is polite but guarded around Rose's family. They're friendly, but he can't help but feel out of place and anxious. His anxiety increases when he hears the house will soon be packed with family friends, fellow progressives, for an annual picnic.

Things start getting strange when Chris tries to make small talk and connect with the black people who work for the family. He discovers that they are stiff and uncomfortable around him. Their politeness is evidently artificial, and he notices that they watch him all the time.

Chris' paranoia increases while he's at the picnic. He's awash with aging white faces, all of whom take uncomfortable levels of interest in him. When he spies a fellow black attendee dressed like he's lived in suburbia all his life, he tries to make small talk. This man is just as awkward and distant as the groundskeeper and housekeeper were. Chris decides to take the man's picture with his phone, and the flash goes off. The man trembles and goes into hysterics and attacks Chris.

Why did he freak out? And why does he look so familiar to Chris, even though they've just met?

Did he dream that Rose's mother hypnotized him into paralysis, or did it really happen? Why is the door to the basement always locked? Is the housekeeper accidentally unplugging his phone charger, or is she doing it on purpose? What's in the box Rose hides in her closet?

Writer and director Jordan Peele created a horror film that tackles cultural appropriation, the fallacy of a "Post-Racial America," the shadow of slavery, and the harm inflicted on minorities by Liberal arrogance.

That last detail is why I believe *Get Out* is this generation's *Night of the Living Dead*. In *NOTLD,* George Romero reinvented the zombie as a metaphor for the generational revolution happening in the '60s—how one generation devours the other. With *Get Out*, Jordan Peele reinvents the on-screen image of racism for the twenty-first century as a wake-up call for his generation, and Romero's too.

We've been conditioned to see racists as visible, hate-filled caricatures in films. When *Get Out* introduces the wealthy and well-meaning progressive into the mix, it's a jolt to our expectations and perceptions. *Get Out* comments on how subtly arrogance, hubris, and complacency has turned former allies who fought against racism into a devious part of the problem.

The new horror for the disenfranchised is in being marginalized by the very people who say they're on their side. Minorities are rendered voiceless, and then they see people who are supposed to be allies cover their inaction with empty platitudes.

I think that's one of the reasons this generation is embracing the film. They can see the problem. They are directly affected by it.

Sure, the topic makes people nervous. That is what horror is supposed to do.

Get Out makes us look at hard truths while still being entertaining. *Get Out* captured the nation's struggle with racial issues, but it's entertainment first. The movie uses horror and humor to create situations that have a recognizable appeal.

But Peele also gives audiences a glimpse into what it's like to be a person of color in America.

I highly recommend *Get Out*.

Green Room (2015)

A road-weary punk band travels by van to a secluded part of the gloomy, rainy Pacific Northwest. Like just about any punk band that ever existed, they're broke, and they are on the precipice of obscurity. They arrive in Portland, Oregon and find out that their gig has been canceled without notice.

A local DJ arranges an impromptu gig at a private club out in the woods outside the city. He swears the owner of this club is a serious businessman who pays up front and doesn't cancel. The band is desperate for cash, so they take the gig.

When they arrive, they discover it's a neo-Nazi skinhead bar. There is a genuine sense of menace from the bar manager and the patrons. It's a quiet danger, one where conversations are short interrogations, and hostility barely hides behind unblinking stares.

Although the clientele makes them uneasy, they refuse to be intimidated, and they play the gig, starting with a rousing rendition of the Dead Kennedys' "Nazi Punks Fuck Off." It does not go over well, but they make it through their set. The manager and the bouncer help them pack their gear to get them out as quickly as possible.

The band is ready to leave, but one of the members has forgotten her cell phone in the green room. One of the band members goes back to the room to get it for her.

He stumbles onto a murder scene.

There's a woman on the floor with a knife stuck in her head, another terrified woman frozen in place, and a skinhead who is ready to kill again. We are dropped into the middle of this situation without any explanation, and part of the horror is slowly learning what's going on as the story reveals itself.

After a flash of panic and violence, the band manages to barricade themselves inside the green room taking the club's bouncer, a giant skinhead, hostage. He's the only thing keeping the others from breaking down the door and executing them all.

The leader of the skinheads is summoned, and he quietly and soberly tells the band that there is no hope, there is no escape, and no quarter will be given. We realize the group didn't just stumble upon a murder. They've stumbled upon a secret every person in that club will die to keep hidden.

The skinheads don't run around swearing in a blind rage. They are quiet and calculating, like wolves. Like a professional army of killers. That makes them, and the movie, feel real.

Green Room is ruthless and pitiless. It's also smart, witty, and it keeps you off-balance. When the movie was over, I was reminded of the tagline on the poster for the original *The Texas Chainsaw Massacre*.

The tagline was, "Who will survive, and what will be left of them?"

That's a question you will ask yourself again and again while you watch *Green Room*.

We Are Still Here (2015)

It's probably apparent that I love movies that isolate characters in single locations. When the movie's story is solid, and the actors are game, what may seem like a limitation brings out the imagination and the focus of the filmmakers.

That brings me to 2015's *We Are Still Here*, a ghost story with a Lovecraftian twist that does it right. It pays homage to classic films like *The Legend of Hell House* (1973) and *The Changeling* (1980), but it has a modern mean streak and a wonderfully surreal take on ghosts.

The story follows Anne and Paul Sacchetti, a middle-aged couple who move to an old house in a small New England town after their adult son dies in a car accident. The house has a history. Spirits live there. The small town has dark secrets.

It's a standard setup, right?

Well, not so fast.

We Are Still Here is quite aware you've seen a few ghost stories. The movie faithfully tells its ghost story with care and style. It doesn't forget to be scary. But that familiar ghost story gives you a false sense of comfort.

Trust me; you don't know what's going to happen.

It's a triumph of low-budget filmmaking, where timing, misdirection, and the power of suggestion creates a slow burn. The final act is absolute insanity. I highly recommend *We Are Still Here*.

The Autopsy of Jane Doe (2016)

I almost didn't watch this movie because of the sordid title. I'm glad I reconsidered. This film is one of the best ghost stories I've ever seen.

The movie starts with a homicide crime scene investigation. There are multiple brutally murdered people inside a locked house. There are no signs of forced entry. In fact, it seems like the victims were trying to get *out* of the house.

Investigators find something even more bizarre in the basement. There is a pit dug in the dirt basement floor. In the hole there is a dead, naked woman. We can't tell if she was halfway buried or halfway exhumed before the carnage started.

She doesn't seem to have a mark on her.

The image of this naked woman in the hole is painterly. She looks like Goya's *Portrait of the Marchioness of Santa Cruz*, except nude. And stone dead. It's the first of many visuals that are truly horrible/beautiful.

The sheriff takes the body to the local coroner for an urgent autopsy. Coroner Tommy Tilden performs the autopsy, and his son, Austin, assists him. Tommy looks at corpses like they are a mystery to solve. The body is the key, the Rosetta Stone, and it always reveals secrets.

But this Jane Doe doesn't reveal anything at first. There are no outward signs of any trauma. The body is fresh, pristine, beautiful. Except for the eyes. The eyes are cloudy, as if she's been dead for several days. Tommy discovers that her wrist and ankle bones are shattered, but the skin is unmarked. It doesn't make sense.

We learn some disturbing facts about dead bodies, the art of the autopsy, and the ugly business of storing the dead.

And you just know these facts are going to come back to haunt us.

While Tommy and Austin race to solve the puzzle before morning, there's a powerful rainstorm outside. It seems to be affecting the lights. And the radio.

And it's about at the time when Tommy takes the scalpel. When he makes the first incision, *The Autopsy of Jane Doe* rises to another level of nightmarishness and compelling visual storytelling.

The chills and, dare I say it, the *joys*, of *The Autopsy of Jane Doe*, come from the movie's surprises.

The film drips with atmosphere and intelligence. The story is focused, tight, and mean in a way only a smart screenplay can be.

Even though a movie with the word "autopsy" in the title will have gore in it, the film shows a lot of restraint. It chooses to use shadows and sound effects in the vein of the movies of producer Val Lewton, like *Cat People* and *I Walked with a Zombie*.

The end of this movie has a twist so cruel, and so unusual, and so clever, it will stun you.

I applauded when I saw it.

I give *The Autopsy of Jane Doe* my highest recommendation.

Surreal Horror Films

One of my favorite films of all time is *Phantasm*, a surreal horror film from the '70s that deals with death and loss, through dreams within dreams and time shifts in the narrative. Good surreal horror films are rare because there's a fine line between surreal and incoherent.

Just like nightmares, surreal horror films are meant to disorient you and disturb you. They are intentionally Expressionistic, more about feel than story logic.

That isn't everybody's cup of tea.

However, if it *is* your cup of tea, like it is mine, the next two films are good examples.

Baskin (2015)

"Hell is not a place you go to. You carry hell with you at all times.

You carry it inside you."

Baskin is a Turkish horror film. It's not for the squeamish or those who need a linear plot.

Within its lucid-dream logic, *Baskin* weaves a powerful spell. The film makes you feel like you've been dragged into a nightmare. There are scenes that pull off nightmare logic so well that I felt my mouth go dry.

Baskin translates to "Raid." A group of Turkish police officers responds to a call for backup at an incident miles away in a remote town.

This film was made during actual riots in Turkey over police brutality, and the officers we follow in the movie are bullies with badges. They take what they want with fear and intimidation.

The town they head to has a bad reputation, and the police are on edge. Before the officers get there, a naked man runs into the road and the police hit him with their patrol van. When they get out to investigate, there is no body. Instead there is a huge mass of squirming frogs. And someone has carved strange symbols on the side of the van.

After many surreal and creepy encounters, the police finally arrive. It is an old, defunct police station and jail. There is a police car outside with its door open and lights flashing. But there is nobody in sight. Nobody responds over the radio.

When the officers enter the abandoned police station, *Baskin* goes into full, grotesque nightmare mode. The movie contains some of the most hellish images I've seen in recent memory.

Baskin is a movie that lingers in your head after it ends, just like a particularly bad dream.

Humor and Horror

Creep (2014)

Horror and comedy is not an easy balancing act, but when it is accomplished, it makes for a memorable movie. Balance is what makes *Creep* so damn good. The film makes you laugh one moment and then makes that laugh freeze in your throat in the next.

Aaron is a videographer who responds to a Craigslist ad for a one-day gig at a residence in the mountains. The house is the kind of tastefully low-key, hidden mansion in the hills that the ridiculously rich own.

He meets the owner, Josef, who has hired him to record various messages for his unborn son. We learn that Josef has brain cancer, and these messages will be given to Josef's son when he's old enough. By that time, Josef will be dead.

Early on, it's evident that Josef is a little weird. He smiles too much, he's a big hugger, and he seems to get attached to people quickly.

Oh, and he likes to play practical jokes to scare people.

What's so great about *Creep* is that it lives right on the line between comedy and horror. Every scene mixes the two in a way that is hilariously uncomfortable. The story and situations grow out of the awkward interactions between the two men.

One guy is a paid professional. He's used to being polite while dealing with eccentrics. The other is a rich guy, oblivious to other people's boundaries. So, there is nervous humor built in. All it takes is one character to step over the line of reasonable behavior to have the movie cross over from comedy into horror.

This is smart, low-budget filmmaking at its best. It's just two guys, in one location. They are all alone in a house in the woods. Well, they are alone, except for the occasional visit from "Peachfuzz."

Who, or what, is "Peachfuzz"?

You'll just have to watch *Creep* to find out.

The Romantic Side of Horror

When we fall in love, we are vulnerable. We risk personal suffering in the hope that it will all work out and we will live happily ever after. But if it doesn't work out, we are in our own personal horror film.

Honeymoon (2014)

The fear of realizing that you never truly know anyone, even your life partner, drives the horror of *Honeymoon*.

The movie opens with the wedding video of newlyweds Bea and Paul. It's full of romantic memories of how they met. The newlyweds are honeymooning at Bea's family cabin on a lake that's surrounded by forest. Bea has spent her summers there as a kid, and she wants to share her memories with Paul.

One night, Paul wakes up to find Bea is not in bed, so he calls out to her.

Nothing.

He searches the cabin, but Bea is gone. He finds the back door wide open. Paul runs into the woods in a panic, and he sees Bea, naked and disoriented. When he takes her inside, she tells him it's stress-related sleepwalking. Paul's not convinced. Bea has never sleepwalked before. But she assures him that she's okay.

The next morning, she wakes up early to fix him a breakfast of French toast and coffee. Except she forgets to batter the bread and it burns in the pan. Bea is embarrassed but insists that she's okay…she's just feeling a little funny.

Paul goes to pour coffee and finds whole coffee beans floating in hot water.

That is the beginning of a terrifying journey into personal dread that gets more frightening and tragic as it goes along. Bea starts to forget the meaning of words, and she is missing memories.

Is there something physically wrong with Bea? What is out there in the woods that terrifies her when the night comes? Watch *Honeymoon* to find out. It's a horror movie so well constructed and so well acted, that you'll want to watch it a second time to catch the clues you missed.

Spring (2015)

Where *Honeymoon* found horror in a relationship falling apart, *Spring* says that with some relationships, the horror gets worse the deeper you fall in love.

We meet Evan, a young man whose life is a total train wreck. His mother has just died of cancer, he has lost his job, and he has just managed to get himself into a brutal and senseless fight that might lead to jail. Evan flees the country and escapes to a beautiful seaside town in Italy. He has no particular plans, but he hopes to either change his life or drink it away.

He meets Louise, a beautiful local woman. She is mysterious, aloof, and flirtatious. Evan is smitten. He takes a job at a local farm to stay in Italy illegally so he can pursue her.

If this movie sounds like a romance, it is. Except there are some complications.

It's obvious that Evan comes with some serious baggage. But it is *nothing* compared to Louise's baggage. Hers might be full of body parts.

Louise keeps secrets from Evan, things about her past that she knows could put him in jeopardy. Evan knows there's something she's not telling him, but he can't let her go. When he finds out the secret she carries, he is horrified. At first, the secret terrifies him. Then he is horrified to realize that he doesn't care; he will risk everything to be with her.

I know, I'm being vague, but there's a reason. Because *Spring* is a real rarity, a horror movie that dares to cover a wide array of emotions honestly and realistically, without losing sight of the horror elements.

It is a gorgeous movie, full of color and life, and contrasts. And it photographs a violent death as beautifully as it does the Italian countryside.

Because love can be equally horrible and beautiful, especially in this movie.

Spring is a wildly original and ambitious horror film that dares you to use your head and your heart. Highly recommended.

Whole Lotta Lovecraft

Monsters come in all dimensions. They also come *from* all dimensions. H.P. Lovecraft created the concept of "cosmic horror," where the horror comes from how insignificant humans are compared to the unknown monsters of an ever-expanding universe. The next film is an excellent example of Lovecraftian horror.

The Void (2017)

The movie starts with a young man and woman being run out of a house by two men armed with shotguns. They fire, and the woman gets the brunt of the shotgun blast. The man is wounded and he runs into the nearby woods.

The armed men calmly walk over to the woman lying on the ground. They pour gasoline on her and light a match.

That's just the first 60 seconds of *The Void*, a gonzo, blood-spattered, head-trip, killer cult, killer monster movie. This ultra-low-budget film is a proud throwback to 1980s horror. They even use practical effects over CGI. *The Void* might pay homage to many of those classic '80s movies, but it is decidedly its own beast.

The plot kicks in when a sheriff's deputy finds the wounded man on the road and rushes him to a nearby hospital. Things get worse, and weirder, when they get to the hospital.

A gathering of hooded cultists surrounds the hospital. A small group of patients, nurses, and doctors, as well as the deputy are trapped inside. The cultists stand like sentinels, and they attack when someone tries to leave the hospital.

All of that happens within the first 10 minutes.

Why are they being forced to stay inside the hospital? The group soon discovers there's something else inside the hospital with them. Some of the nurses and patients start to go insane. Some of them start to change.

What's happening inside the hospital starts to affect the world outside.

And that is, quite literally, not the half of what is going on in *The Void*. This movie proudly disregards budgetary limits as a reason to scale down its ambition. More ideas are floating through *The Void* than the majority of big-budget horror films ever try.

But what most impressed me was the dark, doomsday atmosphere of the film. There is a grit and an immediacy, a real grasp of horror that catches your breath.

Hypnotic Horror Films That Won't Bore You to Death

There's a plague that has infected horror movies. I call it "Shiningitis." It's when a horror movie tries to emulate the claustrophobic tone and deliberate pace of Stanley Kubrick's *The Shining*. Most of these attempts are flat-out dull. They can't duplicate the hypnotic state that Kubrick delivered to audiences, the one that attracts multiple generations to that film. However, sometimes a horror movie finds its own path to a hypnotic state and blows you away. Here are three of them:

The Witch: A New England Folk Tale (2015)

Let's start with *The Witch: A New England Folk Tale*. I think a direct comparison between *The Shining* and *The Witch* is appropriate. Both movies place a family in complete isolation against nature and madness, and both films can be read as either psychological or supernatural horror. Both movies are meticulously shot and deliberately paced. And they are both utterly hypnotic.

The Witch follows a deeply religious family who is banished from their Puritan Village due to the father's heretical views. The issue is that the father believes the Puritans are *too liberal*. So, yeah, he's a piece of work.

He and his family are banished into the wilderness and they have all their belongings on a wagon. He sets out with his wife, his teenage daughter, Tomasin, their son, Caleb, as well as Mercy and Jonas, who are fraternal twins, and an infant named Sam, to build a homestead at the edge of the woods.

What could possibly go wrong?

The father might be a devout man of God, but he turns out to be a shitty farmer and an even shittier hunter. The corn rots and they're starving, all alone in the wilderness. The family is barely holding it together.

Everything unravels one morning when Tomasin plays with Sam at the edge of the woods. She covers her eyes to play "peek-a-boo" with the baby, but when she opens them, the child is gone. He has somehow silently disappeared. This tragedy crashes Tomasin headlong into a wall of grief and superstition, and religious paranoia that seals the family's fate.

This family is obsessed with sin and damnation, and they believe their misfortunes are brought to them by evil forces. Are we watching a family slowly go mad at the edge of civilization, letting their delusions run wild? Or is there evil out there in the woods?

Was it a wolf that took the baby, or was it something much older and darker that lives in the woods and wants to possess them all? Does Black Phillip, the creepy horned farm goat, talk to the twins like they say he does, or is it just a kids' game? Are illnesses curses in disguise, and are fever hallucinations the devil's tongue?

We see the answer soon enough. We see a coven of witches in a cave, performing unspeakable acts to fly in the moonlit sky.

Or do we?

Do we see real events, or is this the manifestation of what the family fears and believes is out there? Are their delusions playing out in front of our eyes like an Expressionistic nightmare? Is reality distorted by the fairytales the family brought with them to the wilderness, or is every fairytale that the family brought with them true?

The movie keeps us guessing by immersing us in a hyperrealistic historical vision that feels authentic and believable. The use of natural lighting and the dirty grit of the wild make the woods they enter feel like real woods.

This immersion in detail and the total commitment of the actors allows the movie to weave a hypnotic spell. You might forget the modern world and sink into a world full of superstition and primal fear. It isn't until the final moments of the film that we find out what is real and what is not.

Or do we? I highly recommend *The Witch*.

The Neon Demon (2016)

When this next movie premiered at the Cannes Film Festival, people either booed it or gave it a standing ovation. And, in all honesty, *The Neon Demon* will kindle both responses in most viewers, and I don't believe this is accidental. This is a beautiful movie about ugly things and it shows how flexible horror can be. That makes it challenging.

The plot follows a young model who runs off to Los Angeles to find fame. Her natural beauty and innocence draw the attention of jaded photographers. It also draws the attention, and jealousy, of the older models in the agency. That kind of attention can be deadly.

The movie opens with a gorgeous model in a stunning dress laying on an antique sofa. It looks very vogue, except for her slashed throat and the blood running down her arm.

It's an illusion for a fetishistic glamour photo shoot. This movie is all about fantasy, the artifice of glamour, and the temporary power of beauty. But it is also about worshipping false idols, and rituals and sacrifices.

Our young model fascinates the top photographers because her beauty is completely natural. Virginal. She stands out because every other model we meet has had cosmetic surgery to their bodies. Once you cut away a part of yourself, you lose your innocence, which is something no surgery can correct.

Our young model gets the showcase role at a prestigious fashion show. With that the ritual begins. Is she transforming into the new Virgin Queen, or is she the new Virgin Sacrifice?

The surface beauty of abstract visuals can't hide the sense of menace underneath the shallow surface of *The Neon Demon*. Once the ritual of fame and glamor begins, the movie becomes a surreal nightmare. In the end, I think you'll be shocked to see how far the film decides to go. Boo it or applaud it, *The Neon Demon* makes my list because it walks the razor's edge of horrible/beautiful.

Starry Eyes (2014)

The movie *Starry Eyes* is similar to *The Neon Demon* in theme, but it tells the story differently. Even though this film has a much lower budget, and got very little promotion, I think it's the better movie of the two.

Starry Eyes follows Sarah, an anonymous actress, through her version of Los Angeles. It's an LA where fledgling movie directors live in abandoned vans, and where waitressing jobs are considered show business by the manager, and where competition for a good shift is just as harsh as a cattle call.

Sarah lives in a run-down motel with a group of wannabe artists who are also wannabe friends. She endures her friends more than she likes them.

Sarah gets an audition for a horror film called *The Silver Scream*. It is being made by a small, but well-regarded film studio named Astraeus Films. At the audition, she meets the casting director from hell and his assistant. They sit there expressionless and barely speak to her.

The audition goes poorly, and Sarah runs into the ladies room. When she gets there, she punishes herself by violently pulling her hair until her neck vertebrae crack. The casting assistant walks in and sees this happen…and she is very intrigued. She offers a second audition if Sarah will allow herself to go to that emotion that made her punish herself.

They want to see "The Real Sarah." Even though she feels vulnerable and ashamed, Sarah agrees. And, when she channels that angry animal, she goes so far that she convulses on the floor.

And they are pleased.

Sarah gets a callback for a screen test. Unfortunately for her, it takes place in a pitch-black room. She is given direction by a disembodied voice. Suddenly, a bright light starts to rhythmically flash.

And then things start to get weird. And violent.

What makes *Starry Eyes* so good is that it is a fleshed-out character study. There is a duality to everyone. Characters may look friendly, but they carry evil deep inside them.

Starry Eyes explores the evil shadow that we all have inside. It says that we are only as nice and as kind as *our options force us to be*. But, if our options were to change, and that evil shadow is permitted to come out, we will allow it. Because it's easy to become possessed when the demon has been with you all along. I highly recommend *Starry Eyes*.

The Many Faces of Horror

It's an exciting time to be a horror fan because there's no single dominant trend to define what modern horror looks like or what kinds of stories will be told. Here are some movies that are entirely different from each other in style, yet they are all brilliant horror films.

Proxy (2013)

Brian De Palma is the crazy, hit-and-miss genius who gave us *Sisters*, and *Carrie*, and *Dressed to Kill*, and *Body Double*. De Palma was an American

Hitchcock who wasn't afraid to be called a pervert. His movies started at the point where Hitchcock would slam on the brakes.

De Palma's perversion wasn't just sexual. He relished in the depravity of the twisted soul, and the deviant lengths one would go to in order to get revenge. Now De Palma isn't making movies like this anymore; he's moved his business into a less bloody neighborhood. But his influence in the horror genre remains.

That brings me to *Proxy*, directed by Zack Parker, the best Brian De Palma film that Brian De Palma didn't direct himself. It's about time someone emulated the director who spent a good portion of his career emulating Hitchcock. Turnabout is fair play.

A pregnant woman walks down the street after having a prenatal exam. Suddenly, someone in a red hoodie jumps out from around a corner and hits her on the head with a brick. The attacker drags her unconscious body into the alley, and he uses the brick to strike her repeatedly on the belly.

This moment is shocking and hard to forget, and we are left asking the question, "Why?"

The baby does not survive, and the woman, named Esther, joins a hospital support group. Esther meets and befriends Melanie, whose husband and son were killed by a drunk driver. These lonely women bond over their tragedies.

One day Esther is at a department store, and she sees Melanie and walks over to say hello. But before she gets there, Melanie starts to change. She starts screaming that someone has taken her boy, and chaos ensues. The security guards try to calm her down, and they scramble to find the lost boy. Melanie runs for the parking lot, and Esther chases after her only to see Melanie change again.

Melanie calmly walks over to an SUV, and she pulls out her little boy. She pinches his arm to make him cry, and she carries him into the mall to complete the bizarre playacting. Esther is stunned, and then she does something unexpected.

She smiles.

You will be asking "why," again and again, as this crazy puzzle box of a movie unfolds. Suffice to say that this insane moment is just the tip of the insanely perverse iceberg that is *Proxy*. This movie starts out Hitchcockian, but by the end, we are in classic Brian De Palma horror mode. You might find yourself rewatching that opening scene to see it with a different pair of eyes.

Right after you pick your jaw up off the floor.

I recommend *Proxy*, and I also say it's high time for a Brian De Palma revival!

The Girl with All the Gifts (2016)

If you had told me back in 1985, when the only recent zombie film was George Romero's *Day of the Dead,* that there would come a time when I'd be sick of zombies, I would have laughed at you. Yet here we are, and zombie fatigue is real.

Imagine my surprise when I found myself recommending one here.

The movie opens with a young girl lying in bed in a prison cell, counting to herself. She hears her corrections officers coming, so she dutifully sits in a wheelchair by the bed. When the cell door opens, she is all smiles and welcomes her jailers by name.

They welcome her with machine guns pointed at her and call her an abortion.

She continues to smile pleasantly as they strap her head and extremities into the chair. When the soldiers take her out of the cell, they join a convoy of other children in wheelchairs. The children are brought to a classroom where they stay strapped in their chairs.

Melanie, the girl from the cell, is the star pupil in this weird class. She tells a heartfelt story to her teacher, who absentmindedly pats Melanie on the head. The soldiers pour into the classroom, locked and loaded. The sergeant in command reminds the teacher that these may look like children, but they are not children. He reminds her of what they are.

The sergeant spits on his forearm to remove a scent-covering gel, and he puts his arm in front of a boy. The boy looks at him innocently. The boy gags. And his jaw muscles crack. And then he is a crazed beast, hissing and snapping his jaws uncontrollably. All the other children around him start to go wild as well, like some crazy chain reaction.

What *are* they?

Welcome to *The Girl with All the Gifts*, a movie about a human outbreak of the very real "zombie fungus" (*Ophiocordyceps unilateralis*) that's found in insects. In the film, it has mutated and jumped species, and it is now out of control. The infected are mindless zombies who spread the disease one bite at a time.

But Melanie and these other kids aren't mindless at all. They are polite and capable of conversation. Until they smell your warm flesh.

What *are* these children?

The scientists don't have a term for it, except that they are second-generation carriers of the illness. These children still interact with their environment, and yet, they are no longer human. They have the fungus inside them, and they will instinctively kill you if they are triggered. They are perfect mimics, and they aim to please you and get you to empathize with them.

All the better to infiltrate you.

Is every human attribute that Melanie expresses just camouflage for a dangerous mutation? Or, is there more to this variation than meets the eye? This question goes from academic to horribly practical as the military base gets overrun and a small band of people escapes, with Melanie in tow.

There are more revelations and mutations to be found in *The Girl with All the Gifts*. But, most of all, there is an intelligent, and surprisingly moving, discussion on what makes something alive, and what makes us human. I highly recommend *The Girl with All the Gifts*.

Here Comes the Devil (2013)

A family goes on a day trip to the Tijuana countryside. The kids, a preteen brother and sister, ask their parents if they can explore the caves in a nearby hill. The mother agrees, but says they need to be back in an hour and a half because it's getting late. She gives them her watch and they climb the hill.

They do not return.

The parents are in a panic as darkness falls. The police tell them that a full-scale search is impossible until morning, so they tell the parents they should get some rest for the arduous day ahead of them.

The next morning, the parents wake up to find out that the police have found the children. The kids just walked out of the hills. They are returned to their parents, but the children are…different. They are withdrawn, and they act strangely, and they only spend time with each other. The children don't remember anything, except waking up in a cave, but the parents fear the worst, that their children were abused by someone in the hills.

Strange things start happening, things that can't easily be explained away. And the parents hear a local legend about those hills—that there is evil up there.

That's the spine of the story to *Here Comes the Devil*, but what makes this movie so creepy is the meat surrounding the bone. The film is drenched in uncomfortable sexuality, and the dread of sexuality when it comes to children.

The events of the movie start with the daughter having her first period. After that, the mother sees male predators in every gas station.

Creepy.

The movie exploits the anxiety parents have when their children hit puberty, when the kids transform into something different and out of their control. Whatever these children are turning into brings with it some nightmarish imagery, and possible visits from a demon, and murder, and torture.

Oh, and I can't forget that there is a madman with a machete who cuts off women's fingers and keeps them in a box. And that's just some of the madness in this movie. I recommend *Here Comes the Devil* for creeping me out and creating a sense of dread that feels like a fever dream.

I Am Not a Serial Killer (2016)

I love a good monster movie. However, they are usually like comfort food on a chilly evening. A large part of the enjoyment is the familiarity. No surprises. But every so often, there's a gem of a movie that defies expectations, and even easy classification. *I Am Not a Serial Killer* is a monster movie that beams with creativity and originality.

The story follows a teenage boy named John who lives in a small Midwestern town. John is diagnosed as a sociopath who also suffers from homicidal impulses. He curbs his impulses with mental exercises and rules of conduct that he and his therapist have created together.

He also works in his mother's funeral home, which satisfies his morbid curiosity.

Then there is a violent murder and mutilation in town. Of course, Mom and the therapist need to ask the tough question. John answers that, no, he did not do this. But he is fascinated with the body and the crime scene.

And then, there is another brutal murder and mutilation. This starts talk around town that this might be the handiwork of an active serial killer.

John is pretty sure he didn't do this. So, he starts to sleuth around, searching for a serial killer with the understanding of how a serial killer thinks. And it's about that time when John begins to notice a drifter around town.

And that's where I'm going to stop. I've only covered stuff that the name already spells out for you because this is another movie that is best when you don't know what's coming.

And you don't know what's coming.

I will say that I was completely caught off-guard with what this movie develops into. The audacity of this film made me laugh. But, underneath the horror and the humor is a story of loneliness. It speaks to the tragedy of never being truly accepted by some of those we love unless we alter ourselves to get the affection we crave. It's the pathos under the audaciousness that makes *I Am Not a Serial Killer* a must-see. Highly recommended.

In Fear (2013)

This movie is a breathtaking psychological horror film that's so immersive you can smell the sweat of the main characters. *In Fear* is as experimental as it is simple in idea. This is such a weird little movie, and I don't know what I can tell you without spoiling it.

It's the story of an English couple who come to Ireland for a music festival, and they get lost on their way to their bed and breakfast. And things go horribly wrong. It's two people driving around, lost, and the sun is going down.

And herein lies the problem writing to praise a movie that has a simple premise where the brilliance is in the execution and the subtlety of the terror. I don't know what else I can tell you that won't give anything away.

I can say that when I saw *In Fear*, it felt so authentic that I immediately looked up the behind-the-scenes information on how it was filmed. I can't talk about *that* either because it might taint your reading of scenes as they unfold. If you intend to watch *In Fear*, don't read anything about it until after you see it.

You're either going to love it or hate it. If you love it, you'll probably be as curious as I was to find out how the director was able to get such genuine performances from the actors. And if you hate it? You can at least take solace that you weren't *in* the movie.

I can say that the movie is intense, and it is claustrophobic, and it is bizarre. *In Fear* is one of my favorites on this list, and it earned its place.

A Dark Song (2017)

Ireland, the land of the Old Religions and Druids, and fairy mounds, has recently been on fire with great horror movies, and *A Dark Song* is one of the best.

A woman rents a country estate for six months, with the purpose of performing a pagan ritual. Her young son was murdered by a group of teenagers, and she cannot continue with her life until she speaks with him one last time. She is obsessed, compelled by grief.

She hires an occultist to perform the ritual, and the two of them will live at the estate for six months. Once locked inside, they cannot leave until the ceremony is completed.

Why six months? That's how long it will take to open the veil between the worlds of the living and the dead, and then to contact the dead, and then to convince them to speak. If you're lucky.

It's that kind of commitment to the movie's universe that makes *A Dark Song* so mesmerizing. In most horror movies, the ritual is a plot point to get to the ghosts, and all it takes is a séance or a bunch of amateurs fumbling with a Ouija board to get the spirit world's attention.

I have no idea what you'd need to do to speak to the dead, but my instincts tell me it takes more than knocking three times on a special door and leaving a plate of the loved one's favorite cheese.

In this film, the entire house is a sacrificial altar, and each room has a symbolic purpose. They painstakingly circle the house with a line of salt to lock themselves inside. To cross that salt line before the ritual is over is to risk death, or worse.

Is this authentic stuff? I have no clue, but I will say that the amount of detail that *A Dark Song* commits to makes you suspend disbelief. This movie is about the physical ritual, but it is also about the hidden emotional rituals that possess our troubled souls.

We have two broken people trapped inside the rituals of addiction, and the rituals of grief, and the rituals of abuse. Are they driving each other mad, or is the emotional fragility proof that the ritual is working? What lengths would you need to go to in order to get the attention of the dead?

And once you get their attention, can you turn it off?

Watch *A Dark Song* to find out. It's a movie that is at times terrifying and, surprisingly enough, life-affirming. Highly recommended.

I hope you take a chance and dive into these films and give yourself that horror restorative. Because I do believe there's a horror resurgence happening, and it is happening under the radar, in small independent films.

Like it always does.

There will always be the odd movie that breaks into the mainstream and creates a fad that gets copied endlessly, but that's temporary. The new classics will be picked by us, through word of mouth.

Before I close, let me leave you with one more movie.

It's a perfect example of stumbling upon gold in them independent movie hills, and how word of mouth creates a new horror classic. I had never heard of this movie, even though it had a big-name star and several dependable character actors in it. However, a friend recommended it to me with the zeal of a Pentecostal preacher.

When I looked the movie up, I found it had played the film festival route. It had a very limited theatrical run after it got picked up by a small independent distributor at a festival, and it was released in January—not a good sign.

With this big-name actor? It must suck. And yet, the name of the movie intrigued me. I decided to rent it and give it a shot.

After I watched it, I called my horror movie friends to tell them they *had* to watch this movie. I'm going to tell you what I told my friends on the phone, and nothing more.

There's a movie you've got to see. It stars Kurt Russell and an ensemble cast. It's a horror movie set in the Old West. The name of the film is *Bone Tomahawk* (2015).

There are cannibals. Just shut up and watch the movie!

SHAMEFUL CONFESSIONS: HORROR FILMS THAT I WOULD CLASSIFY AS OVERRATED

1. *The Shining* (1980): I like the movie a lot, but I am confounded by people who revere it and call it the scariest movie they've ever seen. Never underestimate the power of the name Stanley Kubrick and a Steadicam to elevate a movie in the eyes of cineastes.

2. *It* (2017): A good, solid horror film, but Pennywise nearly sinks it. What's scary about the original idea of Pennywise is that although he looks like a regular clown, he's a Venus fly trap of evil. What he says and does is scary, not what he looks like. No kid in his right mind would go near the drooling, dirty clown in the remake.

3. *The Lost Boys* (1987): Once again, a solid horror movie, and likeable. Maybe that's the problem for me. Horror shouldn't offer you half of its sandwich at lunch. The tone isn't tense or dangerous, and it's so stylized it could be a commercial. Muscle-men playing saxophone on the beach, high fashion—where did they research teenage life to get this?

4. *Cat People* (1982): I like copious nudity as much as the next person, but this film has always hit me as a gorgeous mess. It's beautifully photographed and it has one truly disturbing death scene at a zoo, but other than that I felt the story was unfocused.

5. *House of 1,000 Corpses* (2003): As much as I love and praise Rob Zombie's *The Devil's Rejects* (2005), that's how much I dislike this film. It has no constant tone or even color palette. As violent as the film can be, I think it plays very safe by being a little bit of every type of film. It goes for violence and then gets jokey, and it gets weird for the sake of it. When victims are forced into bunny costumes and made to hop in a field at night only to get stabbed to death, I wonder if there's even a second of this movie that I can believe.

THE AUTHOR AND A FRIEND GHOST HUNTING, 1985

CHAPTER TWELVE

HORROR CAN MAKE YOU HAPPIER AND HEALTHIER,
AND I'M LIVING PROOF

Didn't I tell you the dark side was going to be fun?

One of the things I genuinely love about horror is how inclusive it is. Horror is such a universal storytelling style that something as quintessentially Texan as *The Texas Chainsaw Massacre* can be loved in Japan, and something as Japanese as *Ju-on: The Grudge* can be a hit in Texas. It's a style that can be pure nightmare fuel, or it can be a slow-burn tale of dread, or allegorical social commentary, or even a satire, but it will still be unmistakably horror. There are dozens of horror subgenres out there, and there's bound to be one with which you'll fall in love.

Why do we watch? We watch horror movies because we want to connect to our humanness. We want to know what still scares us. We want to know that we are still shockable in a world where the abominable is the new normal. We want to have a handshake with our shadows and know that we aren't alone in our dark thoughts.

The Health Benefits of a Lifetime of Watching People Die

The guilty pleasure of watching monsters and murderers on screen is its own reward, but let's take a moment to gather together the benefits of embracing horror that is scattered through this book.

We've talked about how horror can make an outsider feel like they belong, and how a horror film can sometimes help us come to terms with real traumas. We also explored how watching a horror movie in a crowded theater is a communal experience that lets us bond with the rest of the audience.

We examined how horror literature allows us to break the rules and trespass into taboo territories to form our own worldview with a level of privacy that only a book can give. We also dove into how the fusion of music and horror allows us not only to exorcise darker emotional demons that can't be reached with words but also to find our tribe with which to share the experience.

Horror gives us a manageable surrogate for anything and everything that we fear. Whether it be world events, or death or disease, a horror movie gives us a sense of control where we normally have none.

Not bad for an art form that usually gets dismissed as being about nothing except machetes and half-naked coeds.

Not that there's anything wrong with that.

And if those reasons aren't enough to sway you into allowing horror into your heart, I swear to you that watching horror movies can also make you happier and healthier.

Even though the tone of this book is playfully tongue-in-cheek, I'm sincere when I say that horror is a beautiful art form, and I do believe that art has the power to change people's lives.

You may have noticed a few recurring themes that come up when I talk about the influence horror can have on a person: coping with trauma and tragedy, renewing a passion for life, indulging playfulness, and finding a sense of belonging in a community. No matter who you are, if you have those things, life is happier and healthier.

And, when you're happy and healthy, you feel compelled to share the joy with others.

I'm living proof.

I wrote this book because I've hit several rough patches in my life. I lost my motivation, and I lost sight of my passion, and I isolated myself. Every time that happened, the thing that snapped me back was somehow connected to my love of horror. I'd reconnect with the first love of my life, and catching just a hint of the excitement that I felt as a kid was the spark that led me out of the woods.

When I was a kid, horror movies helped me navigate a seriously stormy sea. Of course, that was when I was a child, at a time when I had no control over my life. So, for what possible reason would a grown adult male have an epiphany through horror movies? Just how bad do things need to get for an adult to find salvation in the type of film where a severed head scene is always a distinct possibility?

How Exploding Heads Gave Me a New Lease on Life

At the beginning of the 1990s, I was in danger of going off the social radar. I had recently finished four years of military service, and I found myself having a hard time acclimating back into civilian life. A lot of veterans feel some temporary culture shock when they leave active duty, but for some reason, I had a hard time reconnecting. I couldn't shake the feeling that I was alone in the world.

I found myself drifting around. A lot. Even though I had joined the service to get money for college, by the time I got out I had lost my ambition. I was emotionally detached, and I moved from state to state. I took odd jobs and was paid mostly off the books. I had very few friends and talked to very few people. I didn't have anything to say.

Weirdly enough, it was my love of horror movies that got me out of this severe isolation. I drifted into a small college town in Connecticut. I had stopped at a liquor store in a strip mall, and when I came out, I noticed there was a mom-and-pop video store right next door. Once a movie lover, always a movie lover, so I decided to go in and see what they had.

I didn't expect a lot. This place was in the middle of bumfuck nowhere.

I was smitten the moment I found the "Great Directors" display on the back wall. All the heavy hitters were there: Welles, and Ford, and Hawks had movie sections. But there were surprises. Next to the movies of Francis Ford Coppola were the films of John Carpenter and David Cronenberg, and there was no line of demarcation between the auteur and the genre guys.

The collection on display included rare early films, like Carpenter's *Dark Star*, his USC film thesis that got a limited theatrical release. They had a copy of Cronenberg's *Scanners,* a movie about killer psychics who make people's heads explode. George Romero was represented, and they had a copy of his little-seen vampire film, *Martin*. It sat right next to Roberto Rossellini's *Roma: Open City.*

I was dumbstruck. This statement wasn't the work of an average mom-and-pop establishment. This was the work of a horror fan and an avid completist. This was a fellow maniac.

It may seem like a small thing, but that display gave me a joy that I hadn't felt for a long time. It was a flash of recognition like I was an amnesiac who recognizes a prized possession. In the middle of bumfuck nowhere, I suddenly felt like I belonged.

That feeling led to a long conversation with the owner, which led to a job opening, which led to meeting a lot of creative people who had also found that video store to be an oasis. And that led to working on local commercials and learning the basics of camera operation and sound decks.

What are the chances, right?

I could easily have walked out of that store without saying a word to anyone. If it were only Coppola, and Kurosawa, and Welles on that wall, I might not have been compelled to start a conversation. But horror is an art form that has a built-in sense of play; it's a warm welcome from a fellow outsider.

I recognized the fun and passion that went into that display. And, just like that, I found my love for horror films again. And that gave me a voice and something to talk about with others. I found social acceptance through movies where people's heads exploded.

Maybe it's just a coincidence that I walked into that video store and started a series of events that changed the direction of my life, but I have to say that coincidences like that one happen to me a lot.

Multiple Maniacs: The Joy of Convention Family

Years after my comeback in Connecticut, I found myself married and living in the San Francisco Bay Area with a successful career and a comfortable lifestyle.

Yet I found myself in a deep funk.

Although I was successful in my career, it was a high-pressure occupation in the high-tech world. The work was competitive and all-consuming. Before I knew it, a decade had gone by with me evangelizing things that didn't feed my passion.

I realized I hadn't had a conversation with another person about the things that interested me in years.

I still had my passion for horror films, but I had no outlet to share my love for them anymore. San Francisco is a lot of things, but a horror town it isn't. I had no community.

And that's when my long-suffering wife decided to do an intervention.

She did the research and found a horror convention in Chicago that was also a cast reunion for one of my favorite films, the original *Halloween*. This was a smart move on her part, as the fans would skew more towards my age. She researched hotel rooms and air flights. Then she pointed me at the door and told me to go get a battery recharge, and that I better come back happy.

And that's how I found myself flying to a horror convention, alone, in a strange town, trapped in a convention hotel for three days, without knowing a single person there. My goal was simple: I was going there for no other reason but talking to fans about horror movies.

Going to this convention was a calculated risk. I had grown disillusioned with conventions a long time ago. Most conventions are, unfortunately, money grabs. Expensive photo ops with celebrities and long lines for pricey autographs bring more collectors than they do fans.

None of this is conducive to rousing conversations.

The first day was everything I dreaded. I tried to make conversation in one of the many long lines only to realize I was flanked by collectors who struggled to balance the 30 items they wanted to be autographed in their hands. When

I met the celebrities they were gracious, but long lines kept the conversation to, "Who should I make this out to?"

Day two was salvaged when I started talking to the vendors. Some were micro-budget independent filmmakers, and some were painters, or photographers, or sculptors. Most of them were real fans. However, commerce comes first, and our discussions were cut short.

But even with these brief discussions, I could feel the energy charging through me. Not only did I feel comfortable talking with these fans, but it felt like I was *supposed* to be talking with them. It felt important to listen to their stories and to tell them mine. These were tales spoken from the heart that rarely got heard outside of the odd convention.

I hit pay dirt after midnight when 90 percent of the conventioneers were drunkenly staggering through the hotel hallways and parking lots. I noticed a group of fans had moved all the lobby furniture into a quiet corner and were huddled there, deep in an animated discussion. I walked over and asked them if, by chance, they were talking about horror movies. They offered me a seat.

The next thing I remember was the sun coming through the lobby window.

We had talked through the night about horror films and their philosophies. All the conversation was thoughtful, deeply inspired, and liberally peppered with laughter. It was gratifying that the group had realized almost immediately that I was part of the tribe and I was welcomed into the fold. Before the convention was over, many of the members of this "Algonquin Round Table of Horror" exchanged contact information with me and swore to keep in touch.

Astonishingly enough, they did. I was inducted into what is called "Convention Family," a group of people who not only look forward to seeing you at conventions but keep in contact with you throughout the year. Convention

Family are folks who write to send you support on any projects you might be working on. Sometimes we call each other because someone just saw a great movie and they need to share it with everybody. It's not about hoarding knowledge. It's all about sharing the experience. Sharing the joy. Sharing the good health.

How could I not follow these guys around the country to different horror conventions? How could I not fly out to a private gathering at one fan's house for a day-long marathon of bad horror movies affectionately known as "Turkey Day"?

The things you do for Convention Family.

Spreading the Disease

What are the chances, right?

My wife could have picked a local convention for me to attend. I could have said I didn't want to travel. I could have called it quits after that disappointing first day and spent the weekend in my room watching horror movies. I could have walked right past the Algonquin Round Table of Horror in the lobby. They could have invited me to sit with them out of politeness and then ignored me.

Instead, everything fell into place, and I came home with what I longed for: a community that made me feel like I belonged, and one where I could bring as much value to as I received from the other members.

Perhaps it was coincidence again, but I think that if you are inspired to take a chance, to satisfy a nagging curiosity, the odds of things working out increase just by participating. And I think the people I met were willing to take the ride because they were partaking in what they loved, and that makes the journey invariably fun.

If you were to talk to many of the folks I've met over the years who are horror fans, you'd find that their early life stories aren't very happy. There was a lot of struggle. Many felt like outcasts and freaks, and quite a few had lonely childhoods. Some of them had it a lot harder, and some of them are scarred survivors.

Their stories might have started unhappily, but just about all of them have had a happy second act. They found a way to cope, and they found their passion and their community through a love of horror. And most of them are so happy for the second chance at a first-class life, and the biggest joy is spreading the wealth. Spreading the disease.

I found out that most of the people in the Algonquin Round Table of Horror were writing books, or painting, or making short films on the side. This was a level of fandom so intense that it compelled other members to create something themselves.

So, I caught the disease.

I knew that I loved starting conversations with people about horror, so I decided to find a way to reach as many people as I could and share my undiluted love of the genre. I started a podcast called *Hellbent for Horror*.

I wasn't even sure what a podcast was. The best definition I could find was that podcasting was like "radio on demand," and it was the Wild West of broadcasting. It seemed like a great place to start a campaign to bring some context and respectability to something most people considered a mongrel art form.

On my podcast, I talk about the movies, and books, and stories that shaped me, and I extol the virtues of what I consider to be a beautiful art form. It's an ancient mode of storytelling that takes the slings and arrows of the populace and is there for them when they desperately need a handshake with their shadows.

The craziness of the world isn't going anywhere. Your morning commute is still going to be a bear, the price of coffee will continue to rise, and there will inevitably be another horrible dance craze that sweeps the nation. The unknown will always be unknown, and no amount of worrying that you do will give you one more iota of control over any of it.

Why not have some fun with that free-floating stress you've inherited just by walking the planet? Real life problems have a heavy weight attached to them, but horror movies can't hurt you. The fear is temporary, and there is power in facing fear and walking away from it unharmed. It's a diffused bomb. That movie moment can never scare you again—it gets turned into a thrill.

Ultimately, I think horror endures because deep down we need it. We need a stand-in boogeyman. It isn't a social or a cultural need; it's a human need. There's a reason there's a house in every town in the world that kids believe is haunted.

You knew it when you were a kid when you sat in the dark with a flashlight under your chin and told ghost stories to your friends.

ACKNOWLEDGMENTS

There wouldn't be a book if it weren't for my magnificent wife, Lisa Gorski, who believed that there was something to my opinions about horror and art long before I did. Lisa is a life-long science fiction fan and an ardent Trekkie and she has no interest in horror movies whatsoever. If that's not proof of the power of love, I don't know what is.

I want to thank Julie Broad, Jaqueline Kyle, and Tim Testa from Book Launchers for navigating this book through the daunting phases of publishing. Creating a book isn't like sailing a ship on stormy seas. It's more like sailing a ship on dead calm water, with no wind and an empty horizon in every direction. I thank Book Launchers for knowing how to keep the ship moving.

I also want to give special thanks to my copy editor, Cathy Reed, and my content editor, Kelly Ragan. Editors make good books better. Period.

I want to express my deep thanks to Heidi Honeycutt, Samantha Kolesnik, Jovanka Vuckovic, Dr. Rhonda Baughman, Dr. Harold Aurand, KT Lowe, Melody Burke, Ian Carruthers, and Dan Truman for giving their time and their voices to help bring this book to life.

I want to express my gratitude to my Patreon supporters: James Hancock, Andrew Boylan, Bradley J. Kornish, Damien Allen, Dan Schreffler, Dennis Guilmette, Donald England, E.J. Hardin, Jack Warrington, Isaac Thorne, James Kelley, Jann Jones, Jef Reynolds, Jenelle Colie, Joe McGuire, John Arminio, John Beasley, John Colucci, Josiah Pitchforth, Keith Say, Kasey Van,

Laura Burkhalter, Kris Thompson, Tony Dixon, Vanessa Hoar, and others who wish to remain anonymous patrons of my madness. Thank you.

Many thanks to the members of what I call "The Algonquin Round Table of Horror:" Jon Kitley (possibly the most knowledgeable horror fan I've ever met—check him out at www.kitleyskrypt.com), Bryan Martinez (https://www.facebook.com/TheGialloRoom), Dave Kosanke (founder of long-running underground fanzine "Liquid Cheese"), Damien Glonek (co-creator of the "Living Dead Dolls"), Billy and Vanessa Nocera (creators of *Evilspeak Magazine*), Gregg Olheiser, Jill Van, Matt "Putrid" Carr, Jason Coffman (director of the film *Housesitters*), Aaron Christensen (author of the book *Horror 101*), Brian Fukala, and Matt Harding. Thanks for letting me into the "convention family."

And I wanted to say a very special thank you to Mike and Kim Kovarovics, the owners of Video Visions of Storrs, Connecticut (1983-2009). This video store was an oasis for me at just the right time in my life, and I can't thank you enough for making it as cool and as special as it was.

ABOUT THE AUTHOR

S.A. BRADLEY is the host of the popular podcast Hellbent For Horror, exploring all things horror across books, film, comics, and music. Bradley has loved being scared by over 1,600 horror films. He's turned his passion into purpose, sharing his expansive knowledge on dozens of podcasts and in anthologies like *Medium Chill* and *EvilSpeak* magazine. Hellbent For Horror was a 2017 Rondo Hatton Classic Horror Awards nominee for Best Multi-Media Horror Site and was described by director Guillermo Del Toro as "Well researched, articulate and entirely absorbing." Bradley's first book, *Screaming for Pleasure: How Horror Makes You Happy and Healthy*, is a thrilling ride through the horror genre and its intense effect on every generation. He shows how you can be enriched by horror.

Prior to becoming a champion of horror, Bradley served in the U.S. Air Force and was a firefighter. He now lives in the San Francisco Bay Area with his wife and their dog, Fiona, where they can often be found meditating in a death metal mosh pit or dancing around a Northern Californian fire pit drum circle. Get your spook on by following Bradley on Twitter @hellbenthorror or on his website, Hellbentforhorror.com.

INDEX

A

ABC Television's In Concert 68
Absentia 163
AC/DC 86
A Dark Song (2017) 251
A Girl Walks Home Alone at Night
        198
Agoraphobia 96
Alfred Hitchcock's Spellbinders in
        Suspense (1967) 40
Alien (1979) 23
Allison, Deborah, "Great Directors:
        Don Siegel," Senses of Cinema,
        2004 131
All That Jazz (1979) 110
American Gods (2001) 55
American Mary (2012) 175, 190, 191,
        193, 198
American Psycho (2000) 176, 198
Amirpour, Ana Lily 198
Amok Train, aka Beyond the Door III
        (1989) 121
An American Werewolf in London
        (1981) 158
Animal House (1978) 145, 149, 154
Annihilation (2018) 133
Antichrist (2009) 223
Arachnophobia 92
Arachnophobia (1990) 94
Aranza, Jacob 73
Araya, Tom 78
Argento, Dario 213, 214
Arrival of a Train at La Ciotat Station
        18
Arzner, Dorothy 174
Assault on Precinct 13 (1974) 28
At the Mountains of Madness (1936)
        55

Audition (1999) 100

B

Backmasking 68, 69, 70, 73, 74, 76, 77
Barker, Clive 55, 57, 216, 217
Baskin (2015) 233
Battered Women's Movement 207
Baughman, Dr. Rhonda 212, 216, 265
Bava, Mario 66
Belknap, Raymond 86, 87
Benjamin, Roxanne 198
Bergman, Ingmar 109
Best, Amy Lynn 198
Beukes, Lauren 55
Beyond the Realms of Death, song
        (1978) 81
Bigelow, Kathryn 167, 176, 198
Biller, Anna 198
Bill Haley and the Comets' "Rock
        Around the Clock" (1954) 18
Birth of a Nation (1915) 214
Black Christmas (1975) 163
Black Magic: A Tale of The Rise and
        Fall of the Antichrist (1909)
        173
Black Metal 83
Black Mirror (2011) 161
Black Sabbath 65, 66, 77, 82, 83
Black Sabbath (1963) 66
Blackwood, Algernon 55, 56
Blaine, Jamie, Classic Rock Magazine
        66
Blatty, William Peter 48, 55
Blizzard of Oz (1980) 80
Bloch, Robert 40, 55, 57
Blood Bath (1966) 174
Blood Meridian (1985) 56
Body horror 216, 220

Bogdanovich, Peter 134, 135
Bone Tomahawk (2015) 253
Bonnie and Clyde (1967) 206
Boorman, John 215
Bosch, Hieronymus 32
Bottin, Rob 31
Bowen, Marjorie 173
Boyle, Danny 14, 141
Bradbury, Ray 47, 55, 57
Breskin, David 86
Brilliant, Lawrence 99
Broken Monsters (2014) 55
Bugliosi, Vincent, Helter Skelter – The
	True Story of the Manson
	Murders (1974) 70
Burns, Scott Z. 99
Burnt Offerings (1976) 104, 112, 113
Butler, Geezer 66

C

Cabin Fever (2002) 99
Campbell, Ramsey 55, 57
Canby, Vincent 34
Cannibal Holocaust (1980) 38
Cardos, John "Bud" 94
Cargill, C. Robert, Boston Globe 36
Carolyn, Axelle 198
Carpenter, John 26, 27, 28, 29, 31, 34,
	138, 140, 160, 258
Carrie (film, 1976) 207
Carrie (novel, 1972) 47
Cat People (1942) 166
Cat People (1982) 254
Chaney, Lon 159
Chick, Jack 73, 84
Children of the Damned 79
Christie, Julie 1, 7, 9, 12
Church of Satan 73, 74, 79, 85
Cinefantastique 34
Claustrophobia 95
Clover, Carol, Men, Women and
	Chainsaws: Gender in the
	Modern Horror Film (1992) 216
Cocteau, Jean 110
Connell, Richard 41

Contagion (2011) 99
Contemporary Christian Magazine 73
Cooper, Alice 67, 68, 79, 88
Corman, Roger 134, 174
Coscarelli, Don 111
Craven, Wes 120
Crawford, F. Marion 55
Creature Features 5
Creep (2014) 235
Cronenberg, David 160, 216, 220, 221,
	258
Cronin, Justin 56
Cronos (1993) 151
Crossing Over: How Science Is Rede-
	fining Life and Death, National
	Geographic (2016) 108
Crouch, Paul 74, 75, 76
Crusaders (1978) 73
Cundey, Dean 31
Cuneo, Michael 19
	American Exorcism: Expelling
	Demons in the Land of Plenty
	19
Curtis. Dan 112

D

Dahl, Roald 40, 55
Daley, Jason, Outside Magazine 97
Danse Macabre (1981) 131
Dark Forces (book, 1980) 57
Dark Star (1974) 258
Darsa, Alissa, "Art House: An Introduc-
	tion to German Expressionist
	Films," Artnet News, December
	26, 2013 127
Davis, Erik, Led Zeppelin's Led Zeppe-
	lin IV (2005) 76
Dawn of the Dead (1978) 120, 158
Dawn of the Dead (2004) 142
Deadly Friend (1987) 120
Deathridge, John 61
Deep Throat (1972) 206
Deliverance (1972) 215
del Toro, Guillermo vii, 149, 150, 151,
	169

Demme, Jonathan 14, 174
Demonophobia 101
Denis, Claire 223
Denisoff, R. Serge, *Tarnished Gold: The Record Industry Revisted* (1986) 75
Deodato, Ruggero 38
DePalma, Brian 31, 207, 208
Detroit (film, 2017) 167
de Van, Marina 188, 189, 198
Devil Worship: Exposing Satan's Underground (1988) 86
Diabolus in Musica 59
Diamond, King 83
Diaz, Art 80
Dickey, Nathan, *The Devil Has the Best Tunes: The Fundamentalist Crusade Against Rock Music* (2015) 73
Dio, Ronnie James 77
Dirty Harry (1971) 171
Dirty Mary, Crazy Larry (1974) 6, 20
Disturbed's "Down with the Sickness" (2000) 145
Don't Look Now (1973) 1, 7, 14
Don't Look Now (2017) 1, 7, 8, 13, 14, 163, 173
Dougherty, Steven 80
Dracula (1931) 67
Dressed to Kill (1980) 207
Ducournau, Julia 198
Du Maurier, Daphne 45, 55
Dunning, John 209
Dunsmuir Mansion 112
Dwyer, R. Budd 124, 125

E

Ebert, Roger 34, 36, 155, 215
EC Comics 5
Ellison, Harlan v, 55, 57
Escape From New York (1981) 29
E.T. the Extra-Terrestrial 34
Evil Dead 2: Dead by Dawn (1987) 158

F

Fangoria Magazine 36, 94
Fetherlin, Chelsea 212
Field, Allyson Nadia, "Dorothy Arzner," Women Film Pioneers Project, September 27, 2013 174
Fields, R. Douglas, Ph.D., "The Explosive Mix of Sex and Violence," Psychology Today, January 26, 2016 202
Finney, Jack 48, 55, 131
Fosse, Bob 110
Frankenstein (1818) 126
Frankenstein; or The Modern Prometheus (1818) 55
Freed, Rabbi Herb 209
Friday the 13th (1980) 209
Friedkin, William 14, 51, 52, 156
Fugate, Caril Ann 133
Fujiwara, Kei 198
Funk and Wagnall's Encyclopedias 49

G

Gaiman, Neil 55
Garland, Alex 141
German Expressionism 127
Get Out 149, 150, 154, 155, 157, 158, 166, 167, 168, 226, 227, 228
Ghost Story (1979) 48, 54, 55
Gialli 212
Giallo 212, 213
Gibb, Russ 69
Giuliani, Rudolph 143
Going to Pieces: The Rise and Fall of the Slasher Film (documentary, 2006) 208
Golding, William 55
Golem 159
Gotterdammerung (opera, 1848) 62
Graduation Day (1981) 209
Great Tales of Terror and the Supernatural 56
Green Room (2015) 228
Greenwald, Gary 73
Gregorian Monks 59, 60, 80
Grindhouse Purgatory magazine 212

Grow, Kory 71, 86

H

Habit (1995) 162
Halford, Rob 81, 86
Halloween (1978) 29, 35, 209
Hard Candy (2005) 223
Harris, Thomas 56
Hawkins, Screaming Jay 67
Hawks, Howard 4, 29
Heaven and Hell (1980) 77
Heavy Metal 64, 65, 67, 68, 78, 81, 84,
    86, 87, 88, 217
Hellbent for Horror 263
Hellboy (2003) 151
Heller-Nicholas, Alexandra 85
Hellraiser (1987) 104, 158, 216, 217
Henig, Robin Marantz 108
Henry: Portrait of a Serial Killer (1986)
    105
Here Comes the Devil (2013) 248
Herzog, Werner 151
Hickock, Richard "Dick" 133
Highway to Hell (1979) 86
Hill, Joe 55
Hiroshima and Nagasaki 132
Hitchcock, Alfred 4, 39, 40, 45, 46, 134,
    202, 204, 205
Home Box Office 5, 6, 7
Home Movies (1980) 207
Honeycutt, Heidi 180, 198, 265
Honeymoon (2014) 198, 236
Hooper, Tobe 210, 211
Horns (2010) 55
Horrible/Beautiful 22, 23, 24, 26, 28,
    213, 231, 243
Hostel (2005) 104, 147
House of 1,000 Corpses (2003) 254

I

I Am Legend 47
I Am Not a Serial Killer (2016) 249
I Have No Mouth, and I Must Scream
    55

I'm So Tired, song (1968) 68, 69
In Fear (2013) 250
In My Skin (2002) 188, 198
Inside (2007) 163
Intensity (1995) 56
Intolerance (1916) 214
Introvigne, Massimo, Satanism: A
    Social History (2016) 73
Invasion of the Body Snatchers (1956)
    104, 130
Iommi, Tony 66
Iron Maiden 79, 80
Irreversible (2002) 38, 215
I Spit on Your Grave (1978) 215
It (2017) 254
It Follows (2014) 157, 223

J

Jackson, Forrest 74
Jackson, Shirley 48, 55, 57, 187
Jacquet, Catherine, "Domestic Violence
    in the 1970s", NIH, U.S. National
    Library of Medicine, October 15,
    2015 207
Janiak, Leigh 198
Janisse, Kier-La, Paul Corupe, Satanic
    Panic: Pop-Cultural Panic in the
    1980s (2015) 74, 84, 85
Janowitz, Hans 128, 129
Jarman, Derek 152
Jaws (1975) 23, 26, 28, 36, 37, 97, 155
Jeepers Creepers (2001) 163
Jenkins, Philip, The Oxford Handbook
    of New Religious Movements
    (2004) 88
John Dies in the End (2007) 56
Jones, Amy Holden 176
Jones, Duane 136
Jones, Elliot, Secular Music Trouba-
    dours, MUS 101, Santa Ana
    College (2017) 62
Joy, Leona 218
Judas Priest 78, 81, 84, 86, 87
Ju-on: The Grudge 255

K

Kaes, Anton, Shell Shock Cinema: Weimar Culture and the Wounds of War, 2011 127
Kane, Joe, Night of the Living Dead: Behind the Scenes of the Most Terrifying Zombie Movie Ever (2011) 136, 137
Kantor, Igo 94
Karloff, Boris 66, 134
Kasso, Richard "Ricky" 85, 86
Kelsey, Colleen, "The Cult of Stephanie Rothman", Interview Magazine, 2016 174
Kentis, Chris 97
Kent, Jennifer 175, 183, 185, 198
Kermode, Mark, "The Female Directors Bringing New Blood to Horror Films," The Observer, March 19, 2017 176
Ketchum, Jack 56, 194
Key, Wilson Bryan, Subliminal Seduction (1974) 72
Kingdom of the Spiders (1977) 94
King Kong (1933) 154
King, Stephen 42, 43, 44, 47, 55, 57, 121, 131, 176
Kolesnik, Samantha 176, 265
Koontz, Dean 56
Kracauer, Siegfried, From Caligari to Hitler: A Psychological History of the German Film (1947) 129
Krischer, Hayley, "A Battle to the Grave: An Interview with the Soska Sisters," The Hairpin, October 30, 2014 175
Krutnik, Frank, "Un-American" Hollywood: Politics and Film in the Blacklist Era, 2007 131
Kryah, Kevin, "The Cabinet of Dr. Caligari: Dark Relationship with Postwar Germany," The Artifice, May 9, 2015 128
Kubrick, Stanley 14, 240, 254

Kuchar Brothers 152
Kusama, Karyn 175, 186, 187, 198

L

LaBianca, Leno and Rosemary 70
Lambert, Mary 176, 198
Landis, John 158
Lansdale, Joe R. 56
Larson, Bob 74
Larson, Tom, History of Rock and Roll (2004) 65
Lauwers, Gary 85, 86
LaVey, Anton 79
Led Zeppelin 75, 76
Lennon, John 69
Let the Right One In (2008) 162
Lewton, Val 166, 232
Lipkin, Dr. Ian 99
Lord of the Flies (1954) 55
Lovecraft, H.P. 55, 56, 57, 238
Love It to Death (1971) 67
Lovel, Alan, BFI's American Cinema 131
Lowe, Alice 198
Lugosi, Bela 137, 196, 197
Lumiere Brothers 18
Lynch, David 170, 198

M

Machado, Carmen Maria 55
Mainwaring, Dan 131
Man from the South (story, 1948) 40, 41, 55
Manson, Charles 68, 70, 71
Martin (1977) 162
Martin, George 69
M.A.S.H. (1970) 20
Matheson, Richard 47, 57
Matthews, Christopher, "25 Years Later: In the Crash of 1987, the Seeds of the Great Recession," Time Magazine, October 22, 2012 126
Maximum Overdrive (1986) 121
McCarthy, Cormac 56

McCartney, Paul 69
McCauley, Kirby 57
McEwan, Ian 151
McMartin Preschool 83
Medium Chill 212, 267
Mercyful Fate 83
Mesce, Bill, It's Not TV: HBO, The Company That Changed Television: The Green Channel (2013) 6
Metal: A Headbanger's Journey (2005) 78
Metal: Evolution (television, 2011-2014) 83
Meyer, Carl 128, 129
Michael Powell 143, 204, 205, 206
Michelle Remembers (1980) 85
Midnight Spook Shows 67, 68
Misery (1990) 152
Mob Rules (1982) 77
Mr. Robot (2015) 124
Mullholland Drive (2001) 170
My Bloody Valentine (1981) 209
Mysophobia 98, 99
Mystery Plays 61, 80

N

National Lampoon's Animal House (1978) 145, 149, 154
Near Dark (1987) 162, 176, 198
Nelson, Michelle R., "The Hidden Persuaders: Then and Now", The Journal of Advertising (2013) 71
Nelson, Ray 55
Nelson, R. J. and Chiavegatto, S. Molecular basis of aggression, Trends in Neurosciences 24, December 2001: 713-19 201
Newman, Kim, Filmmaker Magazine 141
Newman, Paul 116
Nightmares in Red, White and Blue (2009) 137, 139

Night of the Living Dead (1968) 135, 163
Night Shift (book, 1978) 57
No Country for Old Men (2007) 152, 171
Noe, Gaspar 215
Not After Midnight (1971) 173
No Time for Flowers (1952) 131
Novak, Matt 67
No Wave Cinema 151

O

Open Water (2003) 96, 163
Opera (1987) 213
Organ (1996) 198
Orpheus (1950) 110
Osbourne, Ozzy 59, 65, 80, 86
Ouija boards 50

P

Packard, Vance, The Hidden Persuaders (1957) 71, 86, 87
Pandorum (2009) 98
Pan's Labyrinth (2006) 151
Paranormal Activity (2007) 102
Parker, Zack 245
Pazuzu (demon) 51
Peckinpah, Sam 28
Peele, Jordan 149, 155, 167, 227, 228
Peeping Tom (1960) 205
Pet Sematary (1989) 43, 176, 198
Pet Sematary (novel, 1983) 43, 54
Phantasm (1979) 111
Phantom of the Opera (1925) 154
Picnic at Hanging Rock (1975) 163
Plant, Robert 76
Poe, Amos 151
Poe, Edgar Allen 55, 56
Poltergeist (1982) 34
Post–horror 162
Pretty Polly 63, 89
Prevenge (2016) 198
Price, Vincent 16, 17
Prime Evil (book, 1988) 57

Prom Night (1980) 209
Proxy (2013) 244
Psycho (1960) 4

Q

Quinones, Albert 85

R

Ramirez, Richard 86
Raw (2016) 198
Rebecca (1938) 173
Rec (2007) 163
Red Dragon (1981) 56
Reeve, Andru J., Turn Me On, Dead Man: The Beatles And The "Paul-Is-Dead" Hoax (2004) 69
Reign in Blood (1986) 60
Requiem for a Dream (2000) 100
Return of the Living Dead (1985) 158
Revolution 9, song (1968) 68, 69
Revolver (1966) 68
Richard Cheese and Lounge Against the Machine 145
Rivera, Geraldo 86
Rocky (1976) 19, 20, 21, 22, 26, 37
Roeg, Nicolas 7, 8, 12, 13, 14
Rogak, Lisa, Haunted Heart: The Life and Times of Stephen King (2009) 44
Rolling Stone 37, 66, 71, 86, 175
Roma: Open City (1946) 258
Romero, George A. 135
Rosemary's Baby (1968) 38, 95, 187
Rose, Steve 162, 191
Rossellini, Roberto 258
Roth, Eli 147
Rothkopf, Joshua, Time Out New York 35
Rothman, Stephanie 174, 198

S

Sad Wings of Destiny (1976) 78
Satan 50, 62, 65, 73, 74, 75, 76, 78, 79, 80, 82, 83, 84, 85, 86, 87, 88

Satanic Panic 74, 77, 84, 85, 87
Saw (2004) 166
Scanners (1981) 258
Schechter, Harold, Savage Pastimes: A Cultural History of Violent Entertainment (2005) 64
Sciaraffa, Jessica, "The Relationship Between Violent Media, Pornography, and Cyber Dating Abuse Among Adolescents", The University of Western Ontario, 2015 202
Sedivy, Judy, PhD, Psychology Today 72
Shelley, Mary Wollstonecraft 55
Shivers (1975) 220
Siegel, Don 131
Silence of the Lambs (1991) 14, 152
Silent Night, Deadly Night (1984) 38
Simmons, Dan 47, 55
Singer, Matt, "A New Kind of Monster," The Dissolve, August 21, 2013 134
Slayer 60, 78, 88
Smith, Jacob, Turn Me On, Dead Media: A Backward Look at the Re-enchantment of an Old Medium (2011) 77
Smith, Perry 133
Snow White (1937) 3
Snyder, Zack 142, 143
Something Wicked This Way Comes 55
Sometimes a Great Notion (1971) 116
Sontag, Deborah, New York Times 97
Soska, Jen 191, 198
Soska Sisters 175, 190, 192, 193
Soska, Sylvia 175, 191, 198
Southbound (2015) 198
Spencer, Alan, Starlog Magazine 34
Spielberg, Steven 23, 24, 25, 26, 35
Splatter Movie (2008) 198
Spring (2015) 237
Stained Class (1978) 86
Stairway to Heaven, song (1971) 74, 75, 76, 77

Stanton, Harry Dean 23
Starkweather, Charles 133
Starry Eyes (2014) 243
Star Wars (1977) 16
Stevens, William K., The New York
    Times 124
Stormfront 140
Straub, Peter 48, 55, 57
Streiner, Russ 136
Subliminal messages 76
Suddath, Claire, "Why Did World War
    I Just End?", Time, Oct. 04, 2010
    127
Suspiria (1977) 31, 213
Sutherland, Donald 7, 9, 12

T

Tales from the Crypt 5
Tales of Halloween (segment "Grim
    Grinning Ghost") (2015) 198
Talk Back with Bob Larson 74
TARANTULA! (1955) 4
Targets (1968) 134
Tate, Sharon 70
Taxi Driver (1976) 20
Teeth (2007) 223
The American Nightmare (2000) 137,
    220
Theatre of Blood (1973) 17
The Autopsy of Jane Doe (2016) 231
The Babadook (2014) 157, 183, 198
The Beatles 68, 69, 70
The Birds (film, 1963) 45, 46, 163
The Birds (short story, 1952) 45, 55,
    173
The Blackboard Jungle (1955) 18, 19
The Blair Witch Project (1999) 163
The Body Snatchers (1955) 48, 55
The Box (2017) 194
The Cabinet of Dr. Caligari (1920) 127
The Call of Cthulhu and Other Weird
    Stories 57
The Changeling (1980) 230
The Descent (2005) 95

The Devil's Rejects (2005) 254
The Doll Who Ate His Mother (1976)
    55
The Entity (1982) 101
The Exorcist (film, 1973) 14, 18, 20, 51,
    161
The Exorcist (novel, 1971) 14, 18, 19,
    20, 48, 51, 55, 156, 161
The Fall of the House of Usher (1839)
    55
The Fly (1986) 160
The Fog (1980) 29
The French Connection (1971) 14, 20
The Fury (1978) 31
The Getaway (1972) 6, 28
The Girl Next Door (1989) 56
The Girl with All the Gifts (2016) 246
The Godfather (1972) 20
The Haunting (1963) 14
The Haunting of Hill House (1959) 48,
    54, 55
The Hellbound Heart (1986) 55
The Hollywood Reporter 174
The Howling (1981) 31
The Hunchback of Notre Dame (1939)
    154
The Husband Stitch (2014) 55
The Invitation (2015) 186, 198
The Last Judgment 61
The Last Man (1826) 173
The Last Shark (1981) 121
The Legend of Hell House (1973) 230
The Life and Times of Judge Roy Bean
    (1972) 6
The Lost Boys (1987) 254
The Lottery and Other Stories 57
The Love Witch (2016) 198
THEM! (1954) 4
The Mist (2007) 163
The Most Dangerous Game (story,
    1925) 41
The Neon Demon (2016) 242
The Night They Missed the Horror
    Show (2006) 56
The Number of the Beast (1982) 79

The Outlaw Josey Wales (1976) 214
The Passage (2010) 56
The Poseidon Adventure (1972) 6
The Revenant (2015) 170
The Ritual (2017) 97
The Ruins (2008) 163
The Satanic Bible (1969) 79
The Sentinel (1977) 31
The Seventh Seal (1957) 109
The Seven-Ups (1973) 6
The Shape of Water (2017) vii, 149
The Shining (1980) 14, 254
The Slumber Party Massacre (1982) 176
The Stand (1978) 55
The Stone Killer (1973) 6
The Student Nurses (1970) 174
The Terror (1963) 134
The Terror (2007) 55
The Texas Chainsaw Massacre 2 (1986)
    210
The Texas Chain Saw Massacre (1974)
    38, 104
The Thing (1982) 4, 26, 27, 28, 29, 30,
    31, 34, 35, 36, 37, 160
The Thing from Another World (1951)
    4, 29
The Twilight Zone 161
The Upper Berth (1926) 55
The Velvet Vampire (1971) 174, 198
The Viper of Milan (1906) 173
The Void (2017) 238
The Walking Dead (2010) 140
The Wendigo (1910) 55
The White Album (1968) 68, 69
The Witch (2015) 157, 240
They Live (1988) 138
Time Travel for Pedestrians (1972) 55
Top of the Pops 68
Treaty of Versailles 127
Trinity Broadcasting Network 73, 74
Tritone 59, 61, 62, 63, 64, 66, 89
Troiano, James "Jimmy" 85, 86
Troubadour songs 62
Trouble Every Day (2001) 223
Trypanophobia 100

V

Vance, James 86
Vault of Horror 5
Venom (band) 82, 83
Vicary, James M. 71
Videodrome (1983) 216, 220
Vokey, John R., PhD, Psychological
    Sketches (1994) 72, 76
Vuckovic, Jovanka 175, 194, 195, 196,
    197, 265

W

Wagner, Richard 62
Walkabout (1971) 14
Walker, Michael W. 77
Wall, Mick, Iron Maiden: Run to the
    Hills, the Authorised Biography
    (2004) 80
We Are Still Here (2015) 230
Weimar Republic 128
Weinstein, Deena 78
Welcome to Hell (1981) 82
Wheatley, Dennis 66
White, Adam, "John Carpenter
    condemns neo-Nazis who
    have co-opted his cult 1988
    satire They Live," The Telegraph,
    January 5, 2017 140
Whitehouse, Mary 68
White Lightning (1973) 6
Whitman, Charles 135
Wiederhorn, Jon, Guitar World 82
Wiene, Robert 128
Wilson, R. Reid, PhD 92
Winter, Douglas E. 44, 57
Wise, Herbert 56
Wise, Robert 14, 158
Wizard of Oz (1939) 3
Women in Horror Film Festival 176
Wong, David 56
Wretched (2007) 177, 198
Wyman, Phil 77

X

XX (2017) 194, 197

Y

Yarroll, William H. 74, 76
Yours Truly, Jack the Ripper 40

Z

Zalewski, Daniel, New Yorker Maga-
    zine 151
Zinoman, Jason, Shock Value: How a
    Few Eccentric Outsiders Gave
    Us Nightmares, Conquered
    Hollywood, and Invented
    Modern Horror (2011) 134, 155

Made in the USA
Monee, IL
15 November 2019